To Cindy

from Phyllis Schlafly

THE
Power
OF THE
Positive
Woman

THE Power OF THE Positive Woman

Phyllis Schlafly

ARLINGTON HOUSE·PUBLISHERS

NEW ROCHELLE, NEW YORK

Manufactured in the United States of America

Library of Congress Cataloging in Publication Data

Schlafly, Phyllis.
 The power of the positive woman.

 Includes bibliographical references and index.
 1. Women—United States—Social conditions. 2. Women's rights—United States. 3. Feminism—United States. 4. Women—Psychology. I. Title.
HQ1426.S33   301.41'2'0973   77-4257
ISBN 0-87000-373-9

For my daughters, Liza and Anne

Contents

Preface

The cry of "women's liberation" leaps out from the "lifestyle" sections of newspapers and the pages of slick magazines, from radio speakers and television screens. Cut loose from past patterns of behavior and expectations, women of all ages are searching for their identity—the college woman who has new alternatives thrust upon her via "women's studies" courses, the young woman whose routine is shattered by a chance encounter with a "consciousness-raising session," the woman in her middle years who suddenly finds herself in the "empty-nest syndrome," the woman of any age whose lover or lifetime partner departs for greener pastures (and a younger crop).

All of these women, thanks to the women's liberation movement, no longer see their predicament in terms of personal problems to be confronted and solved. They see their own difficulties as a little cog in the big machine of establishment restraints and stereotypical injustice in which they have lost their own equilibrium. Who am I? Why am I here? Why am I just another faceless victim of society's oppression, a nameless prisoner behind walls too high for me to climb alone?

If I were stymied by a slice in my golf drive, I would seek lessons from a pro rather than join the postmortems in the bar at the "nineteenth hole." If I found a lump on my breast, I would run, not walk, to the best available physician, rather than join rap sessions with other women who had recently made similar discoveries. If my business were sliding into bankruptcy, I would ask advice from those whose companies operate in the black rather than in the red.

Likewise, it would seem that, for a woman to find her identity in the modern world, the path should be sought from the Positive Women who have found the road and possess the map, rather than from those who have not. In this spirit, I share with you the thoughts of one who loves life as a woman and

9

lives love as a woman, whose credentials are from the school of practical experience, and who has learned that fulfillment as a woman is a journey, not a destination.

Like every human being born into this world, the Positive Woman has her share of sorrows and sufferings, of unfulfilled desires and bitter defeats. But she will never be crushed by life's disappointments, because her positive mental attitude has built her an inner security that the actions of other people can never fracture. To the Positive Woman, her particular set of problems is not a conspiracy against her, but a challenge to her character and her capabilities.

I

Understanding the Difference

The first requirement for the acquisition of power by the Positive Woman is to understand the differences between men and women. Your outlook on life, your faith, your behavior, your potential for fulfillment, all are determined by the parameters of your original premise. The Positive Woman starts with the assumption that the world is her oyster. She rejoices in the creative capability within her body and the power potential of her mind and spirit. She understands that men and women are different, and that those very differences provide the key to her success as a person and fulfillment as a woman.

The women's liberationist, on the other hand, is imprisoned by her own negative view of herself and of her place in the world around her. This view of women was most succinctly expressed in an advertisement designed by the principal women's liberationist organization, the National Organization for Women (NOW), and run in many magazines and newspapers and as spot announcements on many television stations. The advertisement showed a darling curlyheaded girl with the caption: "This healthy, normal baby has a handicap. She was born female."

This is the self-articulated dog-in-the-manger, chip-on-the-shoulder, fundamental dogma of the women's liberation movement. Someone—it is not clear who, perhaps God, perhaps the "Establishment," perhaps a conspiracy of male chauvinist pigs —dealt women a foul blow by making them female. It becomes necessary, therefore, for women to agitate and demonstrate and hurl demands on society in order to wrest from an oppressive

11

male-dominated social structure the status that has been wrongfully denied to women through the centuries.

By its very nature, therefore, the women's liberation movement precipitates a series of conflict situations—in the legislatures, in the courts, in the schools, in industry—with man targeted as the enemy. Confrontation replaces cooperation as the watchword of all relationships. Women and men become adversaries instead of partners.

The second dogma of the women's liberationists is that, of all the injustices perpetrated upon women through the centuries, the most oppressive is the cruel fact that women have babies and men do not. Within the confines of the women's liberationist ideology, therefore, the abolition of this overriding inequality of women becomes the primary goal. This goal must be achieved at any and all costs—to the woman herself, to the baby, to the family, and to society. Women must be made equal to men in their ability *not* to become pregnant and *not* to be expected to care for babies they may bring into the world.

This is why women's liberationists are compulsively involved in the drive to make abortion and child-care centers for all women, regardless of religion or income, both socially acceptable and government-financed. Former Congresswoman Bella Abzug has defined the goal: "to enforce the constitutional right of females to terminate pregnancies that they do not wish to continue."

If man is targeted as the enemy, and the ultimate goal of women's liberation is independence from men and the avoidance of pregnancy and its consequences, then lesbianism is logically the highest form in the ritual of women's liberation. Many, such as Kate Millett, come to this conclusion, although many others do not.

The Positive Woman will never travel that dead-end road. It is self-evident to the Positive Woman that the female body with its baby-producing organs was not designed by a conspiracy of men but by the Divine Architect of the human race. Those who think it is unfair that women have babies, whereas men cannot, will have to take up their complaint with God because no other power is capable of changing that fundamental fact. On some college campuses, I have been assured that other methods of reproduction will be developed. But most of us must deal with the real world rather than with the imagination of dreamers.

12

Another feature of the woman's natural role is the obvious fact that women can breast-feed babies and men cannot. This functional role was not imposed by conspiratorial males seeking to burden women with confining chores, but must be recognized as part of the plan of the Divine Architect for the survival of the human race through the centuries and in the countries that know no pasteurization of milk or sterilization of bottles.

The Positive Woman looks upon her femaleness and her fertility as part of her purpose, her potential, and her power. She rejoices that she has a capability for creativity that men can never have.

The third basic dogma of the women's liberation movement is that there is no difference between male and female except the sex organs, and that all those physical, cognitive, and emotional differences you *think* are there, are merely the result of centuries of restraints imposed by a male-dominated society and sex-stereotyped schooling. The role imposed on women is, by definition, inferior, according to the women's liberationists.

The Positive Woman knows that, while there are some physical competitions in which women are better (and can command more money) than men, including those that put a premium on grace and beauty, such as figure skating, the superior physical strength of males over females in competitions of strength, speed, and short-term endurance is beyond rational dispute.

In the Olympic Games, women not only cannot win any medals in competition with men, the gulf between them is so great that they cannot even qualify for the contests with men. No amount of training from infancy can enable women to throw the discus as far as men, or to match men in push-ups or in lifting weights. In track and field events, individual male records surpass those of women by 10 to 20 percent.

Female swimmers today are beating Johnny Weissmuller's records, but today's male swimmers are better still. Chris Evert can never win a tennis match against Jimmy Connors. If we removed lady's tees from golf courses, women would be out of the game. Putting women in football or wrestling matches can only be an exercise in laughs.

The Olympic Games, whose rules require strict verification to ascertain that no male enters a female contest and, with his masculine advantage, unfairly captures a woman's medal, for-

13

merly insisted on a visual inspection of the contestants' bodies. Science, however, has discovered that men and women are so innately different physically that their maleness/femaleness can be conclusively established by means of a simple skin test of fully clothed persons.

If there is *anyone* who should oppose enforced sex-equality, it is the women athletes. Babe Didrickson, who played and defeated some of the great male athletes of her time, is unique in the history of sports.[1]

If sex equality were enforced in professional sports, it would mean that men could enter the women's tournaments and win most of the money. Bobby Riggs has already threatened: "I think that men 55 years and over should be allowed to play women's tournaments—like the Virginia Slims. Everybody ought to know there's no sex after 55 anyway."

The Positive Woman remembers the essential validity of the old prayer: "Lord, give me the strength to change what I can change, the serenity to accept what I cannot change, and the wisdom to discern the difference." The women's liberationists are expending their time and energies erecting a make-believe world in which they hypothesize that *if* schooling were gender-free, and *if* the same money were spent on male and female sports programs, and *if* women were permitted to compete on equal terms, *then* they would prove themselves to be physically equal. Meanwhile, the Positive Woman has put the ineradicable physical differences into her mental computer, programmed her plan of action, and is already on the way to personal achievement.

Thus, while some militant women spend their time demanding more money for professional sports, ice skater Janet Lynn, a truly Positive Woman, quietly signed the most profitable financial contract in the history of women's athletics. It was not the strident demands of the women's liberationists that brought high prizes to women's tennis, but the discovery by sports promoters that beautiful female legs gracefully moving around the court made women's tennis a highly marketable television production to delight male audiences.

Many people thought that the remarkable filly named Ruffian would prove that a female race horse could compete equally with a male. Even with the handicap of extra weights placed on the male horse, the race was a disaster for the female. The gallant Ruffian gave her all in a noble effort to compete, but broke a leg in the race and, despite the immediate attention of top veterinarians, had to be put away.

Despite the claims of the women's liberation movement, there are countless physical differences between men and women. The female body is 50 to 60 percent water, the male 60 to 70 percent water, which explains why males can dilute alcohol better than women and delay its effect. The average woman is about 25 percent fatty tissue, while the male is 15 percent, making women more buoyant in water and able to swim with less effort. Males have a tendency to color blindness. Only 5 percent of persons who get gout are female. Boys are born bigger. Women live longer in most countries of the world, not only in the United States where we have a hard-driving competitive pace. Women excel in manual dexterity, verbal skills, and memory recall.

Arianna Stassinopoulos in her book *The Female Woman* has done a good job of spelling out the many specific physical differences that are so innate and so all-pervasive that

> even if Women's Lib was given a hundred, a thousand, ten thousand years in which to eradicate *all* the differences between the sexes, it would still be an impossible undertaking. . . .
>
> It is inconceivable that millions of years of evolutionary selection during a period of marked sexual division of labor have not left pronounced traces on the innate character of men and women. Aggressiveness, and mechanical and spatial skills, a sense of direction, and physical strength—all masculine characteristics—are the qualities essential for a hunter; even food gatherers need these same qualities for defense and exploration. The prolonged period of dependence of human children, the difficulty of carrying the peculiarly heavy and inert human baby—a much heavier, clumsier burden than the monkey infant and much less able to cling on for safety—meant that women could not both look after their children and be hunters and explorers. Early humans learned to take advantage of this period of dependence to transmit rules, knowledge and skills to their offspring—women needed to develop verbal skills, a talent for personal relationships, and a predilection for nurturing going even beyond the maternal instinct.[2]

Does the physical advantage of men doom women to a life of servility and subservience? The Positive Woman knows that she has a complementary advantage which is at least as great—and, in the hands of a skillful woman, far greater. The Divine

15

Architect who gave men a superior strength to lift weights also gave women a different kind of superior strength.

The women's liberationists and their dupes who try to tell each other that the sexual drive of men and women is really the same, and that it is only societal restraints that inhibit women from an equal desire, an equal enjoyment, and an equal freedom from the consequences, are doomed to frustration forever. It just isn't so, and pretending cannot make it so. The differences are not a woman's weakness but her strength.

Dr. Robert Collins, who has had ten years' experience in listening to and advising young women at a large eastern university, put his finger on the reason why casual "sexual activity" is such a cheat on women:

> A basic flaw in this new morality is the assumption that males and females are the same sexually. The simplicity of the male anatomy and its operation suggest that to a man, sex can be an activity apart from his whole being, a drive related to the organs themselves.
>
> In a woman, the complex internal organization, correlated with her other hormonal systems, indicates her sexuality must involve her total self. On the other hand, the man is orgasm-oriented with a drive that ignores most other aspects of the relationship. The woman is almost totally different. She is engulfed in romanticism and tries to find and express her total feelings for her partner.
>
> A study at a midwestern school shows that 80 percent of the women who had intercourse hoped to marry their partner. Only 12 percent of the men expected the same.
>
> Women say that soft, warm promises and tender touches are delightful, but that the act itself usually leads to a "Is that all there is to it?" reaction. . . .
>
> [A typical reaction is]: "It sure wasn't worth it. It was no fun at the time. I've been worried ever since. . . ."
>
> The new morality is a fad. It ignores history, it denies the physical and mental composition of human beings, it is intolerant, exploitative, and is oriented toward intercourse, not love.[3]

The new generation can brag all it wants about the new liberation of the new morality, but it is still the woman who is hurt the most. The new morality isn't just a "fad"—it is a cheat and a thief. It robs the woman of her virtue, her youth, her beauty, and her love—for nothing, just nothing. It has produced a generation of young women searching for their identity, bored with sexual freedom, and despondent from the lone-

16

liness of living a life without commitment. They have abandoned the old commandments, but they can't find any new rules that work.

The Positive Woman recognizes the fact that, when it comes to sex, women are simply not the equal of men. The sexual drive of men is much stronger than that of women. That is how the human race was designed in order that it might perpetuate itself. The other side of the coin is that it is easier for women to control their sexual appetites. A Positive Woman cannot defeat a man in a wrestling or boxing match, but she can motivate him, inspire him, encourage him, teach him, restrain him, reward him, and have power over him that he can never achieve over her with all his muscle. How or whether a Positive Woman uses her power is determined solely by the way she alone defines her goals and develops her skills.

The differences between men and women are also emotional and psychological. Without woman's innate maternal instinct, the human race would have died out centuries ago. There is nothing so helpless in all earthly life as the newborn infant. It will die within hours if not cared for. Even in the most primitive, uneducated societies, women have always cared for their newborn babies. They didn't need any schooling to teach them how. They didn't need any welfare workers to tell them it is their social obligation. Even in societies to whom such concepts as "ought," "social responsibility," and "compassion for the helpless" were unknown, mothers cared for their new babies.

Why? Because caring for a baby serves the natural maternal need of a woman. Although not nearly so total as the baby's need, the woman's need is nonetheless real.

The overriding psychological need of a woman is to love something alive. A baby fulfills this need in the lives of most women. If a baby is not available to fill that need, women search for a baby-substitute. This is the reason why women have traditionally gone into teaching and nursing careers. They are doing what comes naturally to the female psyche. The schoolchild or the patient of any age provides an outlet for a woman to express her natural maternal need.

This maternal need in women is the reason why mothers whose children have grown up and flown from the nest are sometimes cut loose from their psychological moorings. The maternal need in women can show itself in love for grandchil-

17

dren, nieces, nephews, or even neighbors' children. The maternal need in some women has even manifested itself in an extraordinary affection lavished on a dog, a cat, or a parakeet.

This is not to say that every woman must have a baby in order to be fulfilled. But it is to say that fulfillment for most women involves expressing their natural maternal urge by loving and caring for someone.

The women's liberation movement complains that traditional stereotyped roles assume that women are "passive" and that men are "aggressive." The anomaly is that a woman's most fundamental emotional need is not passive at all, but active. A woman naturally seeks to love affirmatively and to show that love in an active way by caring for the object of her affections.

The Positive Woman finds somebody on whom she can lavish her maternal love so that it doesn't well up inside her and cause psychological frustrations. Surely no woman is so isolated by geography or insulated by spirit that she cannot find someone worthy of her maternal love. All persons, men and women, gain by sharing something of themselves with their fellow humans, but women profit most of all because it is part of their very nature.

One of the strangest quirks of women's liberationists is their complaint that societal restraints prevent men from crying in public or showing their emotions, but permit women to do so, and that therefore we should "liberate" men to enable them, too, to cry in public. The public display of fear, sorrow, anger, and irritation reveals a lack of self-discipline that should be avoided by the Positive Woman just as much as by the Positive Man. Maternal love, however, is not a weakness but a manifestation of strength and service, and it should be nurtured by the Positive Woman.

Most women's organizations, recognizing the preference of most women to avoid hard-driving competition, handle the matter of succession of officers by the device of a nominating committee. This eliminates the unpleasantness and the tension of a competitive confrontation every year or two. Many women's organizations customarily use a prayer attributed to Mary, Queen of Scots, which is an excellent analysis by a woman of women's faults:

> Keep us, O God, from pettiness; let us be large in thought,
> in word, in deed. Let us be done with fault-finding and leave

18

off self-seeking. . . . Grant that we may realize it is the little things that create differences, that in the big things of life we are at one.

Another silliness of the women's liberationists is their frenetic desire to force all women to accept the title *Ms* in place of *Miss* or *Mrs.* If Gloria Steinem and Betty Friedan want to call themselves *Ms* in order to conceal their marital status, their wishes should be respected.

But that doesn't satisfy the women's liberationists. They want all women to be compelled to use *Ms* whether they like it or not. The women's liberation movement has been waging a persistent campaign to browbeat the media into using *Ms* as the standard title for all women. The women's liberationists have already succeeding in getting the Department of Health, Education and Welfare to forbid schools and colleges from identifying women students as *Miss* or *Mrs.*[4]

All polls show that the majority of women do not care to be called *Ms.* A Roper poll indicated that 81 percent of the women questioned said they prefer *Miss* or *Mrs.* to *Ms.* Most married women feel they worked hard for the *r* in their names, and they don't care to be gratuitously deprived of it. Most single women don't care to have their name changed to an unfamiliar title that at best conveys overtones of feminist ideology and is polemical in meaning, and at worst connotes misery instead of joy. Thus, Kate Smith, a very Positive Woman, proudly proclaimed on television that she is "Miss Kate Smith, not Ms." Like other Positive Women, she has been succeeding while negative women have been complaining.

Finally, women are different from men in dealing with the fundamentals of life itself. Men are philosophers, women are practical, and 'twas ever thus. Men may philosophize about how life began and where we are heading; women are concerned about feeding the kids today. No woman would ever, as Karl Marx did, spend years reading political philosophy in the British Museum while her child starved to death. Women don't take naturally to a search for the intangible and the abstract. The Positive Woman knows who she is and where she is going, and she will reach her goal because the longest journey starts with a very practical first step.

Amaury de Riencourt, in his book *Sex and Power in History*, shows that a successful society depends on a delicate balanc-

19

ing of different male and female factors, and that the women's liberation movement, which promotes unisexual values and androgyny, contains within it "a social and cultural death wish and the end of the civilization that endorses it."

One of the few scholarly works dealing with woman's role, *Sex and Power in History* synthesizes research from a variety of disciplines—sociology, biology, history, anthropology, religion, philosophy, and psychology. De Riencourt traces distinguishable types of women in different periods in history, from prehistoric to modern times. The "liberated" Roman matron, who is most similar to the present-day feminist, helped bring about the fall of Rome through her unnatural emulation of masculine qualities, which resulted in a large-scale breakdown of the family and ultimately of the empire.

De Riencourt examines the fundamental, inherent differences between men and women. He argues that man is the more aggressive, rational, mentally creative, analytical-minded sex because of his early biological role as hunter and provider. Woman, on the other hand, represents stability, flexibility, reliance on intuition, and harmony with nature, stemming from her procreative function.

Where man is discursive, logical, abstract, or philosophical, woman tends to be emotional, personal, practical, or mystical. Each set of qualities is vital and complements the other. Among the many differences explained in de Riencourt's book are the following:

> Women tend more toward conformity than men—which is why they often excel in such disciplines as spelling and punctuation where there is only one correct answer, determined by social authority. Higher intellectual activities, however, require a mental independence and power of abstraction that they usually lack, not to mention a certain form of aggressive boldness of the imagination which can only exist in a sex that is basically aggressive for biological reasons.
>
> To sum up: The masculine proclivity in problem solving is analytical and categorical; the feminine, synthetic and contextual. . . . Deep down, man tends to focus on the object, on external results and achievements; woman focuses on subjective motives and feelings. If life can be compared to a play, man focuses on the theme and structure of the play, woman on the innermost feelings displayed by the actors.[5]

De Riencourt provides impressive refutation of two of the

basic errors of the women's liberation movement: (1) that there are no emotional or cognitive differences between the sexes, and (2) that women should strive to be like men.

A more colloquial way of expressing the de Riencourt conclusion that men are more analytical and women more personal and practical is in the different answers that one is likely to get to the question, "Where did you get that steak?" A man will reply, "At the corner market," or wherever he bought it. A woman will usually answer, "Why? What's the matter with it?"

An effort to eliminate the differences by social engineering or legislative or constitutional tinkering cannot succeed, which is fortunate, but social relationships and spiritual values can be ruptured in the attempt. Thus the role reversals being forced upon high school students, under which guidance counselors urge reluctant girls to take "shop" and boys to take "home economics," further confuse a generation already unsure about its identity. They are as wrong as efforts to make a left-handed child right-handed.[6]

The Five Principles

When the women's liberationists enter the political arena to promote legislation and litigation in pursuit of their goals, their specific demands are based on five principles.

(1) They demand that a "gender-free" rule be applied to every federal and state law, bureaucratic regulation, educational institution, and expenditure of public funds. Based on their dogma that there is no real difference between men and women (except in sex organs), they demand that males and females have identical treatment always. Thus, if fathers are not expected to stay home and care for their infant children, then neither should mothers be expected to do so; and, therefore, it becomes the duty of the government to provide kiddy-care centers to relieve mothers of that unfair and unequal burden.

The women's lib dogma demands that the courts treat sex as a "suspect" classification—just as race is now treated—so that no difference of treatment or separation between the sexes will ever be permitted, no matter how reasonable or how much it is desired by reasonable people.

The nonsense of these militant demands was illustrated by

21

the Department of Health, Education and Welfare (HEW) ruling in July, 1976, that all public school "functions such as father-son or mother-daughter breakfasts" would be prohibited because this "would be subjecting students to separate treatment." It was announced that violations would lead to a cutoff of federal assistance or court action by the Justice Department.

When President Gerald Ford read this in the newspaper, he was described by his press secretary as being "quite irritated" and as saying that he could not believe that this was the intent of Congress in passing a law against sex discrimination in education. He telephoned HEW Secretary David Mathews and told him to suspend the ruling.

The National Organization for Women, however, immediately announced opposition to President Ford's action, claiming that such events (fashion shows, softball games, banquets, and breakfasts) are sex-discriminatory and must be eliminated. It is clear that a prohibition against your right to make any difference or separation between the sexes anytime anywhere is a primary goal of the women's liberation movement.

No sooner had the father-son, mother-daughter flap blown over than HEW embroiled itself in another controversy by a ruling that an after-school choir of fifth and sixth grade boys violates the HEW regulation that bars single-sex choruses. The choir in Wethersfield, Connecticut, that precipitated the ruling had been established for boys whose "voices haven't changed yet," and the purpose was "to get boys interested in singing" at an early age so they would be willing to join coed choruses later. Nevertheless, HEW found that such a boy's chorus is by definition sex discriminatory.

The Positive Woman rejects the "gender-free" approach. She knows that there are many differences between male and female and that we are entitled to have our laws, regulations, schools, and courts reflect these differences and allow for reasonable differences in treatment and separations of activities that reasonable men and women want.

The Positive Woman also rejects the argument that sex discrimination should be treated the same as race discrimination. There is vastly more difference between a man and a woman than there is between a black and a white, and it is nonsense to adopt a legal and bureaucratic attitude that pretends that those differences do not exist. Even the United States Supreme Court has, in recent and relevant cases, upheld

22

"reasonable" sex-based differences of treatment by legislatures and by the military.[7]

(2) The women's lib legislative goals seek an irrational mandate of "equality" at the expense of justice. The fact is that equality cannot always be equated with justice, and may sometimes even be highly unjust. If we had absolutely equal treatment in regard to taxes, then everyone would pay the same income tax, or perhaps the same rate of income tax, regardless of the size of the income.

If we had absolutely equal treatment in regard to federal spending programs, we would have to eliminate welfare, low-income housing benefits, food stamps, government scholarships, and many other programs designed to benefit low-income citizens. If we had absolutely equal treatment in regard to age, then seventeen-year-olds, or even ten-year-olds, would be permitted to vote, and we would have to eliminate Social Security unless all persons received the same benefits that only those over sixty-two receive now.

Our legislatures, our administrative departments, and our courts have always had and still retain the discretion to make reasonable differences in treatment based on age, income, or economic situation. The Positive Woman believes that it makes no sense to deprive us of the ability to make reasonable distinctions based on sex that reasonable men and women want.

(3) The women's liberation movement demands that women be given the benefit of "reverse discrimination." The Positive Woman recognizes that this is mutually exclusive with the principle of equal opportunity for all. Reverse discrimination is based on the theory that "group rights" take precedence over individual rights, and that "reverse discrimination" (variously called "preferential treatment," "remedial action," or "affirmative action") should be imposed in order to compensate some women today for alleged past discriminations against other women. The word "quotas" is usually avoided, but it amounts to the same thing.

The fallacy of reverse discrimination has been aptly exposed by Professor Sidney Hook. No one would argue, he wrote, that because many years ago blacks and women were denied the right to vote, we should now compensate by giving them an extra vote or two, or by barring white men from voting at all.

But that is substantially what the women's liberationists are

23

demanding—and getting by federal court orders—in education, employment, and politics when they ask for "affirmative action" to remedy past discrimination.[8]

The Positive Woman supports equal opportunity for individuals of both sexes, as well as of all faiths and races. She rejects the theories of reverse discrimination and "group rights." It does no good for the woman who may have been discriminated against twenty-five years ago to know that an unqualified woman today receives preferential treatment at the expense of a qualified man. Only the vindictive radical would support such a policy of revenge.

(4) The women's liberation movement is based on the unproven theory that uniformity should replace diversity—or, in simpler language, the federalization of all remaining aspects of our life. The militant women demand that *all* educational institutions conform to federally determined rules about sex discrimination.

There is absolutely no evidence that HEW bureaucrats can do a better or fairer job of regulating our schools and colleges than local officials. Nor is there any evidence that individuals, or women, or society as a whole, would be better off under a uniform system enforced by the full power of the federal government than they would be under a free and competitive system, under local control, using diverse methods and regulations. It is hard to see why anyone would want to put more power into the hands of federal bureaucrats who cannot cope with the problems they already have.

The militant women demand that HEW regulations enforce a strict gender-free uniformity on all schools and colleges. Everything from sports to glee clubs must be coed, regardless of local customs or wishes. The militants deplore the differences from state to state in the laws governing marriage and divorce. Yet does anyone think our nation would be improved if we were made subject to a national divorce law devised by HEW?

The Positive Woman rejects the theory that Washington, D.C., is the fountainhead of all wisdom and professional skill. She supports the principle of leaving all possible control and discretion in the hands of local school and college officials and their elected boards.

(5) The women's liberation movement pushes its proposals

24

on the premise that everything must be neutral as between morality and immorality, and as between the institution of the family and alternate lifestyles: for example, that homosexuals and lesbians should have just as much right to teach in the schools and to adopt children as anyone else; and that illegitimate babies and abortions by married or single mothers should be accepted as normal behavior for teachers—and funded by public money.

A good example of the rabid determination of the militant radicals to push every law and regulation to the far-out limit of moral neutrality is the HEW regulation on sex discrimination that implements the Education Amendments of 1972. Although the federal statute simply prohibits sex discrimination, the HEW regulation (1) requires that any medical benefit program administered by a school or college pay for abortions for married and unmarried students, (2) prohibits any school or college from refusing to employ or from firing an unmarried pregnant teacher or a woman who has had, or plans to have, an abortion, and (3) prohibits any school or college from refusing admission to any student who has had, or plans to have, an abortion. Abortion is referred to by the code words "termination of pregnancy."[9]

This HEW regulation is illogical, immoral, and unauthorized by any reasonable reading of the 1972 Education Act. But the HEW regulation became federal law on July 18, 1975, after being signed by the president and accepted by Congress.

The Positive Woman believes that our educational institutions have not only the right, but the obligation, to set minimum standards of moral conduct at the local level. She believes that schools and colleges have no right to use our public money to promote conduct that is offensive to the religious and moral values of parents and taxpayers.

Neuterizing Society

A basic objective and tactic of the women's liberationists is to neuterize all laws, textbooks, and language in newspapers, radio, and television. Their friends in state legislatures are ordering computer printouts of all laws that use such "sexist" words as *man, woman, husband,* and *wife.* They are to be expunged and replaced with neuter equivalents. Some state legislators have acquiesced rather than face charges of "sexism." Others have rejected this effort and labeled it the silliness that it is.

The feminists look upon textbooks as a major weapon in their campaign to eliminate what they call our "sex-stereotyped society" and to restructure it into one that is sex-neutral from cradle to grave. Under liberationist demands, the Macmillan Publishing Company issued a booklet called "Guidelines for Creating Positive Sexual and Racial Images in Educational Materials." Its purpose is to instruct authors in the use of sex-neutral language, concepts, and illustrations in order to conform to the new Macmillan censorship code. (The McGraw-Hill Book Company has issued a similar pamphlet, "Guidelines for Equal Treatment of the Sexes.")

Henceforth, you may not say *mankind,* it should be *humanity.* You may not say *brotherhood,* it should be *amity. Manpower* must be replaced by *human energy; forefathers* should give way to *precursors. Chairman* and *salesman* are out; and "in" words are *chairperson* and *salesperson.*

You are forbidden to say "man the sailboat." The acceptable substitute is not given; presumably it is "person the sailboat." You must not say "the conscientious housekeeper dusts *her* furniture at least once a week"; you must say "*the* furniture," because otherwise you would imply that the housekeeper is a woman—and that would be intolerable. You may not say "the cat washed herself"; it must be "the cat washed itself," because it would be sexist to imply that the cat is female.

The section forbidding sexism in textbook illustrations is even more amusing. According to the Macmillan guidelines, males must be shown wearing aprons just as often as females. Father should be pictured doing household chores and nursing a sick child, mother working at her desk while dad clears the dining-room table, little girls reaching toward snakes instead of recoiling from them, boys crying or preening in front of a mirror, and fathers using hair spray.

Women must be shown participating actively "in exciting worthwhile pursuits," which, by apparent definition, do not include being a homemaker. The guidelines warn that books will not be tolerated that indicate that "homemaking is the true vocation for a woman."

The Macmillan guidelines reach the height of absurdity when they deliver a stern rebuke to the history book that refers

26

to Sacajawea as "an amazing Shoshoni Indian woman" because she led the Lewis and Clark expedition through the Rockies "with a young baby strapped to her back." According to the Macmillan guidelines, the use of the word *amazing* is intolerable sexist propaganda that perpetuates "the myth of feminine fragility." It is a pity that our school children can no longer be told that Sacajawea was "amazing" because the historical fact is that her physical accomplishment was unique.

The Macmillan guidelines reserve their most stinging rebuke for the four-letter word *lady*, terming it "distasteful" specifically because it connotes "ladylike" behavior.

The Macmillan guidelines are not only a good source of laughs, but are a healthy exposure to the hypocrisy of the liberals who pilloried the West Virginia parents who tried to censor obnoxious four-letter words from their children's textbooks. It all depends on which four-letter words you want to censor.

Baby-care doctor Benjamin Spock was one of those whom the feminists targeted as obnoxious because of the alleged "sexism" in his bestselling baby books. His principal offense was that, in advising mothers how to care for their babies, he repeatedly used the pronoun *he* instead of *she*. Obviously, it would be a semantic hurdle of significant magnitude to write a baby book and say "he or she" every time the author refers to the baby. Until women's liberationists became so vocal, normal mothers understood that *he* is used in the generic sense to mean babies of both sexes.

The feminists continued their campaign against Dr. Spock's "sexism" until they finally convinced him that modern liberated society should treat males and females exactly the same. In his latest book he eliminated "sexist" language. The only trouble was, Dr. Spock bought the whole bag of "liberation." He walked out on his faithful wife Jane, to whom he had been married for forty-eight years, and took up with a younger woman. Dr. Spock was truly "liberated" from traditional restraints.

It is no gain for women, for children, for families, or for America to propel us into a unisex society. Our strength is in our diversity, not in our sameness. Among the many social commentators who have always understood and respected the differences between the sexes was Alexis de Tocqueville, a Frenchman who traveled in the United States in the nineteenth century and wrote books still studied in our colleges. In his

Democracy in America, he described "How the Americans Understand the Equality of the Sexes":

There are people in Europe who, confounding together the different characteristics of the sexes, would make man and woman into beings not only equal but alike. They would give to both the same functions, impose on both the same duties, and grant to both the same rights; they would mix them in all things—their occupations, their pleasures, their business. It may readily be conceived that by thus attempting to make one sex equal to the other, both are degraded, and from so preposterous a medley of the works of nature nothing could ever result but weak men and disorderly women.

It is not thus that the Americans understand that species of democratic equality which may be established between the sexes. They admit that as nature has appointed such wide differences between the physical and moral constitution of man and woman, her manifest design was to give a distinct employment to their various faculties; and they hold that improvement does not consist in making beings so dissimilar do pretty nearly the same things, but in causing each of them to fulfill their respective tasks in the best possible manner. The Americans have applied to the sexes the great principle of political economy which governs the manufacturers of our age, by carefully dividing the duties of man from those of woman in order that the great work of society may be the better carried on....

As for myself, I do not hesitate to avow that although the women of the United States are confined within the narrow circle of domestic life, and their situation is in some respects one of extreme dependence, I have nowhere seen woman occupying a loftier position; and if I were asked, now that I am drawing to the close of this work, in which I have spoken of so many important things done by the Americans, to what the singular prosperity and growing strength of that people ought mainly to be attributed, I should reply: to the superiority of their women.[10]

II

Choosing Options and Opportunities

The Positive Woman of bygone years always had power and influence that were the envy of men. But whereas in the past her achievements were often limited by law, by custom, or by the daily drudgery of "women's work," the Positive Woman in America today has a near-infinite opportunity to control her own destiny, to reach new heights of achievement, and to motivate and influence others. Her potential is limited only by the artificial barriers erected by a negative view of herself or by the stultifying myths of the women's liberation movement.

The story is told about the ambitious young man who sought the secret of success from a wealthy merchant. The merchant counseled the youth, "Just keep jumping at all your opportunities." "But," queried the eager young man, "how will I recognize my opportunities?" "You won't," replied the merchant, "you just have to keep jumping."

To which Ann Landers, a Positive Woman, once added, echoing Thomas Edison, "Opportunities are usually disguised as hard work, so most people don't recognize them." She should know. She found the opportunity to build the most widely syndicated column in the world (810 newspapers) in a spot thousands of others had missed.

Rose Totino is a Positive Woman who recognized her opportunities when they were disguised as hard work and turned them into success in the best Horatio Alger tradition. She was the daughter of Italian immigrants, a child of poverty who had only one orange a year, on Christmas Eve. She shared one bicycle with six sisters and brothers and dropped out of school in the tenth grade to go to work at $2.50 per week doing house-work. In 1975 she sold her frozen food and pizza business to the Pillsbury Company for stock worth $22,190,000 and became a Pillsbury corporate vice-president.

Rose grew up with a spirit of loving generosity to her neighbors, always sharing whatever food she and her family had. The big success of her pizza business came in the last ten years, after she accepted Christ and began to witness to the Lord every day of her life. Here is what she says about woman's role:

> I'm not a women's libber. Why should women go from superiority to equality? Women always have been exalted in this country; now they want to be equal. I'm not a feminist. I enjoy being a woman. . . .
> Success is wanting what you get, not getting what you want.

The Positive Woman spends her time, ingenuity, and efforts seizing her opportunities—not whining about past injustices. The American woman today is guaranteed entree on the escalator to achievement by laws, by bureaucratic regulations, by court decisions, by the increased receptivity toward women in business and the professions, and by the reduced responsibilities of women in what has been traditionally known as women's work.

The real liberator of women in America is the free enterprise system, which has produced remarkable inventors who have lifted the drudgery of housekeeping from women's shoulders.

In other countries and in other eras, it was truly said that "Man may work from sunup to sundown, but woman's work is never done." Other women have labored every waking hour—preparing food on wood-burning stoves, making flour, baking bread in stone ovens, spinning yarn, making clothes, making soap, doing the laundry by hand, heating irons, making candles for light and fires for warmth, and trying to nurse their babies through illnesses without medical care.

The American free enterprise system has stimulated inventive geniuses to pursue their talents with the knowledge that they could keep the fruits of their labor and ideas. All Americans reap the profits, but women most of all. The great heroes of women's liberation are not the straggly haired women on television talk shows and picket lines, but Thomas Edison, who brought the miracle of electricity to our homes to give light and to run all those labor-saving devices—the equivalent, perhaps, of a half-dozen household servants for every American woman. Or Elias Howe, who gave us the sewing machine that resulted in ready-made clothing. Or Clarence Birdseye, who invented the process for freezing foods. Or Henry Ford, who mass-produced the automobile so that it came within the price reach of every American, man or woman.

A major occupation of women in other countries is doing their daily shopping for food, which requires carrying their own containers and standing in line at dozens of small shops. They buy only small portions because they can't carry very much and have no refrigerators or freezers to keep a surplus. Our American free enterprise system has given us the gigantic food and packaging industry and beautiful supermarkets, which provide an endless variety of foods, prepackaged for easy carrying, a minimum of waiting in line, and a minimum of cooking.

New York Times Moscow correspondent Hedrick Smith in his book *The Russians* gives graphic eye-witness descriptions of the dreary and unending daily chore of standing in line for everything one buys in the Soviet Union:

> The accepted norm is that the Soviet woman spends two hours in line, seven days a week. Personally, I have known of people who stood in line 90 minutes to buy four pineapples, and 3½ hours to buy three large heads of cabbage, only to find the cabbages were gone as they approached the front of the line. Lines can run from a few yards to nearly a mile. . . .
> Despite such ordeals, the instinctive reaction of a Russian woman when she sees a queue forming is to get in line immediately—even before she knows what is being sold.[1]

It isn't that bad, of course, in other countries. But shopping in other Western countries is incredibly inefficient by American standards. In the United States, women have long since been liberated from the slavery of standing in line for daily food and necessities.

Household duties have been reduced to only a few hours a day, leaving the American woman with plenty of time to moonlight in full- or part-time jobs, or to indulge to her heart's content in a wide array of interesting educational or cultural or homemaking activities.

"You've come a long way, baby," the Virginia Slims cigarette advertisements proclaim under illustrations showing women at the start of this century laboriously hand-scrubbing clothes and hanging them on the line. Militant women's liberationists did not produce automatic washers and dryers. It was the American competitive system that manufactured appliances cheap enough for the average American family to afford.

If the militant women have their way, they will kill the goose that laid the golden egg. Journalist John S. Knight reported that Wilma Scott Heidi, former president of the National Organization for Women, "would prefer to see business develop measures of what serves human needs—social, economic and cultural. She feels that the profit motive must go." The *Los Angeles Times* reported that Gloria Steinem stated at the University of California at Los Angeles: "We seek the elimination of the caste system and the overthrow of patriarchal values that underpin a wide variety of social systems. That would mean the abandonment of hierarchical, authority-based organizations of which the corporation is a prime example."[2]

The wide disparity between the social and economic status of American women and much of the rest of the world was one of the chief reasons why the International Women's Year conference in Mexico City in June, 1975, was an unviable gathering of irrelevant women in search of an improbable community of interest. What possible common ground could a few negative disgruntled American women's liberationists have with women in other parts of the world who have such genuine problems as hunger, lack of sanitation and medical care, a religious system that sanctions polygamy, a social system that requires women to veil their faces from men, or an economic system in which the women do all the manual and agricultural work, while the men reserve their energies for supervising, fighting, and drinking? The chief aim of American women seems to be to get out of the kitchen, while the fondest dream of women in the rest of the world is to acquire an American kitchen.

Not only were the goals of the women at the conference centuries apart, but communication itself was made difficult because many women did not respect customary rules of civilized discourse and resorted to trying to outshout each other or physically grab the microphones.

The Mexico City conference was just an international consciousness-raising session for bitter women from many countries to air their grievances—some real, some exaggerated, some imagined. A positive approach to the genuine problems of women in other countries would be to invite them to the United States so that we can lend them a helping hand up the ladder that American women have already successfully climbed.

American women are also especially fortunate to be the beneficiaries of the Judeo-Christian tradition, which accords a status to women unknown in the rest of the world. Our Judeo-Christian civilization has developed laws and customs that, since women must bear the physical consequences of the sex act, require men to assume other consequences. These laws and customs decree that a man must carry his share by physical protection and financial support of his children and of the woman who bears his children, and also by a code of behavior that benefits and protects both the woman and the children.

This is accomplished by the institution of the family. Our respect for the family as the basic unit of society, which is firmly ingrained in the laws and customs of our Judeo-Christian civilization, is the greatest single achievement in the entire history of women's rights. It assures a woman the precious right to keep and care for her own baby and to be supported and protected in the enjoyment of watching her baby grow and develop.

American women are also the beneficiaries of a tradition of special respect for women that flowered during the Christian age of chivalry. The honor and respect paid to Mary, the Mother of Christ, resulted in a new gallantry of treatment of all women.

This respect for women is not just the lip service that politicians pay to "God, Motherhood, and the Flag." It is not, as some youthful agitators seem to think, just a matter of opening doors for women, seeing that they are seated first, carrying their bundles, and helping them in and out of automobiles. Such good manners are merely the superficial evidences of a total attitude toward women which expresses itself in many more tangible ways.

In some African and Indian societies, the men strut around wearing feathers and beads and hunting and fishing, while the women do all the tiresome, manual drudgery, including tilling the soil, hewing wood, making fires, hauling water, and building dwellings—not to mention cooking, sewing, and caring for babies.

This is not the American way. In America, one of the first significant purchases a man makes is a ring for his bride, and the largest financial investment of his life is a home for her to live in. American husbands work hours of overtime to pay premiums on life insurance policies to provide for their wives' comfort when they are widows (benefits in which the husbands will never share). In India, by contrast, the problem of supporting the widow was taken care of for centuries by inducing her to commit *suttee* (flinging herself on her husband's funeral pyre).

Careers and Jobs

If we were to rank the factors that have influenced the significant shift of American women from domestic duties into other occupations, the reduction in labor required for the daily amenities of eating, washing, and wearing clothes must rank at the top of the list. Women's time was made available for other activities, paid or volunteer. Second in importance was the Great Depression of the thirties, which forced women to seek employment when the men in their families could not get jobs. Third was World War II, when women in large numbers began to fill jobs for which men were unavailable. Fourth, in our modern specialized economic system, women are frankly preferred for many positions in which their skills are superior to men, such as stenographers, telephone operators, airline hostesses, nurses, linguists, and certain factory inspection jobs.

Finally, a network of federal and state laws has enforced the principle of "equal pay for equal work." The federal Equal Employment Opportunity Act of 1972 is completely extensive. It applies to hiring, pay, and promotion, and establishes the enforcement agency called the Equal Employment Opportunity Commission (EEOC).

Under this commission, women have won multi-million dollar settlements against the largest companies in the country. When they won a $38 million settlement against AT&T, women got back pay for not having been paid as much as they should have been, back pay for not having been promoted as they should have been, and even back pay for jobs they did not

34

apply for because they thought they would not get them! What more could any woman want by way of federal legislation to enforce equal employment opportunity!

When women won a $30 million settlement against the big steel companies, they were mandated to fill 20 percent of their production jobs with women. It may be debatable as to whether it is advantageous for women to have 20 percent of the jobs in steel production, but in any event, the jobs are open to women who want them.

Women are now guaranteed access to credit on an equal basis with men. The Equal Credit Opportunity Act of 1974 fully covers this factor so vital in our credit-structured economy.

Likewise, women are guaranteed full opportunity in education on an equal basis with men. The Education Amendments of 1972 abolished discrimination on the basis of sex in all schools and colleges receiving any federal assistance, from kindergarten through graduate school. Not only can women attend law school and medical school, but some schools give women preferential treatment. Women are not barred from any professional or vocational training.

The net result is that the Positive Woman in America today faces a future in which her educational and employment options are unlimited. She can be a coal miner, a truck driver, an architectural engineer, a stockbroker; she can follow whatever career avenue her imagination and ambition lead her to select

Does this mean that every woman is paid as much as she is worth and educated to the limit of her potential? Of course not —any more than this is true of every man. Most women *and* men believe they are underpaid and that their real worth is underrecognized. Unfair discrimination exists in every walk of life. No law ever enjoys perfect enforcement. We have laws against murder, but murders still take place.

The legislative, administrative, and judicial machinery to give women a fair opportunity to reap life's economic rewards is all in place. The Positive Woman can put it in gear and drive forward at the time and place of her own choosing. The negative woman will be forever inhibited from forward movement so long as she keeps her psychological engine in neutral or reverse.

Women approaching employment are divided into the same

35

two basic groups as men: those who seek *jobs,* for which the return is money only, and those who seek *careers,* for which the return is money plus self-fulfillment. Like men, women divide themselves into these two groups on the basis of the obvious factors of education, aptitude, and ambition.

One of the endemic defects of the women's liberation movement is that it is mostly made up of women who think they should be television station managers or vice-presidents of General Motors, or hold positions of similar authority over other lesser mortals. They are living in a make-believe world in which they postulate that the ultimate fulfillment for all women is to spend their adult life in the paid-employment market. The big percentage of jobs in the world—both male and female—fulfill a need for money, but little else. Whether a woman's ambition, training, and skill lead her into a "job" or into a "career" will usually determine how eager she is to enter the paid-employment labor force and then stay in it all her life. It is an impudent presumption of the women's liberationists to assume that *all* women seek or find self-fulfillment in a lifetime in the paid-employment market.

This is because women have another career option available —one that is seldom recommended in "women's studies" courses or seminars—namely, marriage and motherhood. The desire for this career binds those who seek "jobs" and those who seek "careers" with a psychological bond that truly unites women of all disparate groups: educated and unskilled, rich and poor, black and white. The human problems involved in marriage and motherhood are common to women of all groups, but the problems of the job market can never be.

Virginia Slims, a source that must be considered at least friendly to the women's liberation movement, commissioned the Roper Organization to conduct an in-depth survey during 1974 of women's attitudes.[3] The survey showed that a majority of women would like to include both marriage and a career in their life plan, but that, when confronted with having to make a choice of marriage *or* a paid-employment career, only a tiny 2 percent would choose "career." Two-thirds of women feel strongly that "having a loving husband who is able to take care of me is much more important than making it on my own." That is probably an accurate assessment of women's attitudes.

The Virginia Slims statistic was translated into its human dimension by actress Lauren Bacall. She is one of many successful women who have been frank in admitting how her personal priorities impeded her professional career—and she has no regrets:

> I always wanted a career, but I also always wanted a home of my own, a husband, and children. I made up my mind long ago that when I did find them, they would come first. If my career interferes with our domestic life, it's best that I give it up. Bogie loves a home. He likes to come home to his meals, stay home, and share it with his friends.
>
> When I look around at some of the career girls I have met in Hollywood, I don't envy them. They make lots of money. They are famous. But they are the loneliest people in the world. Not all, but some. Big mansions and empty hearts. I don't want to end up the same way. If it's possible to combine a career and home, that's for me. The minute I see that it isn't working out, home I go and home I stay.[4]

Lauren Bacall wasn't lonely. She had Humphrey Bogart.

The women's liberation movement makes much of the fact that, despite laws requiring equal pay for equal work, statistics show that women hold only a small minority of the high-paying executive and professional positions. The statistics are accurate, but the reason is not discrimination. No person, man or woman, rises to those high-income ranks on a forty-hour week. Ask any successful doctor, lawyer, or business executive. They have invariably spent years working nights and weekends, bringing home briefcases bulging with work, and serving clients or customers in a steady stream outside of office hours.

Top business and professional men and women have all paid a big price for their success in terms of long hours every week, missed vacations, canceled social engagements, and a constant sacrifice of time with their families—in addition to the physical and mental strain demanded by the highly competitive rat race that sometimes causes heart attacks, high blood pressure, and early death or physical collapse.

For any man or woman who chooses that life, there is plenty of room at the top. The stakes are high, and it is a personal decision as to whether the rewards of money, power, and prestige are worth the sacrifices and the risks. Many men think they are. The plain fact is that most women don't. Why? It certainly is not because they lack a willingness to do hard and sustained work, and it probably is not even because they lack a capacity for competition. It is because, for most women, something else

37

comes first in their lives—namely, marriage and motherhood—and business or professional success does not rate high enough in their scale of values to permit it to steal so much time from the home. Many talented women may want to have some of both careers, but home remains primary in their scale of values, while a business or professional career is secondary.

The woman's allocation of career priorities necessarily limits the range of her financial return. There is no way, for example, that a married woman lawyer who puts in a forty-hour week or less and who opts out of her career for several years to have babies can ever earn the same income or achieve the same status in the professional world as a topflight lawyer, who typically devotes sixty hours a week to acquiring, serving, and retaining clients. There is nothing discriminatory about this differential. It is simply a matter of personal choice based on the different scales of male and female values. The situation should not cause "remedial" legislation or court action to abolish "discrimination," or whining complaints about how few lawyers or judges are female, but a mature acceptance of the different goals of men and women.

Another element to cope with in the matter of women rising to top executive and professional positions is the preferences of women themselves. The Gallup Poll reconfirmed in April, 1976, what every personnel manager has always known: by a ratio of six to one, women would rather have a man than a woman as their boss. Most women would rather deal with male than female doctors, lawyers, and bankers. Should a company be compelled to make one woman happy by promoting her to "foreperson," but make twenty women unhappy who do not want to accept her as their boss?

In the political field, women's liberationists cry copiously about the fact that women hold only a small minority of seats in Congress, state legislatures, and national, state, and local boards and commissions. The women's liberationists want such "discrimination" eliminated by allocating half the seats or posts to women.

Not only would this be a perversion of the electoral process, it would be based on a wholly faulty analysis. The fact that there may be only 18 women out of 535 members of Congress does not prove discrimination at all. There is no bar in any district or state to a woman's running and being elected, as many have proved by doing just that.

The chief handicap of women candidates today is the bad image of politically active women created by the liberationists. If the Bella Abzugs and other strident "spokespersons" of women's liberation would quietly fade away, dignified and capable women would have a better chance of being elected to public office.

The small number of women in Congress proves only that most women do not want to do the things that must be done to win election—drive all those thousands of miles, shake all those strangers' hands, eat all those third-rate chicken suppers, attend political meetings every night and weekend, subject themselves to press and political attacks that impugn their integrity and their motives, and face probes into personal life and finances. Most women say it isn't worth it.

It's all in your scale of values. For those who freely choose and want the highly competitive political life, it can be a rewarding career. But those who would be successful must be willing to accord a higher priority to the demands of their office and of their constituents than to those of home, family, and children. Ask the wife of any successful male politician and she will confirm that he has, indeed, paid this price.

A few women will make that choice and build a successful career. One who did is Chief Justice Susie Sharp of the North Carolina State Supreme Court. By an overwhelming majority, the voters in November, 1974, elected her the first woman state supreme court chief justice in the country, the culmination of a distinguished career as practicing lawyer, judge, and associate state supreme court justice.

But to think that women want, or should be encouraged, to choose such a full-time professional career in equal numbers with men is to misread what women want out of life. To allocate half the seats in governmental bodies to that small minority of women who choose a political career over home and family—in the mistaken notion that they represent *all* women —would be the world's most grievous abdication of authority by a supine majority to a militant minority.

Yet this is precisely what the militant women's liberationists demand. They shamelessly hurl on Republican and Democratic national nominating conventions, television station managers, and every other entity they feel they can intimidate, demands that women have a 50 percent quota of jobs and positions, and that the 50 percent consist of *their* kind of women.

Their arrogant demands are thinly veiled in such code words as "You must appoint only women who are sensitive to women's issues," or "You must exclude women who are just wives or Aunt Toms."

There is today an increasing number of women who are choosing a business or professional career instead of marriage. If they are Positive Women, they are usually successful and often develop into some of the most interesting of all women. As one in public relations work told me: "I've had three fascinating careers, and I'm planning a fourth after my company retires me. I've never had time to get married."

Such Positive Women have been succeeding for years in the business and professional world largely dominated by men. They did it by competing, not complaining. They've had the personal satisfaction of achievement. Because they are Positive Women, they are not defensive about their womanhood; they show no strain in their friendly relations with women and men. They enjoy being women and meeting the challenge of a man's world. Real estate is one of many fields where women have enjoyed outstanding success.

Furthermore, these Positive Women have the self-confidence that comes from having their peers recognize them as authentic achievers, and not as those who got their degrees or positions only because the college or company had to fill its "affirmative action" quota.

Dr. Dixy Lee Ray is another of the many Positive Women who have chosen a career over marriage and reaped the rewards of success and self-fulfillment. She is the marine biologist who was chairman of the United States Atomic Energy Commission, then the top science official in the State Department, and in 1976 was elected governor of the state of Washington.

An extremely talented and capable woman, Dr. Ray is a rare phenomenon of modern bureaucracy in that she retained her own individuality and her standards of dedication to public service despite the cunning maneuvers of the two most skillful bureaucrats in Washington, D.C., Dr. Henry Kissinger and Dr. James Schlesinger. They failed completely to pull her off course and to use her as an instrument of their power-grabbing purposes as they used so many men and then cowed them into silence. In June, 1975, when Secretary Kissinger deprived her bureau of the responsibility it had been delegated by Congress,

Dr. Ray departed from Washington with a courageous statement that was typical of her personal integrity and professional independence.

Among the Positive Women who have chosen the single life and had highly successful careers are the nuns who are hospital and school administrators. These women executives handle heavier responsibilities, direct the spending of more funds, plan more building and service expansion, and cope with more personnel problems than most businessmen in the country. Daily they prove that women can make outstanding executives if they devote themselves to developing that skill. Of course, it must be pointed out that these remarkable women deliberately chose that career over marriage and motherhood, and they make their work their full-time occupation.

Few women in history have ever known the career fulfillment that Mother Teresa has known. She is the Albanian nun who has made it her mission to minister to the poor and dying in Calcutta, India. The English scholar Malcolm Muggeridge, a convert to Christianity, described the impressive saintliness of this humble nun: "Something of God's love has rubbed off on Mother Teresa." She has become a living legend, acclaimed throughout the world—a career success and a happy woman by any standard. And Mother Teresa has said that men could never equal women in love and compassion.

The women's liberationists make the mistake of asking to be treated like men. This has become so ridiculous that many a man is afraid to show a career woman such customary courtesies as opening doors for her, standing when she comes into the room, or paying the restaurant check, for fear she will cut him down with an acid liberationist retort. The Positive Woman feels no need to be defensive about her womanhood. She wants to be treated like a woman, and she knows that her chance for success in a man's world is increased by requiring men to treat her like a woman.

Thus, a most successful Positive Woman, former Premier of Israel Golda Meir, who spent a lifetime attending men's meetings, once said that no man ever told a dirty story in her presence. Men will respect and follow the leadership of such a woman, whose very demeanor requires men to respect her womanhood. Those whose language asks that they be treated like a man, as, for example, Bella Abzug, are not likely to become leaders of men or women.

41

The Double Career

Can a woman successfully combine marriage and mother-hood with a career or job? Some, such as Katharine Hepburn, say no:

> People say to me, "Too bad you didn't have any children." Well, I'm not dumb enough to think I could have handled that situation because I'm a totally concentrated person. I can do one thing at a time. I'm a One-Track Charlie.
>
> If I had a kid, and the kid was desperately ill, and I had an opening night—what am I gonna do? I would be useless. If your mind is on something else, and you are involved in an emotional relationship—you are useless. If someone needs you, they need YOU!
>
> That's why I think women have to choose. I remember making the decision, "Well, I'll never marry and have children. I want to be a star, and I don't want to make my husband my victim. And I certainly don't want to make my children my victims."
>
> I think this frantic desire to make the sexes the same thing is just—well, they're totally different. I think women have to be realistic to figure out what their position is. It cannot be the same as a man's—it *cannot* be the same. She has to have the child. Nurse the child. Watch the child. Degrading that position is a poor notion, I think.[5]

Another who says no is Joanne Woodward, Academy Award-winning actress and wife of Paul Newman. In a June, 1975, interview, she said one has "to be inhuman or superhuman" to combine a career and motherhood, asserting,

> I don't know one person who does both successfully, and I know a lot of working mothers. . . .
>
> If I had it to do all over again, I would make a decision one way or the other. My career has suffered because of the children and my children have suffered because of my career.

When a mother combines two careers, she remains the psychological parent, that is, the one who always feels a direct personal responsibility for the whereabouts and feelings of each child. "Equal parenting" does not work—the maternal tuning in never turns off. The author of a recent survey of working mothers concluded that "almost all the working mothers I interviewed were overworked and tired; many were lonely. Many found it difficult to pinpoint the cause of their distress."[6]

When a wife takes a job outside the home, she pays a high price in freedom because she actually is working two jobs. The *Chicago Tribune* (February 23, 1976) reported that a team of Northwestern University sociologists found in 1976 that the working wife continues to do 80 to 90 percent of the household duties. Working wives routinely put in eight hours at their job and come home and work five more hours. The feminist movement for equality in household duties has not made much of a dent.

Some Positive Women have nevertheless succeeded at this seemingly impossible task. Among those who come to mind is Anne Morrow Lindbergh, the wife of one of America's twentieth-century heroes, Charles Lindbergh, and mother of six children. During the 1930s, Anne Lindbergh earned a reputation as a flier and adventurer in her own right. She later became an extremely successful author.

Another wife and mother who built a successful career is author-historian and two-time Pulitzer Prize winner Barbara Tuchman. When she addressed her fellow alumnae at Radcliffe College in 1975, she refuted a basic fallacy among women's liberationists—the tendency to blame "society" for their personal problems and shortcomings. It's easy to see why Mrs. Tuchman succeeded with this positive philosophy of life:

> I had no idea that growing up female in America was a position of slavery. Not that I was always happy; I often was very unhappy, even miserable. But I always thought that that was due to personal failings. If a boy didn't invite me to dance or go on a date, I thought that was my own fault, not society's. I didn't know that to be a woman was really a very terrible fate. In fact, I thought we had an advantage. I thought that the capacity to recreate life, to create another life, which was what the Bible gave to God and Nature gave to women, gave us a superiority over men. I don't know why; I just grew up with that idea. I thought it was fine to be a woman. As you can see, I was ignorant. . . .
>
> I didn't feel that anyone was repressing my potential. It's true that I had the good fortune to be economically comfortable, but what I did with it, I did alone; nobody helped me. I never asked for help; it just never occurred to me that someone ought to help me. I didn't need a role model. . . .
>
> I always wonder when I read in the papers and magazines especially this year, International Women's Year, why young women feel their capacities have been repressed and that "they," some unnamed "they," have prevented them from fulfilling their potential. What's to prevent it? If you have energy and the drive, you're going to do something with it.[7]

43

Princess Pale Moon, the Cherokee Indian soprano who has thrilled many audiences, including in 1976 the Olympics and the Republican National Convention, offers pertinent refutation to those women who mistakenly think they can find "dignity" or "self-esteem" in legislation rather than within themselves:

> Poor self-image is the number-one problem of women. It used to be my biggest problem until I realized that the solution is in God's love and in working to fulfill the special mission He has planned for your life.

Pale Moon's number-one career is as a wife and the mother of three sons, Michael Flying Eagle, Robbie Swift Arrow, and John Little Bear.

Miss Frances Knight (in private life, Mrs. Wayne Parrish) has survived and succeeded in the labyrinths of the federal bureaucracy through so many administrations that she has become a living legend. In the sea of red ink that engulfs the federal government, hers is the only agency that ends every year with a healthy budget surplus. She is the career director of the United States Passport Office, and her remarkably efficient operation is further proof that women can rise on their own merits to executive positions.

Surely one of the outstanding Positive Women in the world is Margaret Thatcher, British Conservative Party leader, wife and mother of twins. She was a graduate chemist, then became a lawyer. She was elected to the House of Commons in 1959 and became leader of the opposition in February, 1975, by defeating former Prime Minister Edward Heath.

Mrs. Thatcher is obviously capable, articulate, decisive, and a leader of men and women. What kind of woman is she? Those who know her say that the "most operative" word to describe her is *lady.* She is an old-fashioned, proper, traditional lady. And she cooks breakfast every morning for her husband (in contrast to Mrs. Gerald Ford, who stayed in bed while her husband cooked his own breakfast during the many years he was a congressman).

Many wives have started successful careers after their husbands passed away or their children were grown. Many women in Congress were first elected as widows to serve in the seats previously held by their husbands, and then remained for decades. Among the outstandingly successful ones in recent years were Senator Margaret Chase Smith of Maine, Congresswoman Marguerite Stitt Church of Illinois, and Congresswoman Leonor K. Sullivan of Missouri.

The first person born in the United States to be canonized by the Catholic Church, Elizabeth Seton, was an early nineteenth-century woman who successfully combined all roles in her all too brief life. A wife and mother of five children, she embarked on a new career after her husband's death, founding the Sisters of Charity.

Margery Hurst, often called Britain's most successful businesswoman, began her career after her husband left her when her baby was three weeks old. She began typing at home, opened a public typing office, and then an employment agency for typists. Today she is head of a company with 220 branches all over the world and a value of several million pounds on the London Stock Exchange.

There are many Positive Women today who have been able to combine a career in marriage and in the business, professional, academic, or political worlds. Most of them will tell you that it isn't easy, but it is possible for an ingenious and hardworking woman. The ones who are able to sustain the pace and still find happiness, however, are those who establish a set of priorities under which business or professional demands must always give way to home and family whenever there is a conflict.

Marriage and Motherhood

Marriage and motherhood have always been the number-one career choice of the large majority of women. Are they still a viable career for the modern woman? Do they represent servitude or fulfillment? Are they, as the women's liberation movement would have us believe, an anachronism from a bygone era, the institutionalized serfdom (or "legalized prostitution") from which women must be freed if they are to find their own identity and self-fulfillment?

What is it that the women's liberation movement invites women to be liberated from? An objective reading of the liberation movement literature compels the conclusion that the answer must be marriage, home, husband, family, and children—because, by definition, those are all evidences of the "second-

45

class status" of women. The movement literature paints marriage as slavery, the home as a prison, the husband as the oppressor, family as an anachronism no longer relevant to woman's happiness, and children as the daily drudgery from which the modern woman must be freed in order to pursue more fulfilling careers.

Midge Decter closeted herself for weeks with women's "movement" literature and the result was her *New Chastity and Other Arguments Against Women's Liberation.*[8] She distilled the dreary essence of the basic premises of women's liberation, such as that women are the victims of a vast societal conspiracy spearheaded by male supremacists, and that marriage is the ultimate act of prostitution in which women barter their bodies and services for economic security. Based on firsthand sources, she accurately concluded:

> The biggest of all put-downs of women is the movement's own literature. It's all there, so completely that women don't need any put-down by men. . . . The women's liberation movement does not belong to the history of feminism, but to the history of radicalism.

Long before women's lib came along and made *housewife* a term of derision, it had its own unique dignity. The 1933 edition of the *Oxford English Dictionary* defined a housewife as "a woman (usually, a married woman) who manages or directs the affairs of her household; the mistress of a family; the wife of a householder. Often (with qualifying words), a woman who manages her household with skill and thrift, a domestic economist."

A housewife is a home executive: planning, organizing, leading, coordinating, and controlling. She can set her own schedule and standards and have freedom of choice to engage in everything from children to civic work, politics to gardening. What man on a job can do that?

Marriage and motherhood are not for every woman, but before a young woman rejects it out of hand, she should give it fair consideration as one of her available options.

What does a woman want out of life? If you want to love and be loved, marriage offers the best opportunity to achieve your goal. Men may want, or think they want, a cafeteria selection of lunchcounter sex. But most women continue to want what the popular song calls "a Sunday kind of love." A happy marriage is the perfect vehicle for the Positive Woman. Marriage and

46

motherhood give a woman new identity and the opportunity for all-round fulfillment as a woman.

Are you looking for security—emotional, social, financial? Nothing in this world is sure except death and taxes, but marriage and motherhood are the most reliable security the world can offer.

The Ten Commandments adjure us: "Honor thy father and thy mother that thy days may be long upon the land." In the normal courses of human life, the young and healthy eventually grow old, sick, senile, and helpless. The aged and weary become dependent on the younger generation to provide love, compassion, and material aid—not to speak of the regular checks officially labeled "social security." Motherhood provides children who, in their turn, will honor you in your declining years.

Do you want the satisfaction of achievement in your career? No career in the world offers this reward at such an early age as motherhood. In the business or professional world, a man or a woman may labor for years, or even decades, to acquire the satisfaction of accomplishment. A mother reaps that reward within months of her labor when she proudly shows off her healthy and happy baby. She can have the satisfaction of doing her job well—and being recognized for it.

It is generally conceded that former Israeli Premier Golda Meir is the outstanding career woman of our time. She achieved more in a man's world than any woman in any country—and she did it on sheer ability, not on her looks or her legs. The Gallup Poll repeatedly identified her as "the most-admired woman" in the world. Yet Golda Meir said without hesitation that having a baby is the most fulfilling thing a woman can ever do, and she put down the women's liberationists as a bunch of "bra-burning nuts."

Mrs. Meir is correct. If young women think that there are greater career satisfactions in being elected to important positions, traveling to exciting faraway places, having executive authority over large numbers of people, winning a big lawsuit, or earning a financial fortune than there are in having a baby, they are wrong. None of those measures of career success can compare with the thrill, the satisfaction, and the fun of having and caring for babies, and watching them respond and grow under a mother's loving care. More babies multiply a woman's joy.

Consider another highly successful career woman: Oriana

47

Fallaci, the Italian journalist whose interviews with heads of state are the envy of most reporters and whose financial success in her chosen profession has brought her two homes in Italy and an apartment in Manhattan. When she gave a personal interview to the *New York Times,* she conceded that the crushing disappointment of her life is that she never had a baby. Even though she reached the pinnacle of her profession, career success was not enough for her self-fulfillment as a woman. She still yearns to satisfy her natural maternal urge.

Amelia Earhart has been a longtime heroine of feminists because she lived such an independent and exciting life. Yet when her true story was dramatized on national television in October, 1976, she was shown cuddling another woman's baby —and wishing it were her own.

One of the most successful writers of the twentieth century was Taylor Caldwell. *Family Weekly* asked her if it didn't give her solid satisfaction to know that her novel *Captains and the Kings* was to be seen as a nine-hour television production. She replied:

> There is no solid satisfaction in any career for a woman like myself. There is no home, no true freedom, no hope, no joy, no expectation for tomorrow, no contentment. I would rather cook a meal for a man and bring him his slippers and feel myself in the protection of his arms than have all the citations and awards and honors I have received worldwide, including the Ribbon of the Legion of Honor and my property and my bank accounts.

In unguarded moments, women's liberationists often reveal the womanly desires lurking behind their negative attitude toward men and marriage. One who heard me extol the rewards of marriage and motherhood could not restrain the tears in her eyes even in front of live television cameras. Another, with a glamorous network television job, whispered off camera: "I'd rather be scrubbing floors in my own home than working on this program." A third said, "If you find one of those nice guys who would like to support a wife, please bring him around; I'd like to meet him." A fourth conceded in a public debate, "I envy the happily married woman."

Mrs. Ronald Reagan summed it up in a November, 1975, interview: "I believe a woman's real happiness and fulfillment come from within her home with a husband and children."

Anne Morrow Lindbergh spoke for the big majority of women when she described her own priorities in *Hour of Gold, Hour of Lead:*

> To be deeply in love is, of course, a great liberating force and the most common experience that frees—or seems to free —young people. The loved one is the liberator. Ideally, both members of a couple in love free each other to new and different worlds. I was no exception to the general rule. The sheer fact of finding myself loved was unbelievable and changed my world, my feelings about life and myself. I was given confidence, strength, and almost a new character. The man I was to marry believed in me and what I could do, and consequently, I found I could do more than I realized, even in that mysterious outer world that fascinated me but seemed unattainable. He opened the door to "real life" and although it frightened me, it also beckoned. I had to go. . . .
> The first months of motherhood were totally normal, joy-ful, and satisfying and I would have been content to stay home and do nothing else but care for my baby. This was "real life" at its most basic level.

Marriage and motherhood, of course, have their trials and tribulations. But what lifestyle doesn't? If you look upon your home as a cage, you will find yourself just as imprisoned in an office or a factory. The flight from the home is a flight from yourself, from responsibility, from the nature of woman, in pursuit of false hopes and fading illusions.

If you complain about servitude to a husband, servitude to a boss will be more intolerable. Everyone in the world has a boss of some kind. It is easier for most women to achieve a harmonious working relationship with a husband than with a foreman, supervisor, or office manager.

The women's liberationists point to the Bible as proof that marriage forces women into a subservient role from which they must be liberated. The feminists get livid at any reading of Ephesians 5, wherein Saint Paul says: "Wives, submit your-selves unto your own husbands, as unto the Lord. For the husband is the head of the wife, even as Christ is the head of the church." The fringe group called Saint Joan's Alliance of-ten pickets in front of churches when Saint Paul is scheduled to be read at the Sunday service.

The first answer to these anti-Scripture agitators is that Ephesians also states:

> Husbands, love your wives, even as Christ also loved the
> church, and gave Himself for it. . . . Let everyone of you in
> particular so love his wife even as himself; and the wife see
> that she reverence her husband.

The Positive Woman recognizes that there is a valid and
enduring purpose behind this recognition of different roles for
men and women which is just as relevant in the twentieth
century as it was in the time of Saint Paul.

Any successful vehicle must have one person at the wheel
with ultimate responsibility. When I fly on a plane or sail on a
ship, I'm glad there is one captain who has the final responsibility and can act decisively in a crisis situation. A family cannot be run by committee. The committee system neutralizes a
family with continuing controversy and encumbers it with
psychological impedimenta. It makes a family as clumsy and
slow as a hippopotamus (which might be defined as a race-
horse designed by a committee).

Every successful country and company has one "chief executive officer." None successfully functions with responsibility
equally divided between cochairmen or copresidents. The
United States has a president and a vice president. They are not
equal. The vice president supports and carries out the policies
enunciated by the president. Likewise with the presidents and
vice-presidents of all business concerns. Vice-presidents can
and do have areas of jurisdiction delegated to them, but there is
always one final decision maker. The experience of the ages
has taught us that this system is sound, practical, and essential
for success. The republic of ancient Rome tried a system of two
consuls of equal authority, and it failed.

If marriage is to be a successful institution, it must likewise
have an ultimate decision maker, and that is the husband. Seen
in this light, the laws that give the husband the right to establish the domicile of the marriage and to give his surname to his
children are good laws designed to keep the family together.
They are not anachronisms from a bygone era from which
wives should be liberated in the name of equality. If a woman
does not want to live in her husband's home, she is not entitled
to the legal rights of a wife. Those women who preach that a
a wife should have the right to establish her own separate
domicile do not stay married very long. That "equal right" is
simply incompatible with a happy lifetime marriage.

The women's liberationists look upon marriage as an institution of dirty dishes and dirty diapers. They spend a lot of energy writing marriage contracts that divide up what they consider the menial, degrading chores. The much quoted "Shulmans' marriage agreement," for example, includes such provisions as "Husband does dishes on Tuesday, Thursday and Sunday. Wife does Monday, Wednesday and Saturday, Friday is split. . . ," and "wife strips beds, husband remakes them." If the baby cries in the night, the chore of "handling" the baby is assigned as follows: "Husband does Tuesday, Thursday and Sunday. Wife does Monday, Wednesday and Saturday, Friday is split. . . ." Presumably, if the baby cries for his mother on Tuesday night, he would be informed that the marriage contract prohibits her from responding.

It is possible, in such a loveless home, that the baby would never call for his mother at all. Most wives remember those years of diapers and tiny babies as the happiest of their lives.

Are dirty dishes all that bad? It's all in whether you wake up in the morning with a chip on your shoulder or whether you have a positive mental attitude. One happy wife I know has this poem hanging on her kitchen wall:

> Thank God for dirty dishes,
> They have a tale to tell.
> While others may go hungry
> We're eating very well.
> With home, health and happiness,
> I wouldn't want to fuss;
> By the stack of the evidence,
> God's been very good to us.

If you think diapers and dishes are a never-ending, repetitive routine, just remember that most of the jobs outside the home are just as repetitious, tiresome, and boring. Consider the assembly-line worker who pulls the same lever, pushes the same button, or inspects thousands of identical bits of metal or glass or paper, hour after weary hour; the stenographer who turns out page after page of typing; the telephone operator; the retail clerk who must repeatedly bite her lip because "the customer is always right."

Many people take such jobs because they need or want the money. But it is ludicrous to suggest that they are more self-fulfilling than the daily duties of a wife and mother in the home. The plain fact is that most women would rather cuddle a

51

baby than a typewriter or factory machine. Not only does the baby provide a warm and loving relationship that satisfies the woman's maternal instinct and returns love for service, but it is a creative and growing job that builds for the future. After twenty years of diapers and dishes, a mother can see the results of her own handiwork in the good citizen she has produced and trained. After twenty years of faithful work in the business world, you are lucky if you have a good watch to show for your efforts.

Those who want to be hermits and live in isolation are welcome to make that choice. Most people want and need human companionship in facing life's trials. Family living requires many social compromises, but it is worth the price, especially for women. The loneliness of career success without a family was poignantly described by champion golfer Carol Mann, who told a *New York Times* reporter: "Life is nothing more than a mattress, a box spring, a bathroom, and four walls. You say to yourself, 'Is that all there is?' And you cry a lot." She has banked half a million dollars from golf tournament prizes, but she cries into her pillow as she travels from motel to motel.

The most recent sociological phenomenon to receive the attention of the statisticians is the fact that young women are dropping out of motherhood at a landslide rate; hospitals are closing their maternity wards and school enrollment has dropped by a million and a half in the last five years.

On the average, all young women are having fewer children, four-year-college women graduates are having still fewer, and the graduates of the colleges with the highest academic standards are having the least of all. According to the latest United States Census Bureau report, 17 percent of married women between the ages of twenty-five and twenty-nine are childless. But 86 percent of the married graduates of Radcliffe College (the women's division of Harvard University) in that same age group are childless.[9] Samuel L. Blumenfeld observed in his book *The Retreat from Motherhood:*

> The symptoms are all around us. *Parents* magazine is down to a meager shadow of its former self. *Cosmopolitan,* the magazine of the liberated single woman, is fat and prosperous, and *Playgirl* features center foldouts of nude men. Few of the women's magazines show pictures of infants. The motherly virtues are ignored; the wifely love-making virtues are played up. Pictures of active glamourous women pursu-

ing careers in the man's world are everywhere. Articles about
the woman holding her man with sexual know-how and se-
ductiveness are abundant. Here and there an infant appears.
Husband and wife, and unmarried couples, are now so busy
making love to each other that they have little time for children at all.[10]

Many causes are advanced for the plummeting birth rates;
the million abortions that take place every year, the widespread
use of the Pill, the large influx of women into the labor force.
It is likely that the principal cause is the propaganda of the
women's liberation movement that motherhood is the least
attractive role a woman can choose, and that the work force
offers more rewards and more fulfillment. Many causes are
advanced for the apparent disintegration of the institution of
marriage. It is likely that the principal cause is the refusal of
young women to have babies. Why should a man marry a
woman who refuses to be a mother to his children? He can get
everything else he wants from women at a price much cheaper
than marriage.

In his *Washington Post* column of December 18, 1976, William Raspberry described the present retreat from motherhood
like this:

> A hundred years from now, we'll look back at this period
> and wonder how we got so foolishly and so hopelessly side-
> tracked en route to sexual equality. We'll look back, that is, if
> there is anybody around to look back.
>
> For if the present trend continues, we will reach the point
> where no sane woman would even consider having a baby,
> nor would any sensitive man dream of inflicting pregnancy
> upon her. . . .
>
> The trend seems to be growing most rapidly among those
> women with the most education. And since more and more
> women are seeking higher education these days, we may be
> looking toward a future in which having babies will be con-
> sidered as dumb as sponsoring debutante balls, giving tea
> parties, doing volunteer work and other traditionally female
> enterprises.

The Price of a Happy Marriage

With the high divorce rates of today, is a happy, lifetime
marriage a realistically attainable goal?

Of course it is—if you have a positive mental attitude. In the first place, the odds aren't as bad as you have been led to believe, because they include second and third divorces by the same persons. The percentage of first marriages that last a lifetime is thus much higher than any popularly circulated statistics indicate.

In their attack on marriage and the home, the women's liberationists tell young women that *Cinderella* and all fairy tales in which the girl meets her Prince Charming and they "live happily ever after" are a myth and a delusion. One thing is sure. If you make up your mind that you will never find your "Prince Charming," you won't. If you decide in advance that it is impossible to "live happily ever after," you won't. It all *can* happen to you, however, if you make up your mind that it *will* happen. I *know*—because it happened to me.

A happy marriage is truly a pearl of great price, but it isn't something to be discovered by searching in faraway places. Nor is it like a lucky strike for oil or gold. It is like a garden that yields a good crop when the seed is planted and the ground is cultivated regularly. Marriage is like pantyhose; it is what you put into it that makes the difference.

If the recipe for a happy marriage required rare, hard-to-get ingredients or some sophisticated training, marriage would have died out centuries ago. For a woman to build a happy marriage, she does not need beauty, a good figure, gorgeous gams, a high IQ, a dumb look, money, or popularity with other men. All those qualities may make a man look around and notice her, but none will build or hold a lasting relationship.

The Positive Woman knows that there are two main pillars of a happy marriage and that she has the capability to build both. The first is that a wife must appreciate and admire her husband. Whereas a woman's chief emotional need is active (i.e., to love), a man's prime emotional need is passive (i.e., to be appreciated or admired).

The Positive Woman recognizes this fundamental difference and builds her male/female relationship accordingly. She knows that this does not in any sense make her inferior, but that it is one key to personal fulfillment for both herself and her husband. Knowledge of this factor gives the Positive Woman the power to build and retain that most fragile but most rewarding of all human relationships, the happy marriage.

It is really just as easy as it sounds. Those who fight it, or try to bypass it or suppress it, face endless frustration and battles that lead to bitter dead ends. How often have you thought, as you noticed a contented couple, "What on earth does he see in her?" The answer is always very simple: She knows how to make him feel like a man—and to remember always that she is a woman.

Is this degrading to the wife? Humiliating? Subservient? Or any of the other extravagant liberationist adjectives? How ridiculous! It is just the application of the Golden Rule with a simple male/female variation. Most women think that the prize is worth the price.

A satisfying and rewarding relationship between a man and a woman can last through the years only if she is willing to give him the appreciation and the admiration his manhood craves. There are a thousand ways a woman can devise—public and private, obvious and subtle, physical and intellectual. It makes little difference how—so long as it is personal, pervasive, perennial, and genuine.

Take, for example, two such totally different women as Queen Victoria and Katharine Hepburn. Although poles apart in morals and milieu, they were alike in being extremely strongminded in temperament and independent in action. Both spoke with the voice of authority and were forceful to the point of being domineering in their dealings with their fellow human beings, male and female. Except for one person, that is. Victoria's relationship with her husband, Prince Albert, was that of the dutiful wife, deferring always to her husband's wishes in their domestic partnership.

Recent revelations of Katharine Hepburn's twenty-seven-year love affair with Spencer Tracy (who had a wife) show that, to him alone in all the world, this assertive, headstrong, free-thinking spitfire of a woman was submissive and more abnegating than any wife this side of the Orient. She often sat at his feet when they were together, and metaphorically, she was always there. The bond that pulled them together was the abundance of admiration she lavished on him.[11] A really Positive Woman, she had enough self-confidence that she could afford to accord to her man a preeminence in their personal relationship.

Among the dozens of fallacies of the women's liberation movement is the cluster of mistaken notions that traditional marriage is based on the wife's submerging her identity in her husband's, catering to his every whim, binding herself to seven days and nights a week inside the four walls of the home, stultifying her intellectual or professional or community interests, and otherwise reducing herself to the caricature of the dumb, helpless blonde, or a domestic servant.

What nonsense. It is true (and properly so) that the husband is naturally possessive about his wife's sexual favors, but he is seldom possessive of his wife's mind, time, or talents. A Positive Man is delighted to have his wife pursue her talents and spend her time however she pleases. The more she achieves, the prouder he is—*so long as* he knows that he is Number One in her life, and that she needs him.

A man who fights the competitive battle every day does not want to compete with his wife on the same terms that he competes with other men and women in the business world. He wants the security of knowing that he doesn't have to compete against his wife. However, he is perfectly happy to have her compete against others if she wants to join the competitive world—*so long as* he knows that she admires and needs him.

Actually, the total submersion of a wife's identity in her husband's can become more offensive to the husband than to the wife. Many marriages have gone on the rocks when a wife, with no substantive interests in life other than her husband, nags and complains about the time he spends on his growing career instead of on social or family engagements that include her. The marriage is on firmer footing if she develops her own interests. A successful marriage is possessive in regard to sexual fidelity, but possessiveness about personal identity, allocation of time, and life's ordinary routine can crush all the spontaneity out of a loving relationship.

One way of handling decision making in a marriage is to divide jurisdictions between husband and wife. The story is told about the husband who proudly told his friends: "When my wife and I were married, we agreed that I would make all the major decisions, and she would make the minor ones. I decide what legislation Congress should pass, what treaties the president should sign, and whether the United States should stay in the United Nations. My wife makes the minor decisions —such as how we spend our money, whether I should change my job, where we should live, and where we go on our vacations."

The Positive Woman is skillful enough to draw the jurisdictional line at the most advantageous point in *her* marriage. She

56

acquired the key to her power when she erected that first pillar —admiration and appreciation of her husband as a man, as provider and protector, as the father of her children, and, yes, even as head of the household. The woman who goes into marriage thinking she can make it a mathematically equal fifty-fifty partnership in every decision and activity will come out on the short end every time.

The second pillar of a happy marriage is cheerfulness. No other quality can do so much to ensure a happy marriage as a happy disposition.

Life is full of problems and every one has his or her share. A great part of most people's time and energy is occupied with trying to cope with financial problems, health problems, social problems, and emotional problems—their own and those of their families. You may think that you are the first person in the world who ever faced tragic or intransigent circumstances, but you are not. Everyone's own problems always seem the most momentous, the most insoluble, and the most unjust.

However, no problems have ever been solved by a bad disposition, a gloom-and-doom outlook on life, or cross and angry behavior toward spouse, family, or friends. When an interviewer said to opera star Beverly Sills "You're always so happy —how do you do it?" she told him, no, she isn't always happy, but she is always *cheerful.* She has one retarded child, another child who is deaf, and she herself has been operated on for cancer. But she's always cheerful!

A cheerful disposition can guide you over countless obstacles. A wife's cheerful disposition will draw her husband like a magnet. Why would a husband want to stop off at the local bar instead of coming straight home? Unless he has already become addicted to alcohol, the subconscious reason is probably because everyone there is cheerful and no one is nagging him. If home is to have a greater lure than the tavern, the wife must be at least as cheerful as the waitress. The Bacharach/David lyrics are a good reminder to wives: "Hey, little girl, comb your hair, fix your makeup, soon he will open the door. Don't think because there's a ring on your finger, you needn't try any more."

One of the mistaken pieces of advice often given young people is "be yourself." Maybe you are a hard-to-get-along-with person with an irritable disposition who spends the evening reciting and reliving the troubles of the day and blaming them

57

on others. Don't "be yourself." Be the person you would like to be—a cheerful person who sheds a little sunshine into an otherwise gloomy day, who sees the silver lining in every cloud, who keeps a sense of humor in the face of every reverse. A cheerful disposition will keep a happy marriage decades longer than a pretty face. Men may like to watch a beautiful woman like Greta Garbo in the movies, but she is not the type of woman men marry or stay married to. Men choose and love the cheerful over the beautiful and the wealthy. Miss Garbo never married.

The Middle Years

Does the career of marriage and motherhood give a woman an empty life in her middle years when her children are grown and she is left in an empty nest?

One of Marilyn Monroe's better movies was a delightful comedy called *The Seven Year Itch*. It poked fun at the alleged pitfalls of a marriage during its seventh year, especially when a luscious blonde walks on the scene. The women's liberation movement has caused a "twenty-year itch" that is having a tragic effect. Playing on the terrors and the trauma of the menopausal years and the empty-nest syndrome, the women's liberation movement is precipitating marriage crises and collapses among this age group by cutting otherwise contented women loose from past ties and shipping them out alone onto uncharted waters.

A woman in her middle years who has too much time on her hands because of a successful and indulgent husband and who has not yet found a service or a cause to occupy the place that her children once did is a ripe candidate for the disease called women's liberation. She has plenty of time to feel sorry for herself and to magnify her real or imagined grievances. She stews herself into a belief that her life is too humdrum and routine, that her "personhood" is unfulfilled, and that she can walk out into an exciting Never-Never Land in search of a new identity. The grass is always greener on the other side of the street.

Women's liberationists operate as Typhoid Marys carrying a germ called lost identity. They try to persuade wives that they have missed something in life because they are known by their husband's name and play second fiddle to his career.

Mrs. Billy Graham said that she has never had an identity crisis "although I am known as Billy's wife, when I was growing up I was Dr. Nelson Bell's daughter, and then I was Gigi's mother, Anne's mother, Bunny's mother, Franklin and Ned's mother." She said that the Christian woman "is the most truly liberated. She can be liberated behind a sinkful of dirty dishes or a load of dirty clothes. She is free to do what God has called her to do." Mrs. Graham added that the women's liberation movement is "turning into men's lib because we are freeing them from their responsibilities. I think we are being taken for a ride."

Judge Beatrice Mullaney of Massachusetts, who handled more than 10,000 divorce, separation, and custody cases during her nearly twenty years on the bench, blames the women's liberation movement for soaring divorce rates and the breakdown in American family life. Upon her retirement from the bench she said:

> Women are anxious to exercise the freedom promoted by the women's liberation movement—and the result is dissolution of marriages, homes and families. . . . Women's liberation has gone too far. Instead of giving freedom, it has relieved men of their responsibilities as head of the family. That makes it easier for a man to walk out on his family, and for a wife to get a divorce. The overall result is a relaxing of family responsibilities because one parent is simply unable to control growing children.

The worst thing that such a woman can possibly do is take a "women's studies" or some other sociology or psychology course in college. Some of these courses should be called "How to Break Up a Marriage." The Positive Woman can profitably return to college in her middle years only if she has a positive goal. If she is floundering, in search of a purpose, she should scrupulously avoid "women's studies" and related courses as a psychological red-light district where fundamental values are exchanged for fleeting stimulants at an exorbitant price.

The biggest problem for wives in their middle years is boredom and idleness. It can even be a fatal disease. The rich and successful movie actor George Sanders committed suicide because, according to the note he left behind, "I am bored."

59

Women in their middle years are particularly susceptible to this disease. The duties of motherhood are suddenly lifted. The duties of being a wife have been reduced by the private enterprise system to a few hours a day. This gives her entirely too many idle hours to stew about the minor physical and psychological problems of menopause. One mark of the Positive Woman is that she never allows worry to transform a minor problem into a major one.

The solution for both problems of the middle years is to keep busy. Work is the great cure for most of the ills of the world. Every community is crying for the kind of volunteer work that women can best give: welfare, hospital, educational, cultural, civic, and political. All these avenues provide opportunities for women to perform useful services to the community—and in so doing to become happier, more interesting, and more fulfilled.

A man accosted me in the supermarket one day with the words: "You don't know me, but my wife has been coming to your home to help you with your mailings. I just want to thank you for giving her something useful to do. I hope you don't run out of work so long as she is able to come."

The most pitiful women are the wives who turn to the cocktail party circuit or idle entertainment instead of volunteer service. Such diversions may fill their idle hours, but they cannot fill their empty minds and hearts or their maternal needs.

Alcohol is the great temptation of the middle years. Just as profanity can best be described as the poverty of vocabulary, so alcohol can be described as a confession of the inability to allocate your time to useful endeavors. Have you let your life become such a bore that you can't think of anything more interesting to do than stand around with a drink in your hand? In addition, there is the time lost afterward while your body restores itself to full work capacity. It is estimated that it takes twenty to thirty minutes of sleep to compensate for each ounce of whiskey. Tranquilizers are another unfortunate way that some women anesthetize the pain of idleness.

A woman needs to love and to show that love by serving the object of her affections. A good cause can provide an outlet for her continuing maternal urge in the years between the time when her children go off to school and when she is discovered by her grandchildren.

The women's liberationists show outspoken contempt for

volunteer service. They try to dissuade women from volunteering their time and energies to any cause (unless it serves a liberationist goal). In their inverted scale of values, they judge every service by money, never by love. Yet, the social and cultural services of most communities would collapse if all their volunteers were to walk out.

But the women who quit their volunteer "jobs" would suffer even more. The woman who cheerfully volunteers her time and talents to serve others gains more than her needy beneficiaries. The concept that the giver gains more than the receiver, once popularly dramatized in Lloyd Douglas' novel *Magnificent Obsession,* is true of some men, but even more true of most women. Their best availability for such a "magnificent obsession" is during their middle years.

Some women start a new career in the paid-employment world when their children are grown. It is never too late. James Michener, one of the most successful writers of our time, published his first book when he was forty years old. So did I. Everyone knows wives who successfully started careers in real estate, life insurance, business, and the professions after they were forty.

The lure of the women's liberation movement was most succinctly—if inadvertently—caricatured in the billboard run by the United States Army during its months of intensive recruiting in the early uncertain days of the volunteer Army. "The Army Has Openings For Cooks" was the caption over an enticing picture of a man and a woman, each sporting a high, white chef's cap, standing in front of a pile of potatoes and a pile of apples.

The billboard was a perfect example of the liberation trap: Come, leave your own kitchen, where an ever-loving male chauvinist pig has bought you a refrigerator, a stove, and perhaps a dishwasher. Come, cook in an Army kitchen where some sergeant will tell you how and when to peel the potatoes and the apples, what you must wear during your KP duties, whether or not your hair can be up in curlers, and when you can take your coffee breaks. And then call this "liberation!" Oh, yes, and also take your chances on the possibility that the sergeant may be a woman.

A graphic description of the social devastation wreaked by women's liberation on stable marriages that have endured for two decades, more or less, is given in the book *One Man, Hurt*

61

by Albert Martin. It gives an intimate, firsthand true story of a wife who one day walked out on her eighteen-year marriage, a successful and faithful husband, four sons, and a fine home in search of her identity. The husband didn't want a divorce and couldn't figure out why she did. To anyone who understands the women's liberation movement, however, it is obvious that *that* was the sole cause. As a homewrecker, women's liberation is far in the lead over "the other man," "the other woman," or "incompatibility" of any physical or mental variety.

After the divorce, Mr. Martin felt very sorry for himself and for his motherless sons. But he is convinced that his ex-wife is even worse off than he is, concluding:

> When I think of the horrifying price she has paid for whatever it is she has obtained, my rage turns to sorrow. . . . An extraordinary emphasis on self is happening today across our nation, and this is why we continue to tear our marriages apart, splinter our families, and raise our divorce rates to new heights every year. The very core . . . is the enshrinement of individuality, the freedom of self, at the expense of marital union and social compromise.[12]

Should a woman try to live as fully as her individual potential allows? She will be the loser if she chases this goal at the price of neglecting others within her immediate family. It is no gain for her to pursue personal ambitions to the extent that she becomes a virtual stranger to those who depend on her for nourishment, protection, and inspiration. Women's liberation is eroding the fabric of our families and weakening the ability of our children to function within a basic social unit. It encourages the "do your own thing—nobody cares" attitude among children. It breeds loneliness, not fulfillment.

Women's liberation leads the woman in her middle years into an emotional wasteland that can best be described in a paraphrase of those descriptive words of Rachel Carson, a Positive Woman who had the courage to swim against the tide. As she told it in *Silent Spring:*

> There was a strange stillness. The birds, for example—where had they gone? . . . The feeding stations in the backyards were deserted. . . . It was a spring without voices. On the mornings that had once throbbed with the dawn chorus of robins, catbirds, doves, jays, wrens, and scores of other bird voices there was now no sound; only silence lay over the fields and woods and marsh.

On the farms the hens brooded, but no chicks hatched. . . .
The apple trees were coming into bloom but no bees droned
among the blossoms, so there was no pollination and there
would be no fruit.

The roadsides, once so attractive, were now lined with
browned and withered vegetation as though swept by fire.
These, too, were silent, deserted by all living things. Even
the streams were now lifeless. Anglers no longer visited
them, for all the fish had died.

No witchcraft, no enemy action had silenced the rebirth of
new life in this stricken world. The people had done it
themselves.[13]

The woman in her middle years who has left her family to
follow the siren call of women's liberation will find her springs
equally silent—no happy noises of teenagers and their friends,
no footfall of a faithful husband in the kitchen, no gurgling of
grandchildren eager to be cuddled. She will come "home" to a
cold, lonely apartment whose silence is broken only by the
occasional visits of men who size her up as one with a liberated
view of sex, societal restraints, and the institution of marriage,
and therefore an easy mark for sexual favors for which they
will neither have to pay nor assume responsibility.

This, then, is the false lure of women's liberation: Come,
leave your home, husband, and children and join all those
unhappy females in a new sisterhood of togetherness. In all
history, it is unlikely that so many ever gave up so much for so
little. The only "liberation" that the wife and mother in the
home needs is liberation from the fallacious doctrines of wom-
en's liberation!

Only a woman who has, or somehow allows herself to be
given, a negative view of herself could follow the Pied Pipers
of women's liberation. The Positive Woman is too busy doing
constructive work to brood over her own misfortunes, real
though they may be. She knows that every living human has
his or her own mix of physical, psychological, and financial
problems; but the Positive Woman applies herself to the task of
trying to solve them rather than trying to lay the blame on
others.

The Senior Woman

Useful work, paid or volunteer, can fill the needs of the senior woman just as much it can those of the woman in her

middle years. The greatest need of the senior woman is to feel needed by others, to feel useful, to herself, to her family, and to society.

Since the passage of the Social Security Act, retirement at age sixty-five has generally become mandatory throughout the business world. Some companies enforce an even earlier retirement, down to age sixty. Social Security has conditioned us to believe that everyone is on the shelf at age sixty-five. The psychological effect on men and women reaches even further. Ten years before retirement, many people start to coast downhill because they think it isn't worth trying to climb any more.

In the entertainment world, where there is no mandatory retirement age, men and women over sixty-five seem to retain their youthful appearance and their stamina. Among those who work a twelve- to fourteen-hour day, on energetic schedules that would be tough at any age, are Bob Hope at seventy-three, Henry Fonda at seventy-two, John Wayne at seventy, Lawrence Welk at seventy-four, Helen Hayes at seventy-six, Marlene Dietrich at seventy-four, Gloria Swanson at seventy-nine, Bing Crosby at seventy-three, Arthur Fiedler at eighty-two, and Lowell Thomas at eighty-four.

A continuing capacity for hard work seems to come primarily from a stay-young attitude toward life and a commitment to work instead of to retirement. Some who tried retirement, such as Robert Young and Fred Astaire, are glad to have retired from the boredom of retirement and stepped back—at ages sixty-seven and seventy-four, respectively—into the harness of hard work. Both men said retirement was the most miserable period of their lives.

Jack Benny, who said he was thirty-nine for the last forty years of his life because he considered thirty-nine to be the "maximum age of youth," said shortly before his death at eighty: "I actually do feel I'm thirty-nine years old—and that feeling is what's kept me young." Bob Hope, who puts in a sixteen-hour day when he is doing a tour, thinks it is important to "walk tall" and keep your posture up.

James Cagney, seventy-three, tap dances every day and thinks we should all "work out enough to get out of breath two or three times a day." Buddy Ebsen at sixty-six is an active skier and says "retirement represents the pinnacle of boredom." Mae West credits her vitality to good living and good food, doesn't smoke or drink, and at age eighty-four works out with an exercise bicycle and walking machine. Ray "Wizard of Oz" Bolger, still a fabulous dancer at seventy-three, says: "I'm like a leprechaun. I want to bring joy to people. That's my role in life."

Another striking example of an energetic senior citizen was my friend Larry Lewis, who died in 1974 at the age of 106. He used to say that "retirement is the biggest mistake that business —and individuals—can make."

Larry's fabulous career began at age fifteen when he joined the P. T. Barnum Circus and became a flying trapeze star. Ten years later, he joined Houdini, the famous magician and escape artist, with whom he worked for thirty-three years. Houdini died in Larry's arms in 1927.

At age eighty, Larry started a new career as a waiter at the St. Francis Hotel in San Francisco. He would rise every morning at 4:00 A.M., run six miles through Golden Gate Park, walk to the St. Francis, and then do a full day's work as a waiter. When Larry was ninety-seven, he was hit by a truck as he was crossing a street. The truck driver was killed. Larry had six fractures, but recovered. Three months later, he resumed his daily morning run.

At 105, Larry started another new career as a goodwill ambassador for the Western International Employment Services. Within the year, he logged 30,000 miles in his travels to the company's offices in this country and abroad.

Larry Lewis' secrets for living a long and happy life were hard work, running six miles a day, drinking many glasses of water every day, and avoiding alcohol, tobacco, and heavy meals. Most important was planning never to retire. Larry had a wife who was twenty years younger than he. She kept up with him for a long time, but he finally outlasted her. It was only after her death that Larry collapsed, like the one-horse shay.

A wonderful old Indian named Arthur Young did our yard work for the last two decades of his life. Up through age ninety-six, he put in a full day of heavy and strenuous outside work in spite of a colostomy he had in his sixties. His secret of longevity was his constant vision of the future. He was always planning what he was going to do next month and next year: paint his room, retile his floor, or trade in his tools for better ones. He would still be going strong if the will to live hadn't been taken out of him by the death of his only son.

The most remarkable senior citizens in the United States in 1976 were George Meany, longtime president of the AFL-CIO, and Richard J. Daley, six-term Mayor of Chicago. Mr. Meany at eighty-two and Mayor Daley at seventy-four worked full-time in important and strenuous jobs, at a pace and under tension that would stagger the physical and mental strength of men half a century younger.

The Positive Woman will never let herself be put on the shelf. That doesn't mean that she necessarily must keep a paid job into her seventies and eighties. But it does mean that she must keep active and work hard—or deteriorate and die from "giveupitis." Useful work is available everywhere. The house doesn't exist that couldn't use more cleanup, more fixup, more painting and decorating and remodeling. Every community needs services for which there are no funds to pay. Be useful. Make yourself needed—in your home, in your church, in your community, for your country, and for the younger generation.

And have fun. In 1975 Marian Hart, the "flying granny" of Washington, D.C., flew solo from Washington to Shannon, Ireland, at age eighty-three. She is believed to be the oldest woman to fly solo across the Atlantic. Helen Hayes reminds us how nature helps us to keep the illusion of youth:

> The good thing about growing older is that your eyesight begins to fail first, so that when you peer in the mirror in the morning you can't really see the lines and can convince yourself that you're still young.[14]

The senior Positive Woman looking for a successful role-model should consider the example of Agatha Christie. More people have read her books than those of any author of our era. She wrote more than eighty books that have sold 100 million copies in 103 countries. Translations of her books have surpassed those of every other writer in history, including Shakespeare. She totally dominated the detective story genre.

Miss Christie's play *The Mousetrap* is the most successful and longest-running play in history. Like other playgoers who have seen it in London during its twenty-five years of continuous performance there, I found it an absorbing mystery. It has been performed in forty-one countries and translated into twenty-two languages. The movie based on a book Miss Christie wrote forty years ago, *Murder on the Orient Express,* has already grossed $40 million and is still going strong. Her last book, *Curtain,* is expected to sell 3 million copies.

Because of the way Agatha Christie gave away her royalty rights to various relatives, friends, and charities, no one will ever know how much money her books and plays earned, but it is estimated to be in the tens of millions of dollars, and there is no end in sight. In recent years, she wrote only one book a year because, she said, if she wrote more, she would just "enlarge the finances of Internal Revenue, who would spend it mostly on idiotic things."

How could this plain, small, shy Englishwoman create the ideas and develop the talent that made her the wealthiest writer in the world? She said she thought up the plots of her mysteries while she was washing the dishes!

Agatha Christie's incredible success reminds us that, in an era when many people want to stop working at age sixty-five, a Positive Woman can be original, creative, and highly successful up to age eighty-five.

III

Rejecting Gender-Free
Equality

The Positive Woman will never fall into
the trap of adopting gender-free equality in theory or in practice. The Positive Woman builds her power by using her womanhood, not by denying or suppressing it. The Positive Woman
wants to be treated like a woman, not like a man, and certainly
not like a sex-neutral "person."

The primary legislative goal of the women's liberationists is
ratification of an amendment to the United States Constitution
that reads in full as follows:

> *Section 1:* Equality of rights under the law shall not be
> denied or abridged by the United States or by any State on
> account of sex.
> *Section 2:* The Congress shall have the power to enforce,
> by appropriate legislation, the provisions of this article.
> *Section 3:* This amendment shall take effect two years after
> the date of ratification.

The fundamental error of the Equal Rights Amendment, or
ERA, is that it will mandate the gender-free, rigid, absolute
equality of treatment of men and women under every federal
and state law, bureaucratic regulation, and court decision, and
in every aspect of our lives that is touched directly or indirectly
by public funding. This is what the militant women's liberationists want and are working for with passionate and persistent determination.

The Positive Woman opposes ERA because she knows it
would be hurtful to women, to men, to children, to the family,
to local self-government, and to society as a whole.

68

Pro-ERA speakers go up and down the country reciting a tiresome litany of obsolete complaints about women not having the right to vote, not being able to serve on juries, and not being admitted to law or medical schools. All those past discriminations were remedied years ago, or decades ago, or even generations ago. They have no relevance to present-day America. Pro-ERA speakers paint a picture of American women in "serfdom," treated like "chattel" and trampled on as "second-class citizens," and then offer the Equal Rights Amendment as the remedy for an alleged oppression that exists only in their distorted minds.

Some pro-ERA speakers even claim that the United States Constitution does not treat women as "persons." The facts are clear that the United States Supreme Court back in 1875 in the case of *Minor* v. *Happersett*[1] specifically declared that women are "persons" as well as "citizens" under the Constitution, including the Fourteenth Amendment, entitled to all the rights and privileges of persons and citizens except the right to vote—and women received that right in 1920 under the Nineteenth Amendment.

In July, 1976, thirty-five women's magazines—including those with respectable reputations, women's liberationist journals such as *Ms.*, those that feature the "true confession" type of sensationalism, and pornographic publications—published articles on ERA. Most were blatantly pro-ERA.

Redbook, the magazine that instigated the pro-ERA consortium, featured an article by Cathleen Douglas, fourth wife of three-times-divorced former Supreme Court Justice William O. Douglas. Her article contained a lot of nonsense about a wife's being "considered the 'chattel,' or property, of her husband, with the same legal rights as a goat, a hog or a piece of land."

It is too bad that some women believe such falsehoods. This is the way the women's liberation movement deliberately degrades the homemaker and hacks away at her sense of self-worth and pride and pleasure in being female. The best cure for women who are limited in their own self-esteem is to stop reading women's magazines!

Many people have supported the Equal Rights Amendment in the mistaken belief that it means "equal pay for equal work." The fact is that ERA will add no new employment rights whatsoever. Federal employment laws are already completely sex-neutral. ERA will not add any new rights to those spelled out in the Equal Employment Opportunity Act of 1972, which prohibits all sex discrimination in hiring, pay, and promotion.

If any woman thinks she has been discriminated against, she can file her claim with the Equal Employment Opportunity Commission, and the government will pay the costs. Under this law, women have already won multi-million-dollar settlements against some of the largest companies in the country, including $38 million against AT&T and $30 million against the big steel companies. There is nothing more that ERA can do.

When I debated the leading congressional proponent of ERA, former Congresswoman Martha Griffiths, on the Lou Gordon television show in Detroit, I made the statement that "ERA will do absolutely nothing for women in the field of employment." She replied, "I never claimed it would."

Her concession is similar to those made by other pro-ERA lawyers when they are cross-examined in debates or at state legislative hearings. It is only those who are permitted to make statements without rebuttal or cross-examination (such as Betty Ford) who continue to promote the false illusion that ERA means equal pay for equal work. It can be stated categorically that ERA will *not* give women equal pay for equal work, or *any* employment rights, choices, or opportunities that they do not now have.

A Wife's Right to Support

Americans have the immense good fortune to live in a civilization that respects the family as the basic unit of society. This respect is not merely a matter of social custom. We have a great fabric of federal and state laws designed to protect the institution of the family. These laws are not for the purpose of giving one sex a preference over the other. They were not born of oppression or discrimination, but of vision and enlightened judgment. They are designed to keep the family together and to assure the child a home in which to grow up.

The results of these laws are highly beneficial to the wife. Based on the fundamental fact of life that women have babies and men don't—which no legislation or agitation can erase— these laws make it the obligation of the husband to support his

70

wife financially and provide her with a home. Since God ordained that women have babies, our laws properly and realistically establish that men must provide financial support for their wives and children. The women's liberation movement has positioned itself in total opposition to the entire concept of "roles," but in so doing, they are opposing Mother Nature herself.

The right of a wife to be supported by her husband stems from one or more of three sources: (1) *statute law,* the laws passed by the state legislatures, (2) *common law,* the laws derived from English custom and court decisions, and (3) *case law,* the decisions reached by our state and federal courts in adjudicating controversies. A typical statement of the financial responsibility incurred by the marriage contract is this Ohio law:

> The husband must support himself, his wife, and his minor children out of his property or by his labor. If he is unable to do so, the wife must assist him so far as she is able. If he neglects to support his wife, any other person, in good faith, may supply her with necessaries for her support, and recover the reasonable value thereof from the husband unless she abandons him without cause.[2]

Laws similar to this exist in every one of the fifty states. They vary in details from state to state, but the sum of these laws speaks with a unanimous voice that one of the precepts most firmly ingrained in our legal structure is the obligation of the husband to support his wife. Many states impose criminal penalties on the husband if he fails to live up to his obligation to support his wife. In some states, the wife has the right to require her husband to post a bond to guarantee payment for her support. In most states, the wife has the right to get credit in her husband's name and thereby obligate him for payment for all her necessities, such as food, clothing, housing, and medical and dental care. A wife usually has the right to be supported regardless of any independent income or property she may possess. Federal recognition of these laws appears currently in the 1968 Revenue Ruling, which says simply: "Generally, a husband has a duty to support his wife during their joint lives or until she remarries."[3]

This network of laws gives the wife her legal right to be a full-time wife and mother, in her own home, taking care of her

71

own babies. One of the most comprehensive modern text statements of American law, *American Jurisprudence, 2d,* gives a detailed composite summary of these rights in volume 41 under the heading "Husband and Wife":

> One of the most fundamental duties imposed by the law of domestic relations is that which requires a man to support his wife and family. In some jurisdictions, the duty of support is imposed on the husband by statute. . . . But it exists apart from statute, as a duty arising out of the marital relationship. . . .
> The duty of a husband to support his wife arises out of the marital relationship and continues during the existence of that relationship. This duty of support is consistent with the husband's financial ability, and in accordance with the station in life to which he has accustomed his family. . . .
> The duty of a husband to support his wife and family, arising out of the marriage relationship, exists without reference to the wife's separate estate or independent means, and the husband has no right to resort to her separate estate or means, as a general rule, to support her or the family. A husband's duty to support his wife also exists without reference to what she can earn by her own labor, and he has no right to demand that she earn all that she can in order to contribute to her support. . . .[4]

The law provides for modification of this rule because of extenuating circumstances, such as the illness, incapacity, or unemployment of the husband. But such exceptions do not negate the general primary rule of the husband's obligation to support his wife. As is made clear in the Ohio law quoted above, the wife has some obligation—but that obligation is *not* equal to that of the husband. He has the primary obligation.

The Equal Rights Amendment would invalidate all the state laws that require the husband to support his wife and family and provide them with a home, because the Constitution would then prohibit any law that imposes an obligation on one sex that it does not impose equally on the other. Thus, if ERA ever becomes part of the United States Constitution, all laws that say the *husband* must support his *wife* would immediately become unconstitutional. In the liberationist jargon, such laws are "sexist." ERA would impose a constitutionally mandated legal equality in all matters, including family support. This would be grossly unfair to a woman because it would impose on her the double burden of financial obligation plus motherhood and homemaking. The law cannot address itself to who has the baby, changes the diapers, or washes the dishes.

Most of the fifteen states that have rejected ERA have state laws that give wives superior rights—which they will lose if ERA is ratified. These superior rights, which vary from state to state, include the immunity many states give a wife from her husband's debts, while he has no such immunity from her debts.

ERA proponents cannot dispute the fact that ERA will require all marriage laws to impose equality of financial obligation on husband and wife. The only dispute is over how that equality will be interpreted.

Colorado, one of the few states that have adopted a *state* Equal Rights Amendment as part of their state constitutions, has given us a forecast of what absolute equality means when applied to the marriage contract.

The Colorado state legislature amended the existing law that required a husband to support his wife and children, changing the "sexist" words (such as *man, woman, husband, wife*) into "sex-neutral" words (such as *person, spouse*). Anyone can plainly see that *person* must support *spouse* is not the same thing at all as *husband* must support *wife*.[5]

Under the Colorado law, a wife now shares equally in the obligation to support her family under pain of criminal conviction of a class-five felony. This is what equality means. No longer is it a crime in Colorado for a husband to abandon his wife. This new law took effect July 1, 1973, and is a forecast of what will happen in the other forty-nine states if ERA is ratified as part of the United States Constitution. If the state legislatures fail to amend their laws to require equality, the federal courts will then do it for them.

Women who naively think the Equal Rights Amendment merely means equal pay for equal work are in for a big shock when they find out what "equality" really means. The Colorado law shows the foresight of such eminent legal authorities as Professor Paul A. Freund of the Harvard Law School, who pointed out that ERA would "dictate" a completely new principle of family support that "would be contrary to the law of every state," and then asked the question:

What will be the reaction of wives to the Equal Rights Amendment when husbands procure judicial decisions in its

73

name relieving them of the duty of support because an equal
duty is not imposed on their wives?[6]

And Professor Philip B. Kurland of the University of Chicago
Law School concurred. He wired the Illinois legislature on
June 5, 1972: "It is largely misrepresented as a women's rights
amendment when in fact the primary beneficiaries will be
men. I am opposed to its approval."

Some ERA proponents have introduced bills in state legislatures to anticipate the equality requirement of ERA. Representative Sarah Weddington, pro-ERA leader in the Texas legislature, introduced a bill to change the family support law by the
addition of a phrase to ensure complete equality. The present
Texas law reads: "The husband has the duty to support the
wife, and the wife has the duty to support the husband when
he is unable to support himself." The obligation is thus not
equal. The wife has an obligation only if the husband for some
reason is unable to support himself.

Ms Weddington's proposed bill would amend this law by
means of the italicized words so that it would read: "The husband has the duty to support the wife *when she is unable to
support herself* and the wife has the duty to support the husband when he is unable to support himself."

When is a wife "unable" to support herself? Only the first
week after she has a baby? Or only for fifty-six days afterwards,
the maternity leave granted to women in China? Or only for a
few months afterwards, as women are allowed in European
Communist countries?

Under the Weddington bill, as under ERA, the wife would
lose her present legal right to be supported and her right to be a
full-time wife and mother in the home, and she would be reduced to proving that "she is unable to support herself." It is
hard to see how there could be a more devastating effect on the
family structure and on the present legal rights of the wife.

This Texas bill is not unique. In Illinois, the ERA sponsor,
state Representative Eugenia Chapman, introduced a similar
amendment to change the family support law from "A husband
is liable for the support of his wife, and a wife for the support
of her husband if he is in need of such support and is, or is
likely to become, a public charge," to revised wording under
which the husband and wife would be responsible for each

74

other's support only "*if either* is in need of such support and is, or is likely to become a public charge" (emphasis added). Clearly, this reduces the wife's customary and primary right to financial support to the level where she has a legal right to support *only* if she is "in need" or about to go on welfare.

That this drastic reduction in the rights of the homemaker is the real objective of leading ERA proponents was confirmed by their principal legal authority, Professor Thomas I. Emerson of Yale Law School. In Hartford, Connecticut, in the studio of television Channel 3 on June 23, 1976, I asked him what would happen, under ERA, to the New York state support law which now reads tersely: "Husband liable for support of his wife." He replied, "It cannot remain in that form." I asked him how that law would be changed under ERA. He replied that under ERA the law would have to be changed so that the obligation is mutual, or reciprocal, and each spouse would be liable for the support of the other "if he or she were incapacitated."

I looked at him and said, "But I'm a homemaker, and I'm certainly not incapacitated." He replied, "That's right, you're not."

That is the measure of the homemaker's rights wiped out by the ERA: Her legal right to support for all her years as a wife would be cut down to a right to support *only* for the time that she might be considered to be "incapacitated." It is no wonder that former Senator Sam J. Ervin, Jr., called ERA "the most destructive piece of legislation to ever pass Congress."

No one can predict for sure which kind of "equality" will be enforced by the courts and by legislatures if ERA is ever ratified. The new equality rule may be a requirement that the husband and wife each contribute 50 percent of the income required to support the family, or that each spouse take a paying job for half of each week, or half of each month, or half of each year to provide the financial support of the family. Most ERA proponents concede in debate that *if* the wife takes a paying job, she would then be *obligated* to provide half the financial support of the family.

Some pro-ERA lawyers try to argue that under the sex-neutral language required by ERA the courts will hold that the *principal wage-earning spouse* must support the spouse who stays in the home. This would reduce the wife's rights even further. Taking the pro-ERA argument, this means that, if the husband is lazy and wants to spend his time drinking and

75

watching television, and the wife is a conscientious woman who takes a job to feed her hungry children, then she, as the "principal wage-earning spouse," would acquire the obligation to support her lazy husband, subject to criminal penalties if she failed to support him and pay all his debts.

Whichever of these alternative versions of equality might ultimately become the rule under ERA, it would bring a drastic reduction in the rights of the wife and a radical loosening of the legal bonds that tend to keep the family together.

Some ERA proponents argue that husbands support their wives only because of love, not because of the law. But a relationship that is based exclusively on love, or on sex compatibility, is not apt to survive all those years "for better for worse, for richer for poorer, in sickness and in health, till death we do part." Love is a concept that may embrace many relationships with many different persons. Duty is essential to marriage. The moral, social, and legal evil of ERA is that it proclaims as a constitutional mandate that the husband no longer has the primary duty to support his wife and children.

Far more probable than the prospect of husbands immediately taking advantage of their new liberation from duty is the likelihood that wives will voluntarily leave the home and join the labor force because they see the handwriting on the wall. If ERA deprives wives of their economic security in the home, their natural instinct for survival will impel them to seek economic security in employment seniority.

There are today some 40 million wives who are supported by their husbands. If even half these wives enter the labor market, the most relevant question is, where are the jobs? America today has a very high unemployment rate. If 10 or 20 or 30 million homemakers enter the labor market seeking to protect their own financial future (because ERA has relieved their husbands of that duty), this will be a jolt to our economy worse than any we have ever experienced.

Furthermore, the high divorce rate proves that many husbands have stopped loving their wives. In 1975 American divorces passed the one-million mark. Should a husband have the legal right to stop supporting his faithful wife of twenty or thirty years by the simple expedient of saying, "I don't love her anymore; I love a younger woman"? Even though love may go out the window, the obligation should remain. ERA would eliminate that obligation.

76

Some ERA proponents question the good of criminal penalties as a means of requiring a husband to support his wife. Criminal penalties are a very necessary part of our legal system. We live in a society that recognizes the enforceability of contracts. Most people fulfill their contracts because they believe in the Ten Commandments or, at least, in the rule that honesty is the best policy. Others who might be tempted to violate them are deterred because they know that, at the end of a long trail of expensive litigation, they will either be forced to fulfill their contracts anyway or suffer financial penalties. Most people pay up before they get to court, and most of those who do go to court pay up during litigation before they lose their property by court order.

This certain knowledge that the law will ultimately be enforced is what makes 99 percent of contracts self-enforcing. If you buy a car on time, or lease an apartment, or buy insurance, so long as you fulfill your contract by making your payments on time, no court interferes. The average person knows that, if he fails to make his payments on time, his car will be repossessed, he will be evicted from his apartment, or his insurance will be canceled.

Likewise, in marriage, in most cases, a wife does not need to go to court to get support money from her husband. The husband knows that, if he doesn't support her, his wages may be garnisheed, his bank account may be attached, he may have to post a bond, or, ultimately, go to jail, depending on which state he lives in.

One of the most ignorant arguments made by ERA proponents is that the only way a wife can force her husband to support her is by divorcing him because "the courts don't interfere in ongoing marriages." If a woman divorces her husband, then she is no longer his wife; she has relinquished the rights of a wife. It is only while a woman is a wife in an ongoing marriage that she enjoys a wife's rights.

A wife has many remedies available to her before she takes her husband to court. She can purchase necessaries on her husband's credit and then leave it up to the store to handle the collection. As long as she is a wife in an ongoing marriage, the courts now hold that her husband must pay her expenses.[7] ERA will change all that.

A new law went into effect in July, 1975, that establishes a federally operated parent-locator service in the Department of

Health, Education and Welfare to find disappearing fathers and husbands and compel them to provide support for the wives and children they have abandoned. This parent-locator service has access to most government records, including those of the Internal Revenue Service, the FBI, the Pentagon, the Veterans Administration, and, most important, the Social Security Administration, which can easily locate an absent father in his new job anywhere in the fifty states. The new law eliminates bankruptcy as a means of avoiding support payments and allows federal salaries, retirement benefits, and even unemployment compensation to be garnisheed for support payments. This law has a great potential for helping needy women as well as significantly reducing the high costs of welfare. It would be a great pity if ERA were to cut this program off at the pass by voiding the obligation of husbands to support their wives.

The Virginia state legislature, prior to voting on the Equal Rights Amendment, set up a task force of prominent lawyers from five Virginia law schools to study the effect of ERA on Virginia laws. The task force report, presented on January 15, 1974, is a comprehensive analysis of the effect of the Equal Rights Amendment and constitutes the evidence on the basis of which the Virginia legislature has repeatedly rejected ERA.[8]

The task force report proves that there is nothing whatever that ERA will do to benefit women and that there are no Virginia laws that adversely discriminate against women that ERA will remedy. The report shows that ERA will not give women more employment rights, more property rights, more marital rights, or more family rights. ERA will not help women with respect to jobs or home. ERA has no advantages and many disadvantages.

In the area of domestic relations, the task force report concludes that ERA would require amendments to Virginia law that "would impose further obligations on women, rather than accord them further rights." The report explains that the Virginia statute "imposes a lesser obligation of support upon a wife than upon a husband, manifestly because one is a woman and one, a man. The Equal Rights Amendment would require that this be changed. The obligation to support could not be imposed because of sex."

The task force report does a good job of explaining that, even when the statutes in regard to child support may theoretically

78

read in a sex-neutral way (as is the case in some states), case law still imposes "the primary duty of support upon the father," and no case could be found imposing a joint legal duty of support of children on the mother so long as the father is living. The task force report concludes that, while such an interpretation is valid now, "it would not be under the Equal Rights Amendment."

With one stroke ERA would wipe out the most basic and precious legal right that wives now enjoy: the right to be a full-time homemaker. It is no argument to say that a large percentage of wives are already in the labor force. There is all the difference in the world between free choice and legal obligation. Those working wives were not compelled to take a job by the law or by their husbands, and they have the option to drop out of the labor force at any time.

Congresswoman Leonor K. Sullivan, a Positive Woman and a leader in Congress for many years, eloquently summed up this matter of family support in her speech to the United States Congress explaining why she voted against the Equal Rights Amendment:

> Individual women have supported husbands in indolence or in the pursuit of professional education or in the arts and literature, and individual women have that right, including the right to support the children, too. But I do not wish to see—and to vote for—a constitutional amendment which would require all women to be equally obligated with their husbands to support the family, even though millions of women may choose to do so.[9]

Providing a Home

One of the most valuable property rights that a wife has under present laws is the right to be provided with a home in accord with her husband's means. *American Jurisprudence, 2d,* spells out this right:

> The husband's obligation of support requires him to provide his wife with a place of abode that will be deemed a suitable home when considered in the light of modern standards . . . and the means and earning power of the husband . . . the control of which she need not relinquish or share with others, but a home in which she is the mistress.[10]

79

The marital scandal of the governor of Maryland during 1974 provided an unusual dramatization of this property right in the home. For some months, the voters were treated to the spectacle of the governor's wife living alone in the governor's mansion, while the governor shared an apartment with his girlfriend. The governor's wife was rightfully able to retain possession of the home until her husband granted her a proper settlement.

Another amusing case turned up during 1974 when a husband ejected his wife from their home and replaced her with a Playboy "bunny." The wife had no difficulty obtaining a court order requiring her husband to remove the bunny and restore the wife to her rightful place in the home.

There may be many husbands who would like the company of a Playboy bunny as a temporary diversion, but the law is on the side of the wife—so long as ERA remains unratified.

The Senior Woman

It is one thing for the mod young woman to say she wants to give up the rights of wives and take her chances on equality. It is something else again to change the terms of the marriage contract that older wives entered into years ago. This is what the Equal Rights Amendment would do. When senior women were married twenty, thirty, or forty years ago, marriage meant certain rights and obligations. Nothing, not even a constitutional amendment, should be permitted to change those terms now.

Consider a wife in her fifties whose husband decides he wants to divorce her and trade her in on a younger model. This situation has become all too common, especially with no-fault divorce in many states. If ERA is ratified, and thereby wipes out the state laws that require a husband to support his wife, the cast-off wife will have to hunt for a job to support herself. *No matter* that she has made being a wife and mother her full-time career for twenty to thirty years. *No matter* that she is in her fifties and unprepared to enter the competitive job market. *No matter* that age discrimination deals her a double blow.

The most tragic effect of ERA would thus fall on the woman who has been a good wife and homemaker for decades, and who can now be turned out to pasture with impunity because a

80

new, militant breed of women's liberationist has come along and amended the United States Constitution to alter the terms of her marriage contract. This may be equality, but it certainly is not justice. The *Wall Street Journal* published a pathetic expose with many specific examples of how the combination of easy divorce and the sex equality demanded by women's liberation is creating a "new poverty class" of abandoned senior women.[11]

The Virginia task force report cited above shows the adverse effect ERA could have on senior women. Present Virginia law requires children seventeen years old or over to support their father if he is in need or is incapacitated, but requires them to support their mother if she is in need, no matter what her age or capabilities. The Virginia task force report states that this statute accords unequal and superior rights to mothers and "hence it would not meet the requirements of the Equal Rights Amendment."

Thus, if ERA is ratified, the aged and faithful mother, who has made her family her lifetime career, would have no legal right to be supported in her senior years. She would have to take any menial job she could get or go on welfare if her husband and children did not voluntarily choose to support her.

The Arkansas state legislature also ordered a report on the effects of the Equal Rights Amendment on state laws.[12] When released on August 25, 1974, this report proved to be a devastating indictment of ERA. It shows how ERA will be hurtful to all women, and especially cruel to widows.

The report states that about fifty Arkansas laws would be affected by ERA, "nearly all" of which, according to the *Arkansas Gazette,* "are statutes or state constitutional provisions that protect women in some fashion—advantages in the divorce, inheritance and property and criminal laws and extra protections in working conditions."[13] Among the laws providing advantages to a widow that would be adversely affected by ERA are laws providing her a widow's dower, homestead rights, immunity from her husband's debts, special rights in her husband's real property, and double damages if she is cheated. Among the superior rights of wives that would be adversely affected by ERA are property rights in their homes and the right to dispose of their property without their husbands' consent. The Arkansas report makes clear that under present state law wives and widows have a long list of tangible superior property and financial rights that would be wiped out by ratification of the Equal Rights Amendment.

State and federal statutes and state and federal court decisions contain many instances of special benefits granted by our society to widows. For example, Florida has a law that gives a property-tax advantage to widows, and this superior right was upheld by the United States Supreme Court in 1974.[14] It is a measure of the vindictiveness of the militant women that one of the leading female pro-ERA lawyers joined in this case to try to persuade the Supreme Court to void this widows' advantage. Many pro-ERA lawyers cite the Florida law as an example of discriminatory legislation that ERA will eliminate. They are correct; ERA will wipe out all the superior benefits enjoyed by widows under our laws and court decisions.

The Divorced Woman

The divorced woman does not possess the extensive rights that our laws accord to a wife. By definition, when a woman ceases to be a wife, she no longer enjoys the rights of a wife. Those rights have passed on to or will pass on to her ex-husband's new wife. However, a divorced woman does enjoy certain important rights that she will lose if the Equal Rights Amendment is ever ratified.

The most meaningful right of a divorced woman is the presumption of custody of her children. While not usually a matter of state law, this presumption of custody is a custom that in the past has had almost the force of law. Unless a mother does not want her children or there is a substantial showing that she is morally unfit to have her children, she usually is awarded custody.

The custody of her children is vitally important to a mother as she goes through the traumatic experience of a divorce. The custody of the children is what enables her to secure a reasonably fair divorce settlement from her husband, who usually has the better-income-producing job.

The Equal Rights Amendment would mandate the courts to make their determination on the basis of equality of both sexes in all matters. Equality might mean that the courts would award one child to the mother and one to the father. Or it might mean that the courts would award custody to the father in approximately half the cases, ordering the mother to pay child support.

This has already happened where a local ERA has gone into effect. One of the first examples was a divorce case in Washington, D.C., where on February 24, 1973, Superior Court Judge George W. Draper awarded a husband custody of his three children and ordered the children's mother to pay child support. He based his ruling on a little-noticed change in the District of Columbia code (made three years before) that mandates equality, plus what he called "the improved economic position of women generally in our society." In this case, both parents had government jobs, each earning about $17,000 per year.

So now the divorced woman has her job, but she has lost her three children, ages nine, seven, and five. Any way the courts slice it, "equality" means a reduction of rights that women formerly possessed.

As a matter of justice, if a mother is unfit, refuses to give her children home care, or is the spouse who walks out on the marriage, she should not be given custody of her children. The courts now have ample discretion to make this determination.[15] But a rule based on equality or a sex-neutral rule based on which spouse has the larger income (which some courts are tending to adopt) would be most hurtful to women and a big take-away of present rights.

The second important right now enjoyed by a divorced woman is the right to have a court order her ex-husband to support her minor children. By statute, or by common law, or by case law, a father has always had the legal obligation to provide the primary support of his minor children, regardless of his legal or domiciliary relationship to them or their mother. The Equal Rights Amendment, if ratified, would invalidate any law or court order that imposes the obligation of child support on a father just because he is a father.

The states that have put equal rights amendments into their state constitutions have given us a preview of what will happen nationally if ERA is ever ratified. On March 26, 1974, the Pennsylvania Supreme Court, in the case of *Conway* v. *Dana*, invalidated the presumption that a father, just because he is a man, has the primary liability for the support of his minor children. The supreme court listed all the previous Pennsylvania cases holding that "the *primary* duty of support for a minor child rests with the father." Then the court stated that

83

these cases "may no longer be followed" because "such a presumption is clearly a vestige of the past and incompatible with the present recognition of equality of the sexes." From now on, the court said, the support of children will be "the equal responsibility of both father and mother."[16]

Thus, "equality of the sexes" means that a mother must share equally in the liability to provide the financial support of her children. They call this "equal rights," but for the divorced woman, ERA is truly the "Extra Responsibilities Amendment."

If ERA is ratified as part of the United States Constitution, will this effect be retroactive? No one knows the answer to that question for sure. But we do know that the United States House Judiciary Committee, in its majority report on ERA, states:

> In some cases it would relieve the fathers of the primary responsibility for the support of even infant children, as well as the support of the mothers of such children and cast doubt on the validity of the millions of support decrees presently in existence.[17]

The third important right of divorced women is alimony, when ordered by the court. Alimony is certainly not a right of all divorced women; it depends on the circumstances, the length of the marriage, and other factors. The dictionary defines *alimony* as "an allowance paid to a woman by her husband or former husband for her maintenance, granted by a court upon a legal separation or a divorce or while action is pending." Some states allow alimony to be awarded to husbands or wives, in the discretion of the judge, while other states award alimony to wives only. Such a preferential benefit to women could never be tolerated under ERA.

Some people are developing the attitude, Why should an ex-wife get alimony when she is well able to support herself? It is true that a wife divorced after twenty-five years of marriage may be able to get a job. But in no way can she support herself at the level that she could have supported herself if she had spent those past twenty-five years in the job market instead of in the home. Her alimony is the differential between what she can earn and what she could have earned if she had devoted herself to a career in the labor force instead of in the home.

Effect on the Family

After extensive research into the probable effects of the Equal Rights Amendment, Arthur E. Ryman, Jr., professor of law at Drake University, concluded that ERA will seriously affect marriage both as an economic and as a social institution in America. If ERA is ratified, he wrote, "many states will adopt a wildly permissive approach" that would "degrade the homemaker role and support economic development requiring women to seek careers."[18]

Nearly two years after Professor Ryman's findings were published in the *Drake Law Review* of June, 1973, his conclusion was proved when some ERA proponents began urging that every husband whose wife is not employed outside the home be required to pay double Social Security taxes on the assumed "earnings" of his wife as a homemaker. Led by financial columnist Sylvia Porter, these proponents argued that this double tax should be imposed because, if the husband hired a housekeeper, he would be required to pay Social Security taxes on *her* earnings; therefore, why shouldn't the husband do the same for a wife who performs additional duties above and beyond those ordinarily expected of hired employees? Ms Porter then concluded: "If some change along these lines is not enacted sooner, the Equal Rights Amendment, when finally passed, will require it."[19]

It is not clear whether these new Social Security taxes on the wife would be paid at the 7.9 percent rate of self-employed persons, or at the rate of 5.85 percent for the wife's assumed "earnings" to be matched by another 5.85 percent from the husband as "employer." Nor is it clear what would be the assumed "salary" of the homemaker on which the double Social Security taxes would be paid. Estimates of the financial worth of a homemaker start at $12,000 per year.

Since there are no deductions for Social Security taxes, a tax of 7.9 percent on $12,000 would require husbands to pay $948 annually in additional Social Security taxes. The additional tax could be higher, depending on which rate is charged and what "earnings" the homemaker is assumed to be worth. There will, of course, be no increase in benefits, since wives already draw Social Security benefits on their husband's earnings.

The women's liberationists argue that this tax would give "new dignity" to the role of homemaker. There is no evidence that wives want the alleged "dignity" that comes from paying an additional $948 or more in federal taxes. Most would surely prefer the satisfaction of spending their own money for goods or gifts of their own choosing. Since more than half of United States taxpayers are already paying more Social Security taxes than they pay income taxes, ERA would double the federal tax load of many married taxpayers.

The long-range result of such a far-reaching and costly plan would be to drive many wives and mothers out of the home, just as Professor Ryman forecast. It is easy to forsee that many husbands would say, "Honey, our family budget can't afford another $948 a year in federal taxes. You'll have to get a job and earn your own money to pay the taxes."

The imposition of a double Social Security tax on those families who believe the wife and mother should be in the home is a good example of how the ERA proponents are concocting mischief beyond the reach of most people's imagination!

Another striking example of Professor Arthur Ryman's conclusion that ERA will cause many states to "adopt a wildly permissive approach" that will "support economic development requiring women to seek careers" is given in the report of the Ohio Task Force for the Implementation of the Equal Rights Amendment, issued July 1, 1975.[20] This report takes the radically avant-garde position that the "equality principle" of ERA requires the state to provide child-care services in order that mothers can leave the home and join the work force.

The theory behind such a mischievous implementation of ERA is that it is sex discrimination for mothers to be expected to care for their children and that it is therefore the duty of the government to provide child-care centers so that mothers can be relieved of this sex-discriminatory obligation. Here is how the Ohio task force report states it:

> The equality principle embodied in the ERA requires consideration of a new public policy on the issue of child care. Women who are mothers need to enjoy the same freedoms and opportunities as men who are fathers. Mothers who desire to engage in activities outside the home either on a full or part time basis, must have access to child care services so that they can fulfill these professional, educational or personal goals. . . .

The lack of adequate child care services in the State of Ohio raises ERA problems because the State's failure to recognize a need for insuring adequate child care is founded on sex-stereotyped attitudes about both the "proper" roles of men and women and the "innate" abilities of mothers and fathers. . . .

The Task Force recommends that the state set as a priority during the next biennium the establishment of high quality, universally available child care services that are funded in whole or in part by the State of Ohio.

The task force report makes clear that the expression "universally available" means that child care must be provided for all families "irrespective of their income level." This is not a help-the-needy program. This is a program to get all children out of the home so that the mothers can leave their homes to pursue their "personal goals," whatever they may be.

The Ohio task force report contains an eloquent minority report by Simon Lazarus, Jr., that reads in part:

There is a philosophy pervading this section of the report that downgrades the institution of marriage and the family.

For example, in the section on Child Care, a reader would be led to believe that parents can abdicate their responsibilities for their children even when not financially necessary. In the section on illegitimacy, a reader would be led to believe that the constructs of marriage are not important for the welfare of children. . . .

The Report on Children seems to advocate relieving parents of the responsibility to care for their own children, if the parent or parents so desire.

I concur in the need for high quality child care. This is the responsibility of the parents. . . .

Mr. Lazarus' report is wholly sound and constructive. The only trouble is, it is a minority report, and there is ample reason to anticipate that the federal courts, in interpreting ERA, will take the position of the majority, namely, that ERA compels the government to care for children in order to take that "discriminatory burden" off the backs of the mothers. Elimination of the role of "mother" is a major objective of the women's liberation movement. Wives and mothers must be gotten out of the home at all costs to themselves, to their husbands, to their children, to marriage, and to society as a whole.

What is the connection between ERA and the major antifamily objective of the women's liberation movement, abortion-on-demand? That answer can be decisively given only by the United States Supreme Court—which proved on January 22, 1973, that it is so proabortion that it discovered an alleged right to abortion in the Fourteenth Amendment. For 100 years, no one else had ever seen a "right" to abortion there, and such a right clearly was not intended by those who ratified the Fourteenth Amendment. It will be easier to find the right to abortion in ERA. Here is what leading constitutional authorities have to say about the abortion connection.

In a letter written on September 22, 1975, Senator Sam J. Ervin, Jr., said: "I think there is no doubt of the fact that the ERA would give every woman a constitutional right to have an abortion at will."

In a telegram to state legislators on January 9, 1975, Professor Joseph Witherspoon of the University of Texas Law School said:

> Ratification of the ERA will inevitably be interpreted by the Supreme Court of the United States as an explicit ratification and an approval by the people of the United States of its 1973 decision invalidating state anti-abortion statutes and of its declaration therein that the unborn child is not a human person whose life is protected by the Constitution. . . . Ratification of the proposed ERA will also make it much more difficult for pro-life forces to obtain submission and ratification of a Human Life Amendment.

In a letter written on January 21, 1975, Professor Charles Rice of the University of Notre Dame Law School stated:

> If the ERA were adopted, it would make clear beyond any doubt that the states would be disabled from prohibiting or even restricting abortion in any significant way. . . . I believe that the adoption of ERA would jeopardize, at least with respect to public institutions and personnel, the so-called conscience clauses which give hospitals and medical personnel the right to refuse on grounds of conscience to perform abortions.

Coming from the pro-ERA side of the controversy, Betty Friedan, founder of NOW, when asked on the "Town Meeting of the Air" (May 14, 1975) about the relationship of ERA to abortion and future Supreme Court decisions, replied: "As for reliance on future Supreme Courts—that's the reason we need ERA."

There are at least two legal theories according to which abortion may be established as a constitutional right under ERA: (1) Any restriction of abortion would be "sexist" or sex discriminatory because it impacts on one sex only. The parallel would be drawn from civil rights litigation in which discrimination is proved from the *result* rather than the *purpose* of the law. (2) Since the mandate of ERA is for sex equality, abortion is essential to relieve women of their unequal burden of being forced to bear an unwanted baby.

There is already a clear precedent that it is sex discrimination to deny a woman an abortion. The Education Amendments of 1972 state simply:

> No person in the United States shall, on the basis of sex, be excluded from participation in, be denied the benefits of, or be subjected to discrimination under any education program or activity receiving Federal financial assistance.

Although there is no mention of abortion anywhere in this law, the HEW regulation interpreted it (1) to require any medical benefit program administered by a school or college to pay for abortions for married and unmarried students, (2) to prohibit any school or college from refusing to employ or from firing an unmarried pregnant teacher or a woman who has had, or plans to have, an abortion, and (3) to prohibit any school or college from refusing admission to any student who has had, or plans to have, an abortion. Abortion is referred to by the code words "termination of pregnancy."[21]

If the federal government can read the obligation to finance abortions into the Education Amendments, it will have no difficulty reading abortion into ERA.

Another prong of the attack on the family is the drive to legalize homosexuality. Although usually blanketed in such euphemisms as "the right to be different" or "the right to sexual orientation" or "sexual preference," it is clear that homosexuals and lesbians are seeking not merely the right of consenting adults to act in private. They want the right to "marry" and thereby qualify for joint income tax and homestead benefits enjoyed by husbands and wives. They want the right to adopt children. They want the right to teach in schools.

To extend such rights to homosexuals would be a grave interference with the rights of the rest of our citizens, especially

89

children. It would be an assault on our right to have a country in which the family is recognized, protected, and encouraged as the basic unit of society. It would interfere with the right of an adoptable child to be placed in a home with a mother and a father. It would negate the right of a father to secure custody of his own child from its mother who had become a lesbian.

It would interfere with the right of parents to have their children taught by teachers who respect moral law. Surely the right of parents to control the education of their children is a right of a higher order than any alleged right of, say, the two college-educated lesbian members of the Symbionese Liberation Army to teach our young people. Yet the passage of an ordinance prohibiting discrimination because of "affectional preference" by Dade County, Florida, in January, 1977, forbade even private schools to refuse to hire homosexuals as teachers.

College officials have a right to decide that a dormitory is no place for homosexuals. Firemen, who constantly risk their lives in our behalf, should have the right to make a judgment that their close living and working conditions make a homosexual coworker intolerable.

These are some of the reasons why the various proposed homosexual and lesbian bills are usually rejected by state and local units of government. What homosexuals and lesbians have failed to achieve at the federal, state, and local levels, however, they are planning on accomplishing through the Equal Rights Amendment. While no one can predict with absolute certainty how the United States Surpeme Court will rule on any issue, leading legal authorities are convinced that ERA will legalize homosexual "marriages" and grant them the special rights and benefits given by law to husbands and wives.

One reason for this is the language of the Equal Rights Amendment, which says: "Equality of rights under the law shall not be denied or abridged by the United States or by any State on account of sex." It is precisely "on account of sex" that a state now denies a marriage license to a man and a man, or to a woman and a woman. A homosexual who wants to be a teacher could argue persuasively that to deny him a school job would be discrimination "on account of sex."

ERA would require state legislatures (or the courts, if the legislatures fail to act) to delete "sexist" language from state laws (e.g., *man, woman, husband, wife, male, female*) and replace all such words with sex-neutral language (e.g., *person, spouse*). Thus, a law that defines marriage as a union of a man and a woman would have to be amended to replace *man* and *woman* with *person*. A "marriage" between a "person" and a "person" is not the same thing as a marriage between a man and a woman.

Professor Paul A. Freund of the Harvard Law School testified before the Senate Judiciary Committee:

> Indeed, if the law must be as undiscriminating concerning sex as it is toward race, it would follow that laws outlawing wedlock between members of the same sex would be as invalid as laws forbidding miscegenation. Whether the proponents of the Amendment shrink from these implications is not clear.

And Professor James White of the Michigan Law School testified: "Conceivably a court would find that the State had to authorize marriage and recognize marital legal rights between members of the same sex."

Senator Sam J. Ervin, Jr., who placed both the above statements in the *Congressional Record,* added: "This matter illustrates as well as any the radical departures from our present system that the ERA will bring about in our society."[22]

The Yale Law Journal of January, 1973, published a scholarly discussion called "The Legality of Homosexual Marriage," which persuasively rebuts Senator Birch Bayh and others who try to deny the probable effect of ERA in this important area:

> The Court's decision that the denial of marriage licenses to homosexuals does not abridge existing equal protection law would not save that practice from attack under the proposed Twenty-seventh Amendment. . . . The legislative history of the Amendment clearly supports the interpretation that sex is to be an impermissible legal classification, that rights are not to be abridged on the basis of sex. A statute or administrative policy which permits a man to marry a woman, subject to certain regulatory restrictions, but categorically denies him the right to marry another man clearly entails a classification along sexual lines. . . .
>
> The stringent requirements of the proposed Equal Rights Amendment argue strongly for . . . granting marriage licenses to homosexual couples who satisfy reasonable and non-discriminatory qualifications.[23]

Rita Hauser, New York lawyer and United States representative to the United Nations Human Rights Commission, addressed the American Bar Association at its annual meeting in St. Louis in August, 1970, on the subject of ERA, stating:

> I also believe that the proposed Amendment, if adopted, would void the legal requirement or practice of the states' limiting marriage, which is a legal right, to partners of different sexes.

Senator Sam J. Ervin, Jr., summed up this point when he stated in a speech in Raleigh, North Carolina, on February 22, 1977: "I don't know but one group of people in the United States the ERA would do any good for. That's homosexuals."

When you add up the many ways that ERA will work against the family unit, it appears that it was no exaggeration when Dr. Jonathan H. Pincus, professor of neurology at Yale Medical School, testified in Washington:

> Is the Equal Rights Amendment to be the Tonkin Gulf Resolution of the American social structure? . . . I would predict that the Equal Rights Amendment and many of the other goals of its proponents will bring social disruption, unhappiness and increasing rates of divorce and desertion. Weakening of family ties may also lead to increased rates of alcoholism, suicide, and possibly sexual deviation.[24]

The Husband's Rights

In addition to imposing double Social Security taxes and extra taxes to replace mother-care of children with government kiddy-care facilities, there are many other ways that ERA will hurt men. The right to establish the location of the family home is a necessary and proper right of the husband, since he has the obligation to provide a home for his wife and family. ERA would wipe out all state laws that assure husbands the right to establish the domiciles of their families.

The laws that give the husband the right to establish the domicile are principal targets of the women's liberation movement and are often cited in debate as laws the liberationists want to wipe off our statute books. One's attitude toward these laws is based directly on one's assumptions and scale of values. If you think that the family is a social value to be cherished and encouraged, then the existing laws are good.

ERA will also cost a father the right to have his children carry his last name. Most states do not have laws specifically enunciating this right, but it is enforced by other types of legal restrictions, such as birth certificates, driver's licenses, and other official documents and regulations.[25]

ERA would make any requirement that a child carry his or her father's name unconstitutional because, by definition, it would "discriminate" against the mother on account of her sex. If a constitutional amendment requires us to erase the time-honored lines of paternity and legitimacy, the resulting confusion will strike a severe blow at the family unit. The new legitimacy that this would accord to unmarried parents, and to homosexuals and lesbians who adopt children, would come at the expense of our respect for the institution of the family.

The antifamily and antimen objectives of the women's liberationists are clearly shown in their concerted attack on husbands in their role as family providers. It is not clear whether the women's liberationists are motivated by an antagonism toward men as the "oppressor class" or toward the wives those men are supporting, but the net result is to hurt them both.

This hatred for husbands as family providers first surfaced in the official book of resolutions published by the National Organization for Women, *Revolution: Tomorrow Is NOW:*

> [Resolved] that NOW call on the EEOC [Equal Employment Opportunity Commission] to issue an immediate ruling prohibiting applications that require information on sex, including given name of applicant, and that NOW demand that the EEOC prohibit questions concerning marital or parental plans or status . . . from pre-employment inquiries of any sort.[26]

The first significant success of this radical resolution was the contract that the National Organization for Women forced Detroit's WXYZ-TV to sign. It is similar to contracts NOW is trying to force on other employers. This contract calls for eliminating from employment applications all reference to:

> marital status, number of children, height, weight, and number of persons dependent upon the applicant for support, nor will the above factors be considered as criteria for employment.[27]

The womens liberationists succeeded in putting this principle of discrimination against husbands into federal law when it was incorporated into the Health, Education and Welfare regulation on schools and colleges that went into effect on July 18, 1975. The regulation prohibits any school or college from giving any job preference whatsoever to an employee or applicant for employment who is "the head of household or principal wage earner in such employee's or applicant's family unit."[28]

This is clear and cruel discrimination against a husband and father trying to support his family, and against the wife and mother who chooses to be a homemaker. When considered in conjunction with federally enforced "reverse discrimination," it means that employers are being forced to hire and train inexperienced single women with no dependents in order to achieve some arbitary quota (to remedy alleged past injustices of a generation ago), rather than a more qualified married man with dependents. The employer otherwise faces charges of "discrimination" brought by the EEOC or the battery of high-priced lawyers hired by the women's liberationists. Faced with costly litigation, most employers are acquiescing in reverse discrimination against a husband's right and ability to fulfill his role as provider, and against the right of his wife to be a full-time homemaker.

Roy Willkins, in his syndicated column appearing in the *Kansas City Times* of August 15, 1975, quoted a letter from a woman who pinpointed the issue of how ERA will hurt blacks in the job market:

> "Women's Lib and the ERA will only promote a labor market dominated by double income families, most of whom will be white, and the welfare rolls will be bloated with more and more no-income families, most of whom will be black. The result will be untenable for all thinking people."

So long as we don't tie ourselves up with a constitutional noose called ERA, our legislative and judicial system offers many remedies to these problems. If ERA is ratified, however, we will be stuck with endless mischief because, as part of the Constitution, it will be the "supreme law of the land."

The women's liberation movement also despises veterans and is working hard to eliminate all veterans' preferences from every aspect of our laws, job opportunities, and educational system. It is not clear whether this animosity stems from the liberationist dogma that men are women's natural enemies (most veterans are men), or from a dislike of anyone who served in defense of our country, or simply from an unreasoning determination to get women hired in place of men in as many jobs as possible.

In any event, the foremost women's lib organization, the National Organization for Women, is working to abolish all veterans' preferences. This policy is clearly set forth in three separate places in *Revolution: Tomorrow Is NOW:*

> [Resolved] that NOW oppose any state, federal, county or municipal employment law or program giving special preference to veterans. . . .
>
> NOW has continually opposed laws giving preference to veterans, its most recent effort being directed against the Emergency Employment Act of 1971. These laws continue on the books, largely because of the strong influence of Veterans organizations. . . .
>
> [Resolved] that NOW oppose any state, federal, county, or municipal employment law or program giving special preference to veterans. . . .[29]

This vindictive attitude toward the men who have sacrificed so much and served so gallantly in defense of our country is proof of the desire of the militant women to use political pressure to hurt men. If ERA is ever ratified, the women's liberationists will push to invalidate veterans' preferences on the ground that they are "sexist" because they benefit mostly men.

ERA has sometimes been called a men's-lib amendment. It is true that it will provide some liberation for the offbeat and the deadbeat male—that is, to the homosexual who wants the same rights as husbands, to the husband who wants to escape supporting his wife and children, and to the coward who wants to get out of military service by giving his place to a woman.

But ERA will be tremendously hurtful to the overwhelming majority of men who are decent, law-abiding, moral, and family oriented. It will cost them higher taxes, loss of jobs for which they are qualified, loss of personal fulfillment as providers and protectors of their families, and loss of the essential rights of husbands to establish homes and name their children.

George Gilder demonstrates in his book *Sexual Suicide*[30] that the family is the institution that has civilized the male. It enables female stability and nurture to prevail over masculine mobility and violence. Man's role as family provider gives him the incentive to curb his primitive nature. Everyone needs to be needed. The male satisfies his sense of need through his role as provider for the family. If he is deprived of this role, he tends to drop out of the family and revert to the primitive masculine role of hunter and fighter.

The women's liberation movement to the contrary, there *are* male and female roles. It is just as hurtful to a man to be deprived of his role as provider and protector as it is to a woman to be deprived of her maternal role. It is just as hurtful to a husband to be deprived of his right to have a wife who is a mother for his children as it is to a wife to be deprived of her right to be a full-time homemaker.

Equality in the Military

There may be some dispute about what equality means in some fields, but there is no dispute about what it means in relation to the draft and the military. ERA would positively make women subject to the draft and to all military assignments on an equal basis with men because everything to do with the military is a matter of federal law or regulation, and ERA would prohibit any difference of treatment.

Such a radical change would be contrary to present laws, to our customs and mores, and to the wishes of the overwhelming majority of American citizens. In the twentieth century, young American men were drafted during a total of thirty-three years —including service in four bloody wars—and there was absolutely no demand by women or men for women to be conscripted equally, assigned equally, or sent into battle equally. ERA would tie a constitutional noose around our necks for all future wars.

In order to prove that the Equal Rights Amendment would make women subject to the draft and to combat duty equally with men, one need only to turn to the official United States House Judiciary Committee report to Congress: "Not only would women, including mothers, be subject to the draft but the military would be compelled to place them in combat units alongside of men."[31]

The United States House Judiciary Committee, which held the hearings and heard the testimony, reluctantly voted ERA out on the floor of Congress, but only with the addition of the "Wiggins Clause," which specifically exempted women from "compulsory military service." The Wiggins Clause was stricken out of ERA at the demand of militant extremists, who insisted that women be made subject to the draft just like men. This legislative history makes it crystal clear that ERA will subject women to absolutely equal treatment in and by the military.

The ERA proponents who are lawyers or witnesses at legislative hearings cannot deny this inescapable result of ERA. They freely admit it and say it is what they want. For example, the leading congressional sponsor of ERA, Representative Martha Griffiths, stated: "The draft is equal. That is the thing that is equal. But once you are in the Army you are put where the Army tells you where you are going to go." She is surely correct in that. Once you are in the Army, you do what you are told; and if you are assigned to high-risk or combat tasks, you do them.

Senator Birch Bayh, an avid ERA booster, in a debate with me at the Kennedy Center in Washington, D.C., on March 16, 1977, stated that he thinks women should consider it a "privilege to be drafted and sent into military combat."

The principal piece of scholarship presented to the Congress by Congresswoman Griffiths and Senator Bayh is an article by Professor Thomas I. Emerson in the *Yale Law Journal* of April, 1971. It spells out in specific detail how the Equal Rights Amendment will make women and men subject to equal treatment by the military:

> As now formulated, the Amendment permits no exceptions for the military. Neither the right to privacy nor any unique physical characteristic justifies different treatment of the sexes with respect to voluntary or involuntary service. . . . A woman will register for the draft at the age of 18, as a man does now. . . . Training and combat may require the carrying of loads weighing 40 to 50 pounds, but many, if not most, women in this country are fully able to do that. . . . As between brutalizing our young men and brutalizing our young women there is little to choose. . . . Women will be subject to the draft. . . . Women will serve in all kinds of units, and they will be eligible for combat duty.[32]

At state legislative hearings around the country, ERA witnesses enthusiastically take the position that women should be drafted and placed in combat. They also argue that women cannot achieve their full rights in our society until they are treated absolutely equally with men in every military job. I heard one pro-ERA witness gleefully tell Illinois legislators: "I consider myself a salesperson for the Selective Service Board. I think women should be drafted." And I heard another emphatically tell South Carolina legislators: "Women should not have the choice as to whether to serve in the military or not."

At the Virginia hearings, I listened as one of the legislators asked a pro-ERA witness: "If we did draft women, don't you think we could assign the women to the safe, noncombat jobs, and leave the actual fighting up to the men?" She replied: "Oh no, because that would discriminate against women and deprive us of our equal opportunity to win a Congressional Medal of Honor!" Unfortunately, most Medal of Honor winners are dead, and the overwhelming majority of American women do not think they were mistreated because they did not have an equal obligation to fight jungle warfare in Vietnam and become POWs or MIAs.

The whole argument is ridiculous on its face. ERA is presented as a constitutional amendment that will benefit women —and one has to be kidding to call it a step up for women to make them subject to involuntary military conscription and assignment to combat duty. The witnesses who speak this way so enthusiastically are always either over draft age, or have no daughters, or are too young to know what war is all about, or concede that they personally will be conscientious objectors. They will exercise *their* freedom of choice to avoid military service, but they are willing to inflict involuntary military duty on all other eighteen-year-old girls.

Alan Alda, star of the television program "M*A*S*H," whom ERA proponents imported to Illinois to star as their lead witness at a 1975 state Senate hearing, said he was quite willing for everyone else's daughter to be drafted. But when asked if his three daughters would be conscientious objectors, he replied: "I hope so."

When ERA proponents plead their case before women's groups or in the press—where they are not subject to vigorous cross-examination—they sing an entirely different tune. By sheer hypocrisy of argument, ERA proponents have been able to line up many uninformed women in support of such radical proposals. Let us examine some of the foolish and deceitful arguments used to persuade the general public.

False argument: "Congress now has the power to draft women." This is a prime example of the word-chicanery practiced by ERA proponents. It is true that Congress now has the power to draft women—but for 200 years Congress used this power to *exempt* women. This is the way the overwhelming majority of American men and women want it. If ERA is ratified, however, Congress will no longer have the option. Congress will be constitutionally compelled to draft women on an absolutely equal basis with men whenever conscription is reinstated.

False argument: "There is no draft; we have a volunteer Army." This shows the naivete of the ERA proponents who blithely assume that we have now achieved a utopia in which we will have no more wars and no more conscription. Logic, history, and common sense teach us otherwise. During most of the thirty-three years that we drafted young men in this century, politicians were promising peace. In the years prior to Vietnam, no one could have predicted that we would fight that war with conscripts for eight long years. It is only reasonable to assume that we will have future wars and conscription despite all promises and protestations to the contrary.

False argument: "All women will not be drafted; mothers will be exempt." Of all the arguments used by ERA proponents, this is the most hypocritical. No one ever claimed that "all" women will be drafted. If you are over draft age, or if you have only one eye or one leg, of course you will not be drafted. But girls of the proper age and in good physical condition will be drafted and sent into combat exactly like men. The extent of exemptions varies with the national emergency. When the emergency calls for drafting fathers up through age thirty-five —as was done during World War II—ERA will require mothers to be drafted on exactly the same basis.

False argument: "We need ERA so women in the military can get GI benefits equal to those given men." Women who serve in the military now have the best of both worlds. They have the same pay, the same ranks, the same education benefits, the same housing loans, and the same fringe benefits as men. In 1975 the United States Supreme Court even upheld promotion rights for women that are *superior* to men's.[33] At the same time, women are protected against being sent into combat and from assignment to some of the more high-risk and un-pleasant tasks.

False argument: "Only one percent of men are placed in combat." This is like saying that *only* 55,000 American service-men were killed in Vietnam, or there were *only* 1,000 POWs. No matter how many there are, it is no step forward to require that half of our casualties be women. The fact is that millions of young men were drafted for service in Vietnam, and Penta-gon figures show that 22 percent served in combat.

False argument: "The Selective Service System wouldn't really draft women!" Both Congress and the Selective Service System must obey the Constitution because it is the supreme law of the land. Doubting Thomases should read how Selec-tive Service had made plans to draft women before our country converted to all-volunteer armed forces:

> Selective Service must register young men at age 18 (and young women as well if the Equal Rights Amendment be-comes a part of the Constitution), hold an annual lottery, classify registrants, and maintain viable procedures in the event of inductions. It might be wise as well to call some young people for preinduction examinations so that the Pres-ident would have available an acceptable pool of registrants for immediate induction in an emergency.[34]

False argument: "In this modern technological age, combat duty won't be dangerous; it may mean just sitting at a com-puter at a missile site." Tell that to the hundreds of thousands of young men who fought in Vietnam. The technological/com-puter age was born before the Vietnam War, but that didn't save us from jungle warfare. Those who naively think that "we have learned our lesson in Vietnam, and that will never happen again," should read modern history and learn that the politi-cians made all those same resolves when the Korean War ended a decade earlier. No one has a crystal ball that shows what lies ahead. It makes no sense to tie our hands with a constitutional knot that deprives us of options to deal with future emergencies.

False argument: "The knowledge that women are subject to

the draft will be a deterrent to war." History offers no example of a country's saving itself from attack by the device of conscripting women. The fact that Israel drafts women and had a noble woman as chief of state, Golda Meir, did not deter the Arabs from launching their Yom Kippur attack in October, 1973. Women can even start wars, as Indira Gandhi proved when she ordered India's attack on Pakistan.

False argument: "Other countries draft women, so drafting women should be acceptable in America." The only non-Communist country that drafts women is Israel, and Israel's national emergency is entirely different from any we have ever had. A little country whose national survival is in immediate and acute danger, Israel is forced to use all available manpower and womanpower.

Even so, Israel would never tolerate anything so demeaning to women as the Equal Rights Amendment. Israeli women serve in the armed forces only about half as long as men. Israeli women have automatic exemption if they marry or have a baby. They are not put into combat or into integrated barracks with men. The Israelis tried putting their women into combat for a very brief period in the 1948 war, and they found out what happens to women when they fall into the hands of vicious men. Israel did not make that mistake in any of its three later wars.

The women in Israel are willing to do what is necessary for national survival, but according to a 1973 interview with Ada Feinberg-Sereni, one of eight women members of the Israeli Parliament, the second generation of Israeli women are "trading in their rifles for aprons." She said: "The revival of housewifery seems to be the women's choice. They say, 'We want to do our normal roles—looking after our children and our husbands.'"[35]

By 1976 the *New York Times* reported that Israeli women "are actively cultivating the feminine mystique." A series of interviews produced such genuine womanly comments as: "Kibbutz women aren't interested in equality, they're interested in children." "You can't have men looking after children; they wouldn't know what to do." "Working outdoors ages your skin prematurely." The women said they enjoy "the privileges of being female."

False argument: "The United States Navy has already started putting women in ships, so what's so bad about that?" In enthusiastic anticipation of ratification of ERA, Admiral Elmo R. Zumwalt, Jr., placed 50 women on the U.S.S. *Sanctuary* with 400 men. While the top Navy brass obeyed orders and told the public that this experiment was "working out well," enterprising reporters discovered that there were two on-board pregnancies, that the morale of the seamen was damaged because the female deckhands could get out of heavy work by throwing tantrums or crying, and that many of the girls were disillusioned and had blistered hands from the rigors of deck work.

Sanctuary crew member Sherry Sager, age nineteen, told a reporter: "I got fed up with welding, plumbing, and drilling in a cramped hull with little ventilation. I didn't want to burn and scar myself and lose my fingers." One of Sherry's shipmates, Patty Seasock, also nineteen, said: "I'm bored and I feel restricted. I don't know if I can make it two more years. I'd really like to be a Playboy bunny."[36]

The U.S.S. *Sanctuary* has been retired from service. If ERA is ever ratified, however, shipboard integration would become mandatory. Anyone who knows what it means for servicemen to live in combat or shipboard circumstances understands that the assignment of women on an equal basis is simply contrary to prevailing American standards of morals, mores, and morale.

False argument: "Young college women support ERA and are willing to accept the risks and responsibilities of the military draft just like men." When pressed in debate, nine out of ten of those who blithely make such statements indicate that they would become conscientious objectors or flee to Canada rather than accept induction. To the sincere ones, the answer is simple: "Run, don't walk, to the nearest recruiting office and volunteer. The armed services are looking for good women. It is an honorable career and we wish you well. You have your freedom of choice and we urge you to exercise it. But please don't take from other women their freedom to choose a different career."[37]

All evidence indicates that women who do choose a military career do *not* want complete equality of treatment and job assignment. In May, 1976, the United States comptroller general issued a General Accounting Office report to Congress on "Job Opportunities for Women in the Military: Progress and Problems," which concluded that women are not strong enough to do much of the work required in the physical jobs and generally prefer administrative and medical jobs. In the Navy, for example, women simply could not lift 100-pound sandbags, 94-pound paint cans, and boat lines that weigh up to 7 pounds a foot. In the Marines, women could be trained to climb telephone poles, but not to carry fifty pounds of equipment up with them. The Air Force surgeon general concluded that an average woman has only 60 percent of the strength of the average man.

The GAO report shows the injustice of opening up all military jobs to women: "Men must perform a disproportionate share of the work." Equality in the military is unfair to everyone, the serviceman, the servicewoman, and the American people who are paying the costs.

If the future brings a more dire national emergency than that of World War II, when we faced powerful and ruthless enemies on two far-flung fronts, and such an unforeseen circumstance requires the military services of women, there is no present constitutional bar to using women in any capacity and in any numbers. We now have the flexibility to deal with any future circumstances both in the draft and in job assignment.

But if we ratify the Equal Rights Amendment, we forfeit our options. We would be constitutionally prohibited from sending men and fathers into combat unless we likewise send women and mothers into combat. This is not what the American people want.

Equality in Police Work

The illusion that most women might be able to avoid military service and/or combat duty under ERA because they would not be able to meet the same physical standards that men must pass is dispelled by the record of how the federal courts handled the lawsuits filed by the militant women's liberationists against the local police departments. This proves conclusively that the women's liberationists are not pushing for equality of opportunity, and they are not pushing for the rights of individuals to have their qualifications measured

103

against an objective standard regardless of sex. They are pushing for group rights, for reverse discrimination, and for an equal number of women in all traditionally male-dominated occupations, regardless of the inadequacy of female qualifications.

The drive to sex-integrate police departments shows the double standard of the women's liberationists. While they aggressively push reverse discrimination in order to achieve equality of rank and pay for women in police departments, they are just as militantly *against* equality when it comes to qualifications and tests for admission to the force and promotions after women are on the force. They are pushing their goals at the expense of the effectiveness, the service, and the morale of local police departments.

When the subject of women on the police force first comes up, many people are inclined to have a tolerant attitude and ask, Why shouldn't women be police officers if they can pass the same tests and do the same work as men?

The answer is that the women do not pass the same tests and they do not do the same work, but they are demanding reverse discrimination to achieve equality of rank and pay, regardless.

In Los Angeles, Police Chief Edward M. Davis came up with a plan for what he called a "unisex police force," on which women officers would draw the same assignments so long as they meet the same physical requirements as men. When, under this honest equality, only 2 of 35 women applicants passed the physical-strength tests required of all Los Angeles policemen, compared to 139 of 143 male applicants, female chauvinists began working to upset Chief Davis' plan. They want the qualifications reduced so they can achieve quota-enforced equality on a newly established lower level of ability and lower service to the community.

The militant women won their first big success in Detroit. Three women brought a class-action suit in federal court against the Detroit Police Department and succeeded in persuading the court to issue an injunction ordering the hiring of women on a one-to-one ratio:

(5) . . . The Detroit Police Department [shall] hire at least one qualified female for each male hired into the Department. . . .
(6) . . . The Detroit Police Department [shall] assign all persons who henceforth complete training at the Criminal

Justice Institute to divisions of the Department on a unisex basis, that is, without regard to sex *per se.*

(7) . . . The Detroit Police Department [shall] begin immediately the use of recruiting material which stresses the equal role of men and women in the Detroit Police Department.[38]

The joker in that court injunction is the word "qualified." Compliance with this court order does not by any means indicate that female applicants are qualified on the same basis as male applicants. Height and weight requirements have been scrapped altogether. The feats of strength a person must be able to do before being accepted for recruit school have been drastically reduced. Great changes have been made at recruit school in the physical program that always heretofore included boxing, a two-mile run, combat training, and exercises to develop the strength essential to police work.

Is such combat training necessary for police work? It certainly is for all those subject to job assignment without discrimination, just as the Army gives combat training to all those subject to combat assignment, even though they are not assigned to combat duty all the time. The Detroit Police Department, like any big-city police force, can be considered a paramilitary organization. Big-city policemen are on the cutting edge of the war against crime. FBI Director Clarence Kelley said that thirteen police officers were killed during 1973 in what could be described as urban-guerrilla actions.

Some people have cherished the illusion that women in the police department could have their cake and eat it, too; that is, that they could have the advantages of reverse discrimination and quotas, but still be protected from dangerous or unpleasant assignments because they are women. The experience of the Detroit Police Department in obeying the court order dispels this illusion.

Equality means equal assignment and, under the court order, Detroit policewomen began regularly answering run-of-the-mill police calls, including domestic quarrels, saloon brawls, civil disturbances, shoot-outs, and other guerrilla-warfare city crises.

Detroit Police Chief Philip Tannian issued a detailed ten-point order in compliance with court rulings. It specifies that women be assigned to patrol cars "in the same manner in which they assign male officers." Further, it said, "no patrol beats or scout car territories shall be designated exclusively for or deemed unacceptable for the assignment of male or female officers." Women are not to be assigned only to less-demanding duties, such as school details, station runs, or conveying prisoners.

Court-enforced reverse discrimination for women does not apply only to applicants. The United States district judge subsequently ordered the department to promote a specified number of women in the next training classes. The judge ruled that this number of women must be added to the promotion list regardless of their scores on the examination. This is the practice known as "dipping." It means dipping down past the more qualified applicants in order to accept or promote those with lower scores who belong to some favored group.

Commenting editorially on the Detroit police problems, the *Detroit Sunday News* called the court order "a new kind of bias that has begun to stain American life: reverse discrimination."

This court-ordered reverse discrimination had a predictable effect on the morale, efficiency, and ambition of Detroit police officers. Detroit has always had an excellent program of in-department education and prepromotion classes, which most officers attended in order to qualify for upgrading from patrolman to sergeant and from sergeant to lieutenant. After the federal court order, there was a 75 percent drop in attendance at these classes. Here are two typical comments given to reporters by the discouraged nonattenders:

> I was going to go, but I figured, what the hell. Even if I finished in the top 10 percent on the test, I probably would be passed over for promotion when the Chief went "dipping" on the list.

> Well, they said they weren't going to discriminate against anybody because of race or sex, but they are doing it. They're discriminating against guys like me.

Detroit police officer Susan F. Walker refused the promotion given to her as a result of the court order. She wrote the commissioner: "I don't believe in the policy of 'dipping' for promotion just because we are women. Those guys studied long and hard for the exams, and no one told them the rules would be changed in midstream." Standing on principle cost her a $2,500 yearly pay raise as well as the opportunity to be a supervisory officer.[39]

Early in 1973 a civil rights suit was filed against the San

106

Francisco Police Department and city officials charging that the city discriminates against racial minorities and women. In fall 1973, a United States district judge ordered the city Civil Service Commission to institute hiring quotas to "alleviate, with due speed, the past effects of discrimination and prevent any future discrimination."

The court also ordered the commission to hire three minority officers for every two nonminority officers until 30 percent of the department is comprised of minorities, and to appoint as sergeants one minority for each nonminority officer until 30 percent of the sergeants is comprised of minorities. The court also ordered the commission to devise new written and physical tests on the ground that past tests were discriminatory.

New and less rigorous tests and requirements, which are much less demanding, have already been prepared and put into effect. The obvious purpose of the easier tests is to admit women who cannot meet the previous male requirements. Height requirements were abolished. Formerly, the height requirement was five feet seven inches, but the San Francisco Police Department has now taken at least two applicants of only four feet nine inches. The average height of the female applicants is five foot three. The level of the written test has been likewise reduced. Under the former written tests, about 30 percent of the applicants passed; under the new written tests, up to 80 percent have passed.

Even the reduced test levels did not satisfy the female chauvinists. They returned to federal court to challenge the new physical tests as still too rigorous. They claim that the use of a dynamometer, a grip-testing device, is discriminatory against women. The attorney for the women asked the court to order a new lowered physical test for applicants, saying, "It may be necessary to order ratio-hiring of women."

A federal judge issued an order halting the hiring of new officers for the San Francisco police force pending the approval of new tests, even though the police department was under strength by 128 officers and it was anticipated that the shortage would grow to 170 before new officers could be tested, trained, and put into service. The hiring freeze took its toll in reduced police protection for a city that has been the scene of much violent crime.

San Francisco police officials are concerned about the dangerous lowering of police standards and that in the long run the quality of police protection and service to the community will suffer. They believe that a high quality police force requires at least the maintenance of present standards. Jerry Crowley, president of the San Francisco Police Officers Association, said:

> The whole thrust of this court effort is to minimize the tests to the point they are not tests at all. Their whole attitude is to get these people into the department in sufficient numbers, regardless of how it affects the safety of the community.

Yet the San Francisco police force is under such steady pressure from minorities that one of the senior police captains felt it necessary to appear before a meeting of homosexuals and declare: "We welcome anybody to come out and take our exams—even gays."

In Chicago a federal judge on November 7, 1974, found the Chicago Police Department guilty of racial discrimination in the hiring and promoting of policemen, and he ordered the department to devise a new testing procedure. During the preceding year, the Chicago Police Department did not hire any new officers or promote patrolmen to sergeants because of the pending suit, even though there were 700 vacancies for patrolmen and about 100 for sergeant. The judge's ruling came even though he recognized that "eventually, the shortage of patrol officers will become critical in a city the size and complexity of Chicago." In response to the women's lib movement, the judge even ordered the department to discontinue the use of the term *patrolman* and replace it with *police officer.*

After extensive litigation, the federal court in 1976 imposed rigid hiring quotas on the Chicago Police Department: 42 percent white male, 42 percent minority male, and 16 percent female. But that wasn't all. The court required the department to submit a list to the judge of all persons who were not hired. Could the court enforce its decree? You bet it could. It simply cut off all federal revenue-sharing funds to Chicago until the police department complied.

Press interviews with policemen and policewomen show that the overwhelming majority do not want the unreasoning equality of treatment now being demanded by a few female chauvinists and mandated by court order. Experienced police officers are uneasy about the prospect of the problems that will arise with a four-foot-nine-inch officer out on the street, including assignment to patrols in high crime areas. Typical comments from big-city policemen are:

> Most of the men in the Department, I expect, will not like it for a number of reasons—some personal—but the majority for safety reasons. . . .

> Practically speaking, I doubt any police officer on the street would feel at ease in a tight situation with a woman as a partner. . . .

> When things get down to the nitty gritty, where physical strength is required, men officers believe a patrolwoman just can't hold up her end.[40]

And from policewomen:

> It's absurd to think a woman would want to patrol in Baltimore City, where even men don't want to go.

> I'm five foot two and weigh 110 pounds. No six-foot man is going to stop just because I tell him to.

> I know some women who would be very good on patrol, but to me equal rights doesn't mean women are the same as men—it means equal opportunity. I wouldn't request such an assignment because you can run into a lot of problems and I'm slightly queasy.[41]

Unfortunately, it is no longer a question of whether a policewoman "requests such an assignment." Under court-ordered reverse discrimination, a policewoman has lost her right to refuse dangerous or unpleasant or unsuitable assignments, unless, of course, she chooses to resign from the police force. Some have already done that rather than go out on patrol.

The net result is that, for the sake of the handful of female chauvinists who get their psychological kicks by demanding reverse discrimination and the lawyers who get good fees out of judgments awarded in sex-discrimination cases, the entire community is made to suffer from reduced police protection at a time when we need our police more than ever before. And the woman who wants to make an honorable career out of police work that is commensurate with her physical ability is forced to take assignments that she did not seek and does not want at any price.

San Diego Police Chief Ray Hoobler gave an interview that accurately reflects the concerns of those who want to give

women a fair break in police work and at the same time effi-
ciently perform the police mission of protecting the community. He pointed out that policewomen are excellent in investi-
gative work as plain-clothes detectives, but that their physical
stature creates a problem when they are assigned to other tasks,
such as police ambulances: "Some, not all, don't have the
strength to handle the gurneys. One of our policewomen had
just finished putting down an inebriated man in an ambulance.
She turned around, and he struck her. She resigned the next
day."

Chief Hoobler cited another example of a woman who en-
countered a group of men suspiciously congregated on the
street. She just drove around the block without investigating.
"She admitted this to me," Chief Hoobler said. "Later, she
resigned from the force. She felt patrol work made too large a
demand on her capacities." In answer to the question of
whether policemen resent policewomen, Chief Hoobler said:

> No, but they are concerned. Let us say a policeman finds
> himself in a touchy situation and calls for a covering unit. A
> policewoman arrives. The natural instinct for him is to pro-
> tect her. It's part of our culture. So, in addition to being
> concerned about the situation he is in, he is also concerned
> and apprehensive about the female officer.
> My concern is a double one. I'm concerned about the level
> of police service to the community. And I'm concerned over
> the safety and well-being of our women officers.

The heart of the argument is not whether women can handle
most of the work but "whether they can handle the potentially
violent situations when lives are in jeopardy." Mrs. Sherrie
White, president of the New York Citizens Organization for
Police Support, put it this way:

> Violence is inherent in street patrol. Our objection is that
> we feel that women are not physically capable of handling
> what might be a violent incident on patrol and thus endanger
> the lives of the men who are their partners and of the public
> whom they are protecting.

Another aspect was discussed by Dr. Harvey Schlossberg,
the New York Police Department psychologist:

> In a car, partners share what we call "intimate space." This
> evolves into an "us against them" relationship, which be-

110

comes a deep emotional relationship. Sexual tension has to be there between a man and a woman under those circumstances. If it's not there, I'd wonder why not. . . . Partners often get to the point that one can't make a decision without consulting the other.[42]

Finally, there are the antifamily effects of a completely coed police force. Here are four typical comments made at a 1976 seminar attended by the police chiefs of America's largest cities, as reported by the *Washington Post*:

> After we put 11 women on the street, three of the four married women among them subsequently filed for divorce, and four of the men who had been teamed with women also started divorce proceedings.

> Under the tremendous stress of police work, you learn to depend on your partner. You're there eight hours a night side-by-side. You have to get to know your partner. You translate that to male-female and you get sex.

> If you put two women together in a squad car, they fight. If you put male and female together from 8:00 P.M. to 4:00 A.M., they fornicate.

> We broke up marriages by assigning officers to the vice squad, where the incidence of divorce is three times as high.

Is a fully sex-integrated police force morally justifiable? No, say many of the police chiefs who have had practical experience, because "the basic law of Western civilization is to preserve the family."

More recently, militant women have been demanding jobs in fire departments. Not only is a fireman's work beyond the physical strength of nearly all women, but the work pattern of firemen, involving long hours of living, working, and sleeping together, makes a sex-integrated fire department incompatible with community morals and customs. Ask yourself: When you are rescued from the third floor of a burning building, do you want to be carried down the ladder by a man or a woman? Are you satisfied with the knowledge that a "person" will respond to your fire alarm?

The obvious solution is to stop this foolish search for an impossible equality between men and women in physical jobs, and have a double-track system for policemen and policewomen that allows for reasonable differences in assignment, rank, pay, and the department's need for nonpatrol officers.

111

Such a solution could be practically achieved by a simple amendment to the Civil Rights Act of 1964, under which the sex-equality court orders have been issued.

If the Equal Rights Amendment is ever ratified, however, such an amendment to the Civil Rights Act would be unconstitutional, and there would be no way out of the irrationality of mandating identical treatment for men and women on police forces. There is nothing in the Equal Rights Amendment that requires any minimum standards—all it requires is sex equality. Most Americans would say that the physical strength of the average woman is not adequate protection in the face of the high level of crime in our nation's cities. In addition, ERA will probably require police and fire departments to hire and promote homosexuals, or face charges that the departments are discriminating "on account of sex."

Women in Industry

In business, professional, intellectual, and academic pursuits, women can compete equally with men because they are just as smart. In jobs that require physical labor, women cannot compete equally with men because their physical strength is not equal. For the same reasons that it is unfair to women, to men, and to the community to assign women equally with men to tasks in the military and in police work and fire fighting, it is unfair to treat women the same as men in the millions of manual-labor jobs that keep our industrial economy functioning.

In recognition of the physical differences between women and men—which are self-evident to everyone except women's liberationists—our country has developed a fabric of protective labor legislation. This consists of the network of state laws designed to give women employees particular benefits and protections not granted to men.

This protective labor legislation varies from state to state, but generally includes provisions to protect women from being compelled to work too many hours a day, or days a week, or at night; weight-lifting restrictions; provisions that mandate rest areas, rest periods, protective equipment, or a chair for a woman who stands on her feet all day; laws that protect women from being forced to work in dangerous occupations; and laws that grant more generous workmen's compensation for injuries to more parts of a woman's body than to a man's.

112

Women and unions have worked hard over several generations to achieve such legislation to protect and benefit women who are required to join the labor force because of economic necessity, but who have no academic or professional qualifications.

If ERA is ever ratified, all such protective labor laws will be wiped out in one stroke. ERA lawyers and witnesses do not dispute this fact. Instead, they resort to various diversionary arguments to sidestep the issue.

Congresswoman Martha Griffiths deals with the protective labor legislation issue by saying that all such legislation is already outlawed by Title VII of the Civil Rights Act of 1964. It is true that some labor legislation has been invalidated by the courts under the Civil Rights Act. But not all. Just because the courts have knocked out some good labor legislation is no reason to use the sledgehammer approach and knock it all out.

To any extent that protective labor legislation has been invalidated by the Civil Rights Act, it can be restored by amendment to the act. But anything knocked out by the United States Constitution cannot be restored except by the long and laborious process of another constitutional amendment.

ERA speakers confidently assure their uninformed audiences that "whenever the courts are confronted with a law that truly benefits women, the courts will extend the benefit to men instead of declaring it void." This does not happen in practice. In every case on record, particularly in the states of Washington, California, and Ohio, the courts have thrown out the protections of women and have not extended any benefits to men. Women have lost on every count. Most companies are delighted with the removal of the protections for women because they are generally expensive to management.

Syndicated columnist Georgie Anne Geyer reported from Seattle in December, 1976:

> Once the [Washington] state ERA was passed, the protective legislation for women and children dating from 1913, which restricted such things as enforced overtime work, provided for water and cots in restrooms, limited lifting of weights, etc., was voided.
>
> Fine, all the feminist organizations said, now we will go ahead and procure all of that protection for men, too.
>
> Only that is not what has happened.
>
> "The hearings that ensued were incredible," mused Mary Helen Roberts, executive director of the Washington State

113

Women's Council. "On one side, we had workers talking about 'dying in the streets,' and on the other side, we had businessmen talking about being 'forced out of business.' It was unreal...."

As the protective legislation was voided, women complained of forced overtime because business found it cheaper to pay time and a half than to hire new workers. If work was considered "intermittent in nature," the women got no breaks—for lunch or toilet—at all.

Governor-elect Dixy Lee Ray of Washington was asked on "Meet the Press" on November 7, 1976, if the Washington state ERA had caused problems. She said, yes, it had removed the protective labor legislation from women that had formerly guaranteed them coffee breaks, lunch breaks, the right to leave company property at lunch time, and safeguards against heavy lifting.

The women who appear as ERA witnesses before state legislative committees usually argue that protective labor legislation doesn't really protect but instead keeps women from advancing. This is the cloistered attitude of a business or professional woman who sits at a desk all day in a clean and spacious office and never lifts anything heavier than a few books and papers. She is the type of woman who finds intellectual fulfillment in her job, and she may indeed want the opportunity to work longer hours for more pay and promotions. Protective labor legislation does not apply to her, anyway.

This is not the point of view of the factory woman, who works only to help supplement the family income, who stands on her feet all day in front of a machine, whose work may be sweaty or exhausting, and who is eager to go home to take care of her children. There are millions more factory women than there are business women. And it is grossly unfair to the factory woman to wipe out the legislation that now protects her from a company that may order her to work a second eight-hour shift, an extra four-hour shift, seven days a week, or assign her to heavy lifting, dangerous or unpleasant jobs as male employees are arbitrarily assigned according to the workload of the company.

It is no answer to say that all overtime should be voluntary. Of course, it should! But the fact is that it isn't. With a few minor exceptions, even the most powerful unions have not been able to make overtime for men a matter of choice. But

114

protective labor laws protect women from involuntary overtime, and it is grossly unfair to deny them that protection. Most women in factory jobs have home duties, too. Myra Wolfgang, a Positive Woman who was nationally respected as longtime vice-president of the Hotel and Restaurant Employees and Bartenders International Union, AFL-CIO, as well as an officer of her Detroit Local 705 and a member of the Michigan Women's Commission by appointment of three governors, testified repeatedly against ERA because of its harmful effects on the working woman:

> Hours-limitations laws for women provided them with a shield against obligatory overtime to permit them to carry on their life at home as wives and mothers. While all overtime should be optional for both men and women, it is absolutely mandatory that overtime for women be regulated because of . . . [their] double role in our society. . . .
>
> It's one thing for a middle class feminist to talk about the "psychological uplift" of the Equal Rights Amendment. She can afford a brief high. Her working sisters will have to pay for her "fix." When the National Organization for Women calls the passage of the Equal Rights Amendment "a giant step for womankind" they are not all wrong. They just have their directions mixed up. The giant step is a backward one.[43]

Only if ERA is permanently rejected will women in industry be able to work out a solution whereby overtime for women is a voluntary option. If ERA is ratified, there will be no way to achieve this.

It is no answer to say that the factory woman has the right to reject heavy and dangerous work. She may have this right in theory, but not in practice. Take, for example, a period of unemployment and layoffs. When a company lays off workers, it reassigns those remaining to other jobs as needed by the company. In states where the courts have ruled that there can be no sex discrimination in job assignment, women are now being placed on jobs for which they never applied, do not want, and consider too heavy or dangerous or hazardous to their health. If they refuse to take such jobs, they get a black mark on their records. If they resign, they cannot draw unemployment compensation.

If ERA is ever ratified, the women in the lower economic classes, the women who do the manual jobs, will get the short end of the stick. The best one-sentence description of ERA was given by Mrs. Jean Noble, executive secretary of the National Council of Negro Women, who said:

> I call the Equal Rights Amendment the liftin' and totin' bill. More than half of the black women with jobs work in service occupations; if the Amendment becomes law, we will be the ones liftin' and totin'.[44]

At one state legislative hearing, a business woman appearing as a pro-ERA witness confidently argued that protective labor legislation is obsolete and unnecessary in this technological age, so women no longer need a law that requires a company to provide chairs. It comes with exceedingly poor grace for one who sits at a comfortable desk to brush off the legal right of a woman who stands on her feet all day to be provided with a chair.

Naomi McDaniel, the Positive Woman who founded Women of Industry, an organization of labor union women opposed to ERA, is an eloquent witness for the woman who has a double role in our society as wife/mother and factory worker. Mrs. McDaniel has eight children and works the night shift at a General Motors plant in Dayton, Ohio. In her testimony at many state legislative hearings she said:

> Women who work at desks or blackboards, where the heaviest loads they lift may be a pile of papers or a few books, are not representative of factory production workers who need protection of present laws, such as those limiting loads women must lift. The uninformed but noisy minority of ERA proponents—smooth-talking college women who have never even seen a factory production line—parrot the claim that some women can lift up to 75 pounds, and should have the "opportunity" to work alongside men.
>
> In their eagerness to, perhaps, get their boss' job as office manager, they are most generous in giving away those precious distinctions so badly needed by their harder-working sisters on the assembly line. While they point out that mothers easily lift 50-pound children, they do not realize or do not care that this is not like lifting 50 pounds every 60 seconds on an assembly line all day long. We Women in Industry know better than anyone else that we are simply not physically equal to men, but ERA permits no distinction.[45]

When the women's liberationists ridicule the "restroom argument," they are simply proving that ERA is an elitist upper-

116

middle class cause that has no relevance to the big majority of working women. The restroom argument is meaningful to the woman who works in industry. She knows that the women's restrooms are much pleasanter places than the men's and are often equipped with couches. They are places where she can escape for a few moments of rest each day from the drudgery of a manual labor job. She knows that protective labor legislation has mandated rest periods and rest areas for women, and that this is part of her right to be treated like a woman. In the states where the courts have voided all protective labor legislation, company after company has enthusiastically cut operating costs by removing the couches and reducing the size of women's restrooms.

The patronizing attitude of some business and professional women shows that they neither understand nor represent the needs or desires of women who work in industry or in manual-labor jobs. President Nixon's Council on the Status of Women, which endorsed ERA, was wholly dominated by business and professional women and had no representation from women in industry.

Ms Wilma Scott Heidi, former president of the National Organization for Women, answers the protective labor legislation issue by arguing that such legislation usually doesn't protect women in hospitals, hotels, and mercantile establishments. Quite apart from the fact that there is no comparison between hospital, hotel, and retail store work and work in steel mills, glass factories, and oil refineries, her argument is the typical sour grapes approach of the woman's liberationist. We should extend protective benefits to all women who need them—not take benefits away from anyone. But, again, this can only be done in the absence of ERA.

Some young and inexperienced proponents of ERA have argued that, if certain jobs are so hard, dangerous, and unpleasant, men should not be required to do them, either. Such an argument is out of touch with realities.

There are thousands of jobs in industry that are strenuous, hard, unpleasant, dirty, and dangerous that men can and will do and for which they receive good wages, but which women don't want to do and should not be compelled to do. To abolish these jobs would eliminate thousands of necessary and well-paying jobs that produce products Americans want and would significantly reduce our standard of living. Eliminating

117

them would benefit neither women nor men. But legislation can and should protect women from being forced to take such jobs.

It is not only in factories but in retail stores and supermarkets that women are feeling the brunt of unwelcome equality. For example, in 1976 the government issued orders to many supermarkets and liquor stores that all clerks must be paid the same wage *and* perform the same duties, including unloading trucks filled with cases weighing thirty to fifty pounds each. You can guess how enthusiastic women clerks in their fifties and sixties are about this new equality. Yet, their appeals to be exempted from such enforced equality have fallen on deaf ears.

Congressman Emanuel Celler, who was chairman of the House Judiciary Committee that held the hearings on ERA, summed up the reasons why he voted against it:

> In all the swirling arguments and differing interpretations of the language of the proposal, there has been very little thought given to the triple role most women play in life, namely, that of wife, mother and worker. This is a heavy role indeed, and to wipe away the sustaining laws which help tip the scales in favor of women is to do injustice to millions of women who have chosen to marry, to make a home, to bear children, and to engage in gainful employment as well. . . . I refuse to allow the glad-sounding ring of an easy slogan to victimize millions of women and children.[46]

Equality in Education

Speakers promoting the Equal Rights Amendment sometimes cite education as one area of discrimination against women. The fact is that there is absolutely nothing that ERA can do to benefit women in the field of education, and there is a great deal of mischief that it would cause. ERA will not give women more educational opportunities, more pay, or more promotions.

The principal reason why this is so is that there is nothing good ERA can add to the federal Education Amendments of 1972 and the other laws and executive orders that prohibit discrimination on the basis of sex. They are all-extensive, all-inclusive, and, as implemented by the Department of Health, Education and Welfare, already go altogether too far.

The Education Amendments of 1972 prohibit discrimination on the basis of sex in admissions, scholarships, hiring, promotions, and all other aspects of academic work in all schools and colleges that receive any federal assistance, from kindergarten through graduate school. The operative section of Title IX of the Education Amendments is:

> No person in the United States shall, on the basis of sex, be excluded from participation in, be denied the benefits of, or be subjected to discrimination under any educational program or activity receiving federal financial assistance.

Women can go to law schools, medical schools, and all other types of graduate schools. They have full and equal access to all state universities, scholarships, and academic positions.

The Education Amendments of 1972, however, did make a few exceptions to the rule against sex discrimination, and these exceptions would be wiped out if ERA were ever ratified. The Education Amendments specifically exempt admissions to undergraduate institutions of higher education (although everything else connected with these colleges is subject to the nondiscrimination mandate).

There are at least a hundred colleges that have chosen to remain single-sex, including Smith, Wellesley, Bryn Mawr, and Mount Holyoke, believing that there is a place in our pluralistic society for some all-women's colleges. They argue that graduates of women's colleges are more likely to be career achievers than women graduates of coed colleges.[47]

Although these are private colleges, the long arm of federal money reaches into their operations and makes them subject to federal regulations. If ERA were ratified, they would be forced to make a choice: Go fully coed or give up all "federal assistance." These colleges are highly dependent on federal assistance of one kind or another, particularly for scholarship aid. It is unrealistic to think that any college or university that has been the recipient of federal assistance would make the decision to give up that annual income.

Is this what ERA proponents want? You bet they do. Their witnesses come into the state legislative hearings and say, "We don't believe any school or college should be permitted to receive any tax funds, or even to hold tax-exemption, if it discriminates on the basis of sex."

Since the United States Supreme Court decision of *Runyon* v. *McCrary* on June 25, 1976, it must be assumed that ratification of the Equal Rights Amendment would probably mean that *all* private schools (elementary and secondary, as well as college) would become subject to a constitutional mandate prohibiting "sex discrimination" and would be forced to go coed, whether they want to or not.

Runyon v. *McCrary* involved two elementary schools in Virginia that were charged with discriminating on the basis of race. The schools were wholly private. They received no public money of any kind. Apparently they did not even have tax-exempt status. But the Supreme Court, in a seven-to-two decision, held that they are forbidden to discriminate on the basis of race and that they must admit blacks.

The Supreme Court decision was based on a section of an 1870 law entitled "Equal rights under the law." As Justice White stated in his dissent, it is completely clear that both the language and the legislative history of this law prove that it was intended and designed to abolish race discrimination "under the law" only. It was *not* intended to cover private relationships.

But the majority of the Supreme Court stretched the law to include the private acts of wholly private schools. For more than 100 years, no one else had ever detected that meaning in the 1870 law. The Supreme Court ruled in *Runyon* v. *McCrary* that the mandate against race discrimination is so important that it prohibits even private acts of discrimination, and it takes priority over the First Amendment freedom of association, the Fifth Amendment right of due process, the constitutional right of privacy, and the right of parents to select private schools.

Practically every pro-ERA lawyer states—even boasts!—that ERA will impose a national standard that will apply the same strict legal standard to sex as we now apply to race. (In legal jargon, this is called making sex a "suspect" or impermissible classification, just like race.) The agitating women's lib lawyers (in NOW, the ACLU, the EEOC, and HEW) are following the same pattern of bureaucratic regulation and court litigation followed by the "civil rights" lawyers.

The surest way to predict what the ultimate effect of ERA will be is to ask yourself this question: Are we permitted to make this difference or separation based on race? If your answer is no, then—if ERA is ratified—you will not be permitted to make the same difference or separation based on sex. If ERA applies the *Runyon* v. *McCracy* rule to sex, no private school will be permitted to bar any pupil on the basis of sex; all private schools will be compelled to go coed—probably with "affirmative action" ordered by HEW.

Another piece of mischief that ERA would do in the educational world if it is ever ratified is that it would prohibit fraternities and sororities from functioning on college campuses. Two years after Congress passed the Education Amendments of 1972, the Department of Health, Education and Welfare issued eighty pages of proposed regulations "to effectuate Title IX of the Education Amendments of 1972." In regard to fraternities, sororities, and other campus organizations, these HEW regulations stated:

> A recipient [any college, university, or state receiving any federal assistance] may not, in connection with its educational program or activity, *support or assist* any organization, agency or person which discriminates on the basis of sex.

The HEW regulations then gave this specific example of the application of this rule:

> A recipient educational institution would be prohibited from providing financial support for an all-female hiking club, an all-male language club, or a single-sex honorary society.

Since most fraternities admit only men, and most sororities admit only women, by definition, they discriminate on the basis of sex.

As soon as fraternities and sororities began to feel the impact of these HEW regulations, they went into action and issued memorandum alerts to their memberships warning of the probable effect of the threatening ramifications.[48] Some 9,000 letters descended on HEW. Senators and congressmen began feeling the heat.

The sponsors of the Education Amendments of 1972, including Senator Birch Bayh and Congresswoman Edith Green, raised their hands in astonishment and said they didn't mean all this! Congresswoman Green said that Title IX "wasn't designed to do any of this nonsense."

Health, Education and Welfare Secretary Caspar Weinberger indicated sympathy with the complaints of fraternities and sororities, but stated that Congress would have to pass specific legislation before he would change the regulations. He felt that the Education Amendments of 1972 required these regulations, including their application to fraternities and sororities.

Congresswoman Edith Green quickly persuaded a Senate-House conference committee to approve an amendment to the HEW appropriations bill ordering HEW not to apply sex-discrimination rules to college and high school fraternities and sororities, Boy Scouts, Girl Scouts, Campfire Girls, YMCAs, YWCAs, and Boys' Clubs. Certainly the majority of Americans have no wish to wipe out the single-sex nature of fraternities and sororities. These organizations are entitled to their freedom of association.

While congressmen, fraternities, and sororities valiantly tried to bring some sanity into this picture, the women's lib groups complained that the HEW regulations did not go far enough! In many states, the state committees set up to study the HEW regulations are dominated by members of the National Organization for Women, who stridently demanded more and faster sex integration in every aspect of the entire educational process. Four women's groups filed suit against the government demanding more aggressive enforcement of the laws and regulations against sex discrimination.

If the Equal Rights Amendment is ever ratified, the fraternity-sorority exemption passed by Congress would immediately become unconstitutional and invalid. All the effort expended by the fraternities and sororities to persuade Congress to pass legislation exempting them will be to no avail—if ERA is ever ratified. As every informed person knows, Congress can amend any law by the simple expedient of passing an amendment by majority vote. But Congress cannot amend or change a constitutional amendment once it has been sent out to the states for ratification. The only way a constitutional amendment can be changed or modified, or exemptions added to it, is by the long, agonizing process of passing another constitutional amendment (as we did to repeal the Prohibition Amendment).

The furor about fraternities and sororities provided two important lessons: (1) An absolute rule against discrimination on the basis of sex has consequences that are ridiculous, unreasonable, and unwanted by the majority of Americans. (2) A law whose language sounds desirable or innocuous can easily become a fearful weapon of regulation and control in the hands of the bureaucrats who implement it and the courts that enforce it.

When the Equal Rights Amendment was being passed by Congress and during its early months of ratification by the states, the proponents solemnly assured everyone that it referred only to federal and state laws and to employment and higher educational opportunities for women, and that it would not interfere in the "private sector." This is probably why such essentially private organizations as fraternities and sororities did not then recognize the threat to their very existence in the disarming language of ERA.

The Department of Health, Education and Welfare labored another year to develop its final regulation implementing the Education Amendments of 1972. The unisex advocates within and outside the department argued strenuously for total commitment to the coed mandate (except in those areas expressly prohibited by law).

There was just one problem. In order for the HEW regulation to go into effect with the force of federal law, it had to be signed by the president. The militants knew that there would be no way they could deceive former All-American football player Gerald Ford into believing that women are the equal of men on the football field. As a concession to practical necessity, therefore, the final HEW regulation specifically exempts football, wrestling, boxing, ice hockey, and rugby from its order requiring the sex integration of all sports in schools and colleges.

The unisex militants look upon this as a temporary tactical concession. They know that, if ERA is ratified, there can be no exceptions because the language of the amendment is absolute; even contact sports would not be exempt.

The total effect of ERA on sports was also shown by a decision of the Commonwealth Court of Pennsylvania under the *state* Equal Rights Amendment already in effect. The court ruled that girls must be permitted to practice and compete with boys in all high school athletics, specifically including football and wrestling. In a five-to-one decision, the court ruled that a Pennsylvania Interscholastic Athletic Association bylaw prohibiting coeducational competition violates the Equal Rights Amendment to the Pennsylvania constitution. The court saw no difference between football and wrestling and other sports, holding that the mandate of ERA is absolute and must apply to all sports.[49]

This decision is the logical result of the strict ban on sex differences required by the language of the Equal Rights Amendment. It is a good example of the nonsense that results when we are constitutionally required to treat men and women with exact legal equality in everything touched by public funding, including our educational system.

School and college athletics provide a good example of how the Health, Education and Welfare bureaucrats expand their own authority in order to achieve their goals of restructuring our educational system. The National Collegiate Athletic Association and others have contended that athletics should be exempted from federal sex-discrimination rules because sports programs receive little or no direct federal aid. The new HEW regulation, however, takes the position that, if the school or college receives federal aid for *any* program or activity, it is irrelevant whether the athletic program itself receives federal aid. The HEW regulation states that athletics "constitute an integral part of the educational process of schools and colleges and, as such, are fully subject to the requirements."

The American Medical Association Committee on the Medical Aspects of Sports came out strongly against the growing demands of the women's liberation movement for girls to participate in sports with boys, stating:

> It is in the long-range interest of both male and female athletes that they have their own programs. During pre-adolescence there is no essential difference between the work capacity of boys and girls. . . .
> However, following puberty, most boys uniformly surpass girls in all athletic performance characteristics except flexibility, mainly because of a higher ratio of lean-body weight to adipose tissue.
> If girls demand equal rights to compete on boys' teams, boys are likely to request the same rights in return. . . . Boys will win a majority of the positions on girls' teams, which would result in virtual elimination of girls' programs.[50]

ERA is a two-edged sword. If the girls have a right to try out for boys' teams, then boys have a right to try out for girls' teams.

A good example of the result of such an arbitrary rule is what happened in the 1975 girls' bowling tournament in Illinois. An

Illinois circuit court issued a coed ruling similar to the HEW regulation. Dixon (Illinois) High School offered football for boys, but bowling for girls. The boys decided they would take advantage of the court ruling and compete for places on the girls' bowling team. Boys won four out of five places on the team. Then, at the girls' state championship bowling tournament held in Peoria, Illinois, in February, 1975, the Dixon boys easily walked off with the title. Everyone was angry and the tournament was a farce.

If there is *anyone* who should be against forcing girls and boys to compete together in everything, it should be those concerned about women's athletics! The girls will be the big losers under the "gender-free" coed mandate. At high school and college levels, the boys who are cut from the varsity teams can switch over and compete on the girls' teams. In many sports, this will take away the facilities and the funding that are starting to open up for women in school and college athletics.

The HEW regulation is already starting to cause endless mischief by mandating a fifty-fifty coed ratio in every school, college, class, and extracurricular activity, and by forcing role reversals on our students in order to fulfill this goal. The purpose of the Education Amendments of 1972 was to guarantee equal educational opportunities for women; that law was not intended to force all boys and girls into a coed mold for every activity, every hour of the day. But that is the impact of the HEW regulation.[51]

By fall 1976, elementary and secondary schools were being compelled to revise their athletic programs to conform to the HEW guidelines requiring coed sports. Under protest from parents, some schools were resorting to makeshift compromises under which girls and boys would use the gymnasium at the same time, but at different ends! The predictable results were inconvenience to the teachers, confusion among the students, and alienation of the parents.

The HEW regulation on sex discrimination is offensive to the big majority of American women and men. It reflects the narrow view of the women's lib militants who are determined to force their goals on our educational institutions whether the rest of us like them or not. It is a good forecast of the narrow, dogmatic women's liberationist regulations that will pervade our entire system if ERA is ever ratified.

In addition to the coed gym classes, HEW precipitated one

125

controversy after another by its enforcement of arbitrary and absolute rules against sex discrimination.

HEW announced that the high school good-citizenship program, Girls' State and Boys' State, long sponsored by the American Legion, would have to be sex integrated. Although no public funds finance this project, HEW claimed control because the Legion is permitted to put its posters on school bulletin boards. Congress had to pass another amendment specifically exempting Girls' State and Boys' State.

In 1976, HEW created a series of headlines when it banned father-son and mother-daughter events from public schools because they discriminate on account of sex. President Ford put a stop to that nonsense with an "irritated" phone call. On August 26, the United States Senate voted eighty-eight to zero to exempt father-son and mother-daughter school activities from federal sex-discrimination laws, thus providing another example of how bureaucratic mistakes can be remedied by legislation—*so long as* our hands are not tied by a constitutional amendment that permits no exceptions.

But the militant absolutists demanding total gender-free education were not daunted. HEW issued orders calling for an end to all separate boys' and girls' choirs and glee clubs. In some areas, the parochial schools were told that it is discriminatory to require girls but not boys to wear school uniforms, and that uniforms would either have to be abolished *or* made compulsory for girls *and* boys. Otherwise, the parochial schools would lose their milk and remedial-reading subsidies.

As was aptly noted in an editorial in one of the country's leading newspapers:

> Once you unleash the social-engineering imaginations of the haughty HEW bureaucrats, there's no end to the mischief they can work. With simple rules they can force their wills upon society—under threat of court action or withholding public funds if you don't capitulate.[52]

The arbitrary HEW regulations are causing enormous expense and confusion because of their detailed requirements for paperwork, maintenance of files, hiring of additional employees, advertising in newspapers and magazines to prove nondiscrimination, expensive recruitment programs at schools approved by HEW, extensive grievance procedures, and assurances of nondiscrimination required from subcontractors

—all of which must be subject to HEW approval, beforehand and afterwards.

The disarray already wrought in higher education by reverse discrimination was exposed by the Carnegie Commission on Higher Education. Its July, 1974, report showed that the HEW reverse discrimination policy was lowering educational standards and undermining faculty quality, that some women appointees do not have the proper qualifications for the university positions to which they have been appointed, and that sometimes they are even paid more than white male faculty members at the same level. Despite the impractical and unjust nature of such reverse discrimination, most colleges and universities submit to the HEW rule and spend large sums of money preparing statistical reports proving that they have recruited and hired the necessary women, for they dare not risk losing millions of dollars in federal funds.

The HEW regulation prohibits schools and colleges from setting and maintaining standards of morality among their students. It prohibits a school or college from refusing admission to unwed pregnant students and to those who have had or plan to have an abortion.[53] Depending on the ultimate interpretation of the rule that bars treating "persons differently on the basis of sex," the HEW regulation may even prohibit schools and colleges from refusing to admit prostitutes, homosexuals, and lesbians.

Brigham Young University is one of the very few universities that have dared to run the risk of losing federal aid by challenging such regulations. Dr. Dallin H. Oaks, BYU president, in announcing that his university would not follow regulations prohibiting actions based on marital or parental status or pregnancy or termination of pregnancy of present or prospective students or employees, stated:

> Where we believe the regulations are unconstitutional or illegal and where they prohibit or interfere with the teaching or practice of high moral principles, we will not follow them.

Unfortunately, there was no great rush to follow President Oaks' example. As the old saying goes, most people don't look a gift horse in the mouth. Acquiescence is the price of federal aid.

The final HEW regulation implementing the Education Amendments of 1972 went into effect on July 18, 1975, and now governs 16,000 school districts and 2,700 colleges and universities. It brings arbitrary federal control into our schools and colleges to a degree never intended by Congress or authorized by the Education Amendments of 1972.[54] As long as we are dealing with HEW regulations and federal laws, there is always hope that rational changes and amendments can remedy mistakes. Under ERA, however, no law passed by Congress could do anything to prevent the nonsense that will be required.

It is now clear that the ERA proponents, armed with the immense power of the federal bureaucracy and the federal courts, will use every legal technicality and loophole to achieve full sex integration at every level, public and private, whether or not it is desired by the general public or by the persons directly involved. Thus, the sex-integration pushers have been waging war in the courts on Little League baseball, the Jaycees, Kiwanis, and other men's service clubs, veterans' associations, men's bars (such as the famous Mory's at Yale), the Boy Scouts, and men's business and social clubs. In 1976 the militants succeeded in getting the Internal Revenue Service to rule that no business-tax deduction would be allowed for dues to clubs that do not admit women on an equal basis.

There is another area that is specifically exempted from the ban on sex discrimination in the Education Amendments of 1972—religious seminaries. If the Equal Rights Amendment becomes part of the Constitution, it will invalidate all portions of existing legislation in conflict with it. Since ERA allows no exceptions from its strict rule of sex equality, how will this impact on seminaries?

The women's liberation movement is making a determined drive against churches and seminaries that allegedly discriminate on the basis of sex. The National Organization for Women, in its *Revolution: Tomorrow Is NOW,* makes the following demands: (1) that churches and seminaries immediately drop their "sexist" doctrines that assign different roles to men and women, (2) that seminaries recruit, enroll, financially aid, employ, and promote women theologians and theological students on an equal basis with men, (3) that federal statutes be amended and enforced to deprive churches of their right to discriminate on the basis of sex, and (4) that tax exemption be withdrawn from any church actively opposed to abortion.[55]

Although churches and seminaries do not receive any government financial assistance, they do hold a very important federal benefit: exemption from income tax. This is a highly valuable advantage, not only for the church or seminary itself, but also for the individuals who contribute to it and are able to deduct those contributions on their income tax returns.

In 1971 the Internal Revenue Service ruled that "a private school that does not have a racially nondiscriminatory policy as to students does not qualify for exemptions."[56] This ruling was upheld by the courts even when the school involved was a private religious school that received no government money and that tried to assert its First Amendment rights.[57] As was noted earlier, in 1976 the United States Supreme Court went much further and prohibited *all* private schools from ever discriminating in admissions on the basis of race.[58]

Will ERA impose the same ruling on seminaries that are "sex discriminatory"? No one can be sure how the Supreme Court will decide. But we can be sure that the women's liberationists will litigate to use the power of the federal government to force churches to ordain women and admit them in equal numbers to seminaries.

The women's liberationists have access to an impressive roster of high-priced lawyers to fight their causes through the courts. The Equal Rights Amendment—with its total bar on sex discrimination—will give them the constitutional basis to litigate to achieve their objective of forcing churches and synagogues to ordain women and to admit them to total equality and sameness of treatment in churches, seminaries, and religious schools and organizations.

This opens up a whole new area of undesirable and unwanted effects of ERA. Some churches today are ordaining women as ministers, and that is their right. Other churches and synagogues do not ordain women as ministers, priests, rabbis, or bishops, and it should be their right not to do so without losing their tax exemption. If it is part of their religious faith that God has assigned different roles in this life to men and to women, and that these different roles are basic both to the ministerial mission and the family unit, the federal government should not force them to conform to the unisex demands of the militant liberationists.

The Federal Grab for Power

The Equal Rights Amendment reminds me of the story about a salmon swimming off the coast. As it sees a succulent piece of fish floating toward it, it says to itself, "High protein content; what's wrong with that? Delicious aroma; what's wrong with that? Just the right size; I can take it in one mouthful. What's wrong with that?"

What is wrong with it, of course, is that there is a hook in it. The hook in ERA is Section 2, which reads: "Congress shall have the power to enforce, by appropriate legislation, the provisions of this article." Any area that Congress has the power to legislate on, the federal agencies have the power to administer and execute, and the federal courts have the power to adjudicate.

Section 2 is a big grab for vast new federal power. It will take out of the hands of the state legislatures and transfer to Washington the last remaining piece of jurisdiction that the national politicians and bureaucrats haven't yet put their meddling fingers into. This means every type of law and regulation that pertains to differences between the sexes—including marriage, marriage property law, dower, inheritance, divorce, child custody, prison regulations, protective labor legislation, insurance rates, and abortion regulation—will become the province of the federal government.

Why anyone would want to send the Washington politicians, bureaucrats, and judges all that new jurisdiction is difficult to understand. They cannot cope with the problems they now have.

ERA proponents often say, "Isn't it terrible that the various states have different laws pertaining to women? We should have uniform rules for women's rights all over the country." Congresswoman Martha Griffiths, while testifying before the Missouri state hearing on ERA on January 28, 1975, admitted under cross-examination: "The intent of Section 2 is to make state laws uniform."

ERA supporters simply don't understand the system of government we have in the United States, which divides governmental powers between federal and state governments. It is our system to allow state legislatures to establish different taxes, different property laws, and differences in criminal codes. This diversity is one of the principal reasons why we have kept our freedom. All states don't have to levy the same taxes as New York does, or permit wide-open gambling as Nevada does, or become meccas for quickie divorces as some states have done.

We are far better off to keep the matters concerned with marriage in the hands of state legislatures. Does anyone think it would be progress or that women would be better off if, for example, we had a national divorce law implemented by HEW?

In defending Section 2, ERA proponents often say, "Don't worry about Section 2 because many other constitutional amendments have similar sections." There are seven constitutional amendments that have sections giving Congress the power to enforce them by appropriate legislation. A study of these amendments makes clear that *every one did, indeed, transfer power from the states to the federal government.* Five of the seven pertain to voting rights: the Fifteenth Amendment, giving blacks the right to vote, the Nineteenth Amendment, giving women the right to vote, the Twenty-third Amendment, giving a vote in the electoral college to the District of Columbia, the Twenty-fourth Amendment, guaranteeing the right to vote without a poll tax, and the Twenty-sixth Amendment, giving eighteen-year-olds the right to vote.

It is obvious that every one of the these amendments did, indeed, constitute a transfer of power to the federal level. For example, prior to the Nineteenth and Twenty-sixth amendments, many states had given the vote to women or to those under twenty-one years of age. After the Nineteenth and Twenty-sixth amendments were ratified, the states no longer could exercise any legislative option. The five voting rights amendments each granted only one specific power, so that is all the federal government received. The Thirteenth and Fourteenth Amendments, however, are open-ended and have brought about extensions of federal power never dreamed of by their authors.

Professor Paul A. Freund has testified about the endless litigation that ERA would cause, and about who would have the final authority:

> If anything about this proposed Amendment is clear, it is that it would transform every provision of law concerning women into a constitutional issue to be ultimately resolved by the Supreme Court of the United States.[59]

131

Who knows what the Supreme Court will do? The United States Supreme Court has rendered all sorts of unpredictable decisions in the areas of crime, education, busing, security risks, pornography, abortion, and states' rights.

In the leading case of *Katzenbach* v. *Morgan,* the United States Supreme Court interpreted Section 5 of the Fourteenth Amendment, which has wording identical to Section 2 of the Equal Rights Amendment. The court ruled that, under Section 5 of the Fourteenth Amendment, a federal law can preempt any matter covered by Section 1, so that the states simply lose their power to legislate on that subject. This case decided that, because of Section 5, Congress now has the power to nullify a state law which the states were specifically empowered to enact by three provisions of the Constitution and to substitute for it a federal law which Congress was forbidden to enact by the same three provisions of the Constitution.

The dissenting opinion in *Katzenbach* v. *Morgan* summed up very well the far-reaching effect of this Supreme Court decision, stating:

> To hold, on this record that [the Voting Rights Act of 1965] overrides the New York literacy requirement seems to me tantamount to allowing the 14th Amendment to swallow the State's constitutionally ordained primary authority in this field.[60]

In six other decisions handed down since January 1, 1968, the United States Supreme Court applied a drastically new interpretation of Section 2 of the Thirteenth Amendment, which also has the same wording as Section 2 of ERA.[61]

Therefore, the clause in ERA that gives Congress the "power to enforce, by appropriate legislation" means that ERA will swallow the states' present primary authority in everything that involves the rights of women.

Senator Sam J. Ervin, Jr., summed up the problem very well when he told the United States Senate on March 22, 1972:

> If this Equal Rights Amendment is adopted by the States, it will come near to abolishing the States of this Union as viable governmental bodies. I think it will virtually reduce the States of this Nation to meaningless zeroes on the Nation's map. I think it will transfer virtually all the legislative power of government from the States to Congress. . . .
> I believe that the Supreme Court will reach the conclusion that the ERA annuls every existing federal and state law mak-

ing any distinction between men and women, however reasonable such distinction might be in particular cases, and forever rob the Congress and the legislatures of the 50 states of the constitutional power to enact any such laws at any time in the future.

ERA will prevent us forever from making reasonable differences between men and women based on factual differences in childbearing and physical strength. ERA will force upon us the rigid, unisex, gender-free mandate demanded by the women's liberation movement, and it will transfer the power to apply this mandate to the federal government and the federal courts, where average citizens have no control.

ERA proponents try to allay the fears of those who worry about the long-term effect of ERA's Section 2 by saying that Section 3 gives the state legislatures two years in which to bring their state laws into line. Estimates of the number of state laws in each state that would have to be changed under ERA range from 200 to 1,000. If the state legislatures don't conform within the two-year period, then the federal government (either through Congress, or the bureaucracy, or the courts) will step in and require equality on terms that the federal government establishes. A two-year delay in enforcement cannot change the fact that ERA means a tremendous transferal of power from the states to the federal government.

This tremendously far-reaching shift of power out of the hands of state and local governments was accurately foreseen and enthusiastically welcomed by the National Organization for Women in its original testimony before the Senate Subcommittee on Constitutional Amendments, May 5, 1970:

> Until the Equal Rights Amendment is passed, the U.N. Convention on the Political Rights for Women cannot be passed; to do so would be to infringe on States' rights as guaranteed by the 10th Amendment; namely, that "the powers not delegated to the U.S. by the Constitution" . . . "are reserved to the States" . . . "or to the people."
>
> If the U.S. is to retain its place of leadership among the nations, the Equal Rights Amendment must be passed. The Equal Rights Amendment as part of the U.S. Constitution would then delegate certain powers to the U.S. (that were formerly reserved to the States), and subsequently the ratification of the U.N. Convention on the Political Rights for Women would then be possible under this new constitutional amendment.[62]

133

Federal Lobbying to Ratify ERA

The militant women who are determined to erase all differences of treatment between the sexes in order to force us to conform to a "gender-free" society, are not willing to compete fairly in the marketplace of ideas. The record proves that, in any fair contest, their radical notions cannot attract the support of any significant percentage of persons. So they have worked tirelessly to acquire public monies in order to cram their programs down our throats whether we like them or not. For many years, they have been doing this to the tune of tens of thousands of taxpayers' dollars through the various federal and state commissions on the status of women.

Despite all the public money the women's liberationists spent to promote the Equal Rights Amendment and other lib objectives, ERA was defeated in nineteen out of twenty states during 1975 and not ratified in a single state in 1976. So, they retaliated with a new tax-financed gimmick to promote their special interests. Its chief characteristic is the huge dimension of its monetary waste.

Step number one was to persuade President Ford to issue Executive Order Number 11832 on January 9, 1975, setting up the National Commission on International Women's Year (IWY), and then to appoint all pro-ERA members. This was fairly easy, since pro-ERAers had a lobbyist in the White House who boasted in the press about how she gets her way by "pillow talk."

Betty Ford's radical views—favoring abortion (the Supreme Court ruling was "a great, great decision"), tolerating fornication (if eighteen-year-old Susan should have an affair, Betty "wouldn't be surprised"), and accepting drugs (if Betty were young now, she'd try pot)—made her the darling of the women's lib movement.[63]

The members of the Commission on International Women's Year appointed by President Ford included Alan Alda (the television actor who has reaped reams of free publicity rapping for ERA), Pat Carbine of *Ms.* magazine, Martha Griffiths (the principal ERA sponsor in Congress), Barbara Walters, Barbara Bergmann (a college professor who said, "We're not here to glorify homemakers. We're here to try to change a way of life. . . ."), Congresswoman Bella Abzug, and Senator Birch Bayh (who is still so unstrung by a debate with me that he admitted

134

in 1975 that he "wanted to commit mayhem, live and in full color"), and Jill Ruckelshaus, a proabortionist and pro-ERAer known to many as the "Gloria Steinem of the Republican Party."

In April 1975, the IWY commission held its first meeting and officially resolved to make ratification of the Equal Rights Amendment its "highest priority." The commission pledged "to do all in our capacity to see that the Equal Rights Amendment is ratified at the earliest possible moment."[64] Members of the commission and its employees have since spoken at legislative hearings, before private organizations, and on television and radio to urge ratification of the Equal Rights Amendment.

Under the White House patronage of President and Mrs. Ford, the IWY commission opened an office in the State Department and hired a staff of thirteen, headed by Catherine East, a $37,000-a-year bureaucrat from the Council on the Status of Women in the Labor Department, where she has been promoting ERA for years. Betty Friedan writes in her latest book that Ms East was the "pivot of the feminist underground" in Washington, D.C., and that, as "midwife to the birth of the women's movement," she "cajoled" Friedan into starting the National Organization for Women.[65]

With the approval of the president, the IWY commission gathered in more than $300,000 of current operating cash in grants from other federal agencies.[66] The commission then spent part of its time and energies lobbying through Congress an appropriation of $5 million for the purpose of staging a women's conference in every one of the fifty states, to be followed by one large national conference in 1977.

The Legislative History

The Equal Rights Amendment was first introduced into the United States Congress in 1920. It was born of the women's suffrage era, and it addresses itself to the problems of that time. For fifty years, Congress had the good judgment to leave it decently buried in committee. During much of that time, ERA had attached to it the "Hayden Clause," which read: "Nothing in this Amendment will be construed to deprive persons of the female sex of any of the rights, benefits, and exemptions now conferred by law on persons of the female sex."

In 1971 a small band of militants stormed up and down the

corridors of Congress and demanded that ERA be discharged from committee and passed. ERA came out of the House Judiciary Committee only with the attachment of the Wiggins Clause, which read:

> This article shall not impair the validity of any law of the United States which exempts a person from compulsory military service or any other law of the United States or of any State which reasonably promotes the health and safety of the people.

On October 12, 1971, the Wiggins Clause was stricken on the House floor at the demand of the pro-ERA militants.

In the Senate, Senator Sam J. Ervin, Jr., offered nine other amendments to ERA, all of which were defeated on March 21–22, 1972. They constitute an impressive legislative history of what ERA is intended to accomplish. They reveal the radical changes in our society that ERA will compel. These seven amendments would have restricted the reach of ERA:

Amendment 1065: "This article shall not impair, however, the validity of any laws of the United States or any State which exempt women from compulsory military service." Defeated: 73 nays, 18 yeas, 9 not voting.

Amendment 1066: "This article shall not impair the validity, however, of any laws of the United States or any State which exempt women from service in combat units of the Armed Forces." Defeated: 71 nays, 18 yeas, 11 not voting.

Amendment 1067: "This article shall not impair the validity, however, of any laws of the United States or any State which extend protections or exemptions to women." Defeated: 75 nays, 11 yeas, 14 not voting.

Amendment 1068: "This article shall not impair the validity, however, of any laws of the United States or any State which extend protections or exemptions to wives, mothers, or widows." Defeated: 77 nays, 14 yeas, 9 not voting.

Amendment 1069: "This article shall not impair the validity, however, of any laws of the United States or any State which impose upon fathers responsibility for the support of their children." Defeated: 72 nays, 17 yeas, 11 not voting.

Amendment 1070: "This article shall not impair the validity, however, of any laws of the United States or any State which secure privacy to men or women, boys or girls." Defeated: 79 nays, 11 yeas, 10 not voting.

Amendment 1071: "This article shall not impair the validity, however, of any laws of the United States or any State which make punishable as crimes sexual offenses." Defeated: 71 nays, 17 yeas, 12 not voting.

These amendments were offered as substitute texts for ERA:

Amendment 472: "Neither the United States nor any State shall make any legal distinction between the rights and responsibilities of male and female persons unless such distinction is based on physiological or functional differences between them." Defeated: 78 nays, 12 yeas, 10 not voting.

Amendment 1044: "Equality of rights under the law shall not be denied or abridged by the United States or by any State on account of sex. The provisions of this article shall not impair the validity, however, of any laws of the United States or any State which exempt women from compulsory military service, or from service in combat units of the Armed Forces; or extend protections or exemptions to wives, mothers, or widows; or impose upon fathers responsibility for the support of children; or secure privacy to men or women, or boys or girls; or make punishable as crimes rape, seduction, or other sexual offenses." Defeated: 82 nays, 9 yeas, 9 not voting.

On March 22, 1972, after the rejection of all these amendments, ERA was passed in strict, uncompromising, absolute form and sent to the states for ratification.

In the pro-ERA euphoria that followed, ERA was ratified rapidly in some thirty state legislatures—in many cases without any hearings or debate. Then the tide began to turn. Ratification slowed to a snail's pace by 1974. Of the thirty-five states that have ratified ERA at this writing, three have rescinded: Nebraska, Tennessee, and Idaho.[67] The remaining fifteen states have repeatedly rejected ERA. To become part of the United States Constitution, ERA must be ratified by thirty-eight states by March 22, 1979.

ERA would have died a natural death by 1977 if it were not for the artificial respiration provided by the pro-ERA media, massive amounts of federal spending, and White House lobbying activities. Although Article V of the Constitution gives the ratification power exclusively to the state legislatures, pressure and phone calls from President and Mrs. Carter and their employees demanded that state legislators knuckle under and ratify ERA.

American women recognize ERA as a fraud.[68] There is *no*

affirmative case for the Equal Rights Amendment. There is no law that discriminates against women. ERA does not give women *any* rights, benefits, or opportunities that they do not now have.

IV

Spinning the Fabric of Civilization

It is on its women that a civilization depends—on the inspiration they provide, on the moral fabric they weave, on the parameters of behavior they tolerate, and on the new generation that they breathe life into and educate. It is no accident of an artist's fancy that the Statue of Liberty is a woman, that the Scales of Justice are held by a woman, that Winged Victory is a woman. Those three essential bulwarks of civilization are personified in Woman—quite apart from her more widely recognized pictorializations as Beauty and Mother.

The Positive Woman accepts her responsibility to spin the fabric of civilization, to mend its tears, and to reinforce its seams. No matter how wide or how narrow is the scope of her influence, this is her task.

If her influence is limited to her immediate family, she knows that, after all, nothing is more important than building the morals and integrity of the family unit, especially its children, and she addresses herself to that. If circumstance and talent extend the scope of her influence to her club or school or business or community or state or nation, she accepts the responsibility. God has a mission for every Positive Woman. It is up to her to find out what it is and to meet the challenge. Only in so doing can she achieve that inner serenity that brings all-round fulfillment in this uncertain world.

Surveying America after our bicentennial, it would be easy to conclude that we may become another of the many civilizations that perished after discarding the moral standards that bound their people together. One out of every two marriages

139

now ends in divorce. Venereal disease has risen to epidemic levels and is one of the most common illnesses of the nation. Abortion, the killing of unborn babies, is our third most popular operation, ranking right behind tonsillectomies and appendectomies. Militant homosexuals and lesbians are popular lecturers on college campuses and guests on television and radio programs.

All kinds of crime continue to increase, especially violent crime, teenage crime, and female crime. The most notorious criminals of recent years have been women—Patty Hearst, Sara Jane Moore, Squeaky Fromme, and Bernardine Dohrn.

Anyone who considers movies, books, and television the mirror of a society's morals could easily become depressed. It is as though fast-buck promoters are determined to prove the validity of Alexander Pope's famous couplets:

> Vice is a monster of so frightful mien,
> As to be hated needs but to be seen;
> Yet seen too oft, familiar with her face,
> We first endure, then pity, then embrace.

Our leading newspapers compete vigorously with each other in large daily advertisements for pornographic X-rated movies and stage shows. Talented and beautiful actresses play the roles of prostitutes. Crime and vice are depicted as more rewarding than virtue and family life. Newsstands outdo each other in stocking their shelves with pocketbooks and magazines featuring hardcore violence and perversion. *The Happy Hooker* and its imitators sell millions of copies, describing the alleged rewards of a career of vice.

The most vivid dramatization of what has aptly been called the war on the family was provided by the NBC television network on "Of Women and Men," a three-hour special aired on January 9, 1975. It was a thorough television portrayal of the lifestyle, the morals, the religion, and the male-female relationships so stridently promoted by the advocates of women's liberation, the sexual revolution, and the Equal Rights Amendment. "Of Women and Men" was antimarriage, antimonogamy, antimorality, and anti-Bible.

In all the three hours, there was not a single voice *for* monogamous, lifetime marriage as a satisfactory male-female relationship, *for* the family as the basic unit of our society, *for* motherhood as a fulfilling role for women, or *for* the Ten Com-

mandments as a code of conduct that binds our society together. The 100 interviews did not include a single example of
a happy or stable marriage.

Sex without marriage was presented as the accepted way of
life for all ages, from the high school students whose weekend
dates are in closed vans outfitted with wall-to-wall carpeting
and overhead mirrors, to the man and woman in their seventies
who frankly described sharing an apartment and enjoying sex
without benefit of marriage. In between, twenty-five-year-old
Erica enthusiastically discussed how she enjoys sex with a
variety of single and married men, especially group sex, and is
considering homosexuality. The message came through loud
and clear from "anchor persons" Barbara Walters and Tom
Snyder that a world of "serial marriage" and sex without marriage is coming fast and should be cheerfully welcomed.[1]

The task of the Positive Woman is to resist these trends and
mend the rips in the fabric of civilization as far as her influence
and energy can reach.

The "Fourth R": Right and Wrong

The most dramatic rise in crime and immorality has been in
the schools and colleges. Elementary and secondary schools
spend an enormous sum for security against violent crimes and
to repair damage from theft and vandalism. Murders inside
high schools are no longer rare. Knifings, shootings, beatings,
and rapes take place inside public high schools.

When President Gerald Ford spoke to a teachers' meeting on
October 29, 1976, he received tremendous applause when he
said he wanted to do something about the problem of pupils
threatening teachers with knives. Male teenage gangs have
taken control of some urban schools, where they intimidate the
teachers, terrorize the pupils, and shake down almost everyone.[2] Stealing is so common that it is seldom reported. Girls in
some areas are afraid to go alone to the girls' restrooms. On
many college campuses, women are advised to carry a shrill
whistle, not go out alone at night, and keep their doors locked
at all times.

The big cities have reported a large rise in the number of
vicious criminals who are only twelve to sixteen years old.
These adolescent criminals prey particularly on senior citizens

141

—those least able to defend themselves against murderers, muggers, and robbers. The youthful hoodlums show no fear of arrest or remorse when they are caught.

The drug situation in the schools is a national scandal. Mind-affecting substances of all varieties (hard and soft, stimulants and depressants) are available in and near many schools, peddled even to grade school children. The National Institute of Alcohol Abuse reports that 28 percent of the nation's teenagers are problem drinkers. One of the most alarming aspects is the increasing number who are experimenting with a combination of alcohol and depressant drugs.[3] Some estimates are that up to 40 percent of those seeking treatment at drug referral centers have mixed alcohol with other drugs. The majority of students appear to have built a psychological block that precludes their even listening to scientific evidence on the harmful long-term effects of marijuana.[4]

Promiscuity among high schoolers and even junior high schoolers has become a way of life. Illegitimate pregnancies, abortions, and venereal disease among high school students occur at a shocking rate. Court decisions and HEW regulations make it difficult or even impossible to fire teachers who are homosexuals, lesbians, or pregnant but unmarried.

Another major problem on college campuses today is cheating, even among "A" students. Some students, not content with getting the best grades they can steal, resort to an imaginative variety of dirty tricks, including sabotaging the lab experiments of fellow students and stealing journals containing assigned reading.

Despite all evidence to the contrary, the liberal dogma remains unshaken that crime is caused by poverty and lack of education, and that therefore crime can be eliminated by spending more tax dollars, sharing the wealth, and giving everybody a college education. The liberals remind me of a story told about the philosopher Hegel. When informed by a colleague that the facts did not tally with his theories, Hegel sternly replied, "All the worse for the facts."

The United States spends more per student on education than any other nation. Our magnificent education facilities, school buildings, gymnasiums, laboratories, college campuses, endowments, and scholarships are the envy of the world. Yet something is lacking. The missing ingredient is moral training.

The police can protect us against a tiny fraction of criminals so long as nearly all the people respect God's Commandments and cooperate in a system of legal and social sanctions against violators. When they don't, the system comes apart.

Children are not born with a sense of right and wrong. These concepts, both in general and in specifics, must be affirmatively taught to each child. They are no longer taught in the public schools as a result of years of so-called progressive education that began with John Dewey. The Dewey theory was that right and wrong are relative rather than certain, there are no absolutes, discipline must give way to permissiveness, and standards of conduct and achievement must be replaced by "life-adjustment" education.

One of the easiest ways to demonstrate the fact that moral training has been stricken from education is to compare the old McGuffey readers,[5] which our grandparents studied, with today's elementary school readers. The McGuffey stories taught the time-honored virtues—love of God, patriotism, thrift, honesty, respect for elders, where there's a will there's a way, the Golden Rule, true courage, manliness, kindness to the less fortunate, obedience to parents, the value of prayer, the consequences of idleness and truancy, crime doesn't pay, and why virtue and love are worth more than material riches. The old McGuffey readers taught morals, religious faith, and family love.

Modern readers, on the other hand, are completely different. The characters merely run and play, they look up and look down, they hear the duck quack and the cat meow. Their lives are utterly devoid of the standards, the values, the morals, the inspiration, and the ideals of the McGuffey characters.

It is not enough for our schools to teach reading, writing and 'rithmetic; the most important "R" of all is right and wrong. Moral education should be taught from the earliest grades. This includes the moral precepts of the Ten Commandments, especially "Thou shalt not steal" and "Thou shalt not covet thy neighbor's goods," as well as other rules of good conduct, such as "Honesty is the best policy." Our students should be taught that lying, stealing, cheating and murder are both crimes and sins that cannot be excused by past economic, geographic, or racial injustices, no matter how grievous.

Moral education is a basic necessity for civilized living. To abdicate this obligation is to resign our schools and our cities to the law of the jungle, and to allow ourselves to be terrorized by young savages. Many innocent victims of crime are paying the bitter price for our failure to teach the Ten Commandments or to permit the daily acknowledgment of the Divine Creator, whose moral laws should be obeyed.

It was the United States Supreme Court that administered the coup de grace to moral education in the public schools by removing God, prayer, Bible reading, and all religious education. It is still a mystery to most Americans how the United States Supreme Court could say that prayer violates the First Amendment, when all that amendment says is that "Congress shall make no law respecting an establishment of religion." Allowing teachers to lead their pupils in a voluntary nondenominational morning prayer or grace before lunch is certainly not establishing a federal religion. Justice Hugo Black simply rewrote the First Amendment to inject into it a new meaning that for 173 years no president, no Congress, and no court had ever detected.

In writing the opinion banning prayer from the public schools, Justice Black not only ignored the clear language of the Constitution, but he also ignored American history. The men who wrote the Constitution and the First Amendment were educated in schools where daily prayers were recited. Prayer has always been a part of our official public life, beginning with the Declaration of Independence. The Supreme Court and other federal courts open each day with this prayer: "God save the United States and this honorable Court." The United States government has always supported chaplains to lead prayers in Congress, for the armed services, in our military academies, and in our prisons. In 1892 the Supreme Court unanimously declared in *Church of the Holy Trinity* v. *United States* that our history provides a mass of organic utterances that "this is a religious nation."[6]

The trouble with some Supreme Court Justices is that, once they are appointed, they begin to think they have been anointed as high priests to rewrite our Constitution and laws. Justice Robert H. Jackson once stated the Supreme Court's attitude rather bluntly in these words: "We are not final because we are infallible, on the contrary, we are infallible only because we are final."

However, the Supreme Court is not final. The truly final authority is in the people through amendments to the United

144

States Constitution. It is time to pass a constitutional amendment to undo the mischief the Supreme Court has wrought in many areas, and there is no better place to start than by restoring prayer and moral training to our schools.

It is probable that what the majority of Supreme Court justices thought they were doing was to guarantee neutrality as between those who believe in God and those who do not believe in God. The trouble is that nature abhors a vacuum, and when all pro-God religious teaching was prohibited, the gap was filled in many schools by the affirmative teaching of Secular Humanism, which denies the Bible and divine revelation and teaches that man's reason is all we need to accomplish everything.

The "First Humanist Manifesto," published in 1933, has had great status with many educators because it was endorsed by the father of progressive education, John Dewey. The "Second Humanist Manifesto," published in 1973 and signed by many leading educators, states:

> As in 1933, humanists still believe that traditional theism, especially faith in the prayer-hearing God, assumed to love and care for persons, to hear and understand their prayers, and to be able to do something about them, is an unproved and outmoded faith. . . .
>
> We find insufficient evidence for belief in the existence of a supernatural; it is either meaningless or irrelevant to the question of the survival and fulfillment of the human race. As non-theists, we begin with humans not God, nature not deity. . . . We can discover no divine purpose or providence for the human species. While there is much that we do not know, humans are responsible for what we are or will become. No deity will save us; we must save ourselves. . . . There is no credible evidence that life survives the death of the body.[7]

The evidence of a Divine Architect who established the laws of physics, chemistry, heredity, and life itself, with man and his intellect infinitely superior to animal species, is too plain to reject. There must have been a Divine Engineer who arranged the unique combination of sunlight, air, water, a tilted earth to provide four seasons, a rotating earth to prevent extremes of heat and cold, and a moon just the right distance away to furnish the tides to keep our oceans fresh.

Nevertheless, it has become fashionable in many schools to use supplementary reading and even textbooks that are anti-

God, antimoral, anti–private enterprise, and antipatriotic. Many such books promote a tolerance of violence, theft, adultery, obscenity, profanity, and blasphemy.

One notorious example of immoral teaching materials is the National Science Foundation curriculum project for ten-year-olds called "Man: A Course of Study," or MACOS for short. It is full of references to adultery, cannibalism, killing female babies and old people, trial marriage, wife-swapping, violent murder, and other abhorrent behavior of an almost extinct tribe of Eskimos. When the MACOS program was completed at a cost to the taxpayers of nearly $7 million, more than fifty publishers refused to market it because of its objectionable content. The National Science Foundation then subsidized a promotion scheme in direct competition with regular textbook publishers so that 1,700 schools could buy it at cut-rate prices.

Parents are now starting to fight back. Some are taking the legislative route. Although they have not yet achieved passage of a prayer amendment to the United States Constitution, they won significant victories in 1976 when Congress cut funds for future MACOS-type projects and the House voted for a prohibition against the use of federal funds to promote Secular Humanism.

Other parents are going the judicial route by bringing suit under the First Amendment to stop the teaching of the religion of Secular Humanism in the public schools. Since the Supreme Court has declared Secular Humanism to be a religion,[8] the same First Amendment that the Supreme Court claims bars pro-God religious teaching must necessarily be held to bar all anti-God religious teaching.

Evidence that parents' protests are having an impact surfaced when United States Education Commissioner Terrell H. Bell called on textbook publishers to print only "materials that do not insult the values of most parents." He mentioned the Bible, McGuffey's readers, and *The Wizard of Oz* as examples of books that both tell interesting stories and teach worthwhile values. Continuing, he said:

> Parents have a right to expect that the schools in their teaching approaches and selection of instructional materials, will support the values and standards that their children are taught at home. And if the schools cannot support those values, they must at least avoid deliberate destruction of them.[9]

146

Other parents are organizing private schools. Hundreds of private schools have been organized all across the country. There are two problems that parents face, however, in transferring their children to private schools. One of these is the financial burden on schools of complying with unduly restrictive and burdensome state regulations designed to protect the public school monopoly and prevent competition from private schools. Parents have been winning landmark court cases to free private schools from such discriminatory regulations.[10]

The other factor is the double and discriminatory financial burden on parents. They pay high taxes to build and maintain public schools that have failed to do the job, and they pay private school tuition that they are forbidden to deduct from their taxable income. The solution to this situation is passage of an amendment to the income tax law that permits individuals to deduct from their taxable incomes payments for tuition to any school or college of the taxpayer's choice. This is a practical and economical solution that would end the present discriminatory system and give Americans of all classes and races an alternative when the public school to which their children are assigned is not doing a good job.[11]

Time is running out on America as an orderly and safe society if we continue to permit our schools and colleges to be citadels of atheism and moral neutralism. It is more important for our schools and colleges, year in and year out, to teach and train students to obey the laws of God and country than it is to impart any other knowledge. If we don't insist on this before the schools receive our money, we might as well resign ourselves to the fact that schools and college campuses are training grounds for criminals.

There is no more important task for the Positive Woman today—be she mother, teacher, or taxpayer—than to insist on moral training for all American children, and to permit and encourage religious training for as many as will accept it.

The First Three Rs

There is manifest in the country—to my knowledge, for the first time in our history—an active loss of enchantment with our schools . . . from kindergarten through graduate school. . . . Americans in significant numbers are questioning the purpose of education [and] the competence of educators.

147

So said Dr. Sidney P. Marland, Jr., United States assistant secretary for education.[12] He is correct. Americans are disenchanted with our schools. And why shouldn't we be? We have seen the cost of education soar seven times faster than the population and the quality of education fall lower and lower.

There is an old aphorism which asks the question: "Are you working on the solution, or are you part of the problem?" In education, federal spending is not only not working on the solution, but it is part of the problem. Even an American Institute for Research evaluation reported that participants in federal education programs gained less than nonparticipants and that federal expenditures failed to result in any improvement in reading or other cognitive skills.

What American parents and taxpayers have intuitively sensed about the failure of the schools to teach our children the fundamentals is proven by the statistical record. The Scholastic Aptitude Test (SAT), the principal admissions examination used by most colleges, has reported a steady thirteen-year decline in the scores of high school students. Every year from 1963 to 1976 showed a significant drop in average scores in both the verbal and the mathematical tests. The SAT scores are an embarrassment and a puzzlement to the educators who have been telling us that students have been getting smarter. The SAT scores prove that students simply do not do as well in verbal and mathematical skills as they did in former years.

One cause could be that children now watch television instead of reading books. A more basic cause is that, when the educationists eliminated phonics from the teaching of reading and substituted the look-say method, and when they replaced drilling in multiplication tables with the new math, they handicapped our students as much as if they had put a blindfold over one eye of every child. When a student hasn't been taught phonics, he cannot spell and he has an artificially limited vocabulary. When a student hasn't memorized addition sums and multiplication tables, he cannot solve the simple arithmetic problems that confront him in everyday life.

Progressive educationists seem to adhere stubbornly to the dogma that anything new must be superior to whatever is old.[13] It isn't, and the SAT scores prove it. What education needs is a fresh willingness to replace the failures of the present with the successful teaching techniques of the past.

Every fall, millions of six-year-olds start to school, eager to learn to read. Three months later, they are bored and disorderly, for they still haven't started to learn. Instead, they are subjected to volume after volume of boring, repetitious, stupid books, in which they are taught to memorize a few dozen words by guessing at them from accompanying pictures. This is called the whole-word, or look-say, method. The children are inflicted with endless pages of: "Look up, look down; 'quack, quack,' said the duck"; and similar nonsense.

Three years later, many children still cannot read, and many more cannot read well. They limp along from year to year, frustrated and discouraged. When they get to high school, they have had so many years of what is called the controlled vocabulary that they cannot read the classics; so they are fed great literature that has been rewritten in the vocabulary of the elementary grades.

Some are even worse off. In the summer of 1976, a St. Louis television station aired an interview with a twenty-year-old boy who went all the way through the public school system and received his high school diploma—without learning to read or write. After then realizing how handicapped a functional illiterate is in the job market, he took an adult remedial reading course. Jerry Doyle isn't retarded or stupid; he is merely untaught. On television he told how he was never given any grades in school; he was just promoted year after year. The school's attitude was "Here's your diploma, now get lost."

Washington, D.C., residents were shocked in August, 1976, when the newspapers reported that the valedictorian of an inner-city high school was denied admission to George Washington University because his Scholastic Aptitude Test scores were only half as good as they should have been. The highest-ranking graduate of one of the public schools in our nation's capital hadn't been taught enough to get into a home-town university. As the George Washington University admissions dean said, "He's been conned. He's been deluded into thinking he's gotten an education."

This kind of result has been fostered by school administrators who frankly state that students who cannot read should be awarded high school diplomas anyway, that diplomas should be based on attendance and not on academic achievement. Under this system, there are no standards for graduation from public high schools. The psychological frustration this causes cannot help but breed social problems. The students are led to

149

believe they are prepared to face life, but when they apply for a job they cannot even fill out a job application.

I used to think that the dollar bill was the piece of paper whose value has slumped most in the past ten years. It now appears that this dubious honor has been won by the high school diploma.

You can measure the decline in reading skills by comparing current readers with the old McGuffey readers. The McGuffey readers are about two years advanced over modern readers of the same grade level in all reading skills, including vocabulary, comprehension, spelling, writing, pronunciation, grammar, and intellectual and spiritual content.

It was in 1955 that Rudolf Flesch's book *Why Johnny Can't Read* became an overnight bestseller and shook the educational world by exposing how the progressive educationists had eliminated the teaching of phonics from the first grade. He conclusively proved that phonics is the indispensable key to learning to read the English language.[14]

As a result of Flesch's book, a few phonics lessons were reintroduced into the schools, but phonics is still not generally used as the basic method at the start of first grade. I followed Flesch's advice and personally gave all my six children the first grade at home, using a 100 percent phonics system.[15] My project was a total success. Parents teach their children to ride a bike, to swim, to cook, to sew, to drive a car, and many skills. Why not teach your children to read—the most important skill of all—and give them the key to a sound education?

In our current era of consumerism, it is a wonder that Ralph Nader or some public-interest law firm hasn't investigated the shoddiest consumer product on the market today—the teaching of writing by the public schools. When Detroit automobile dealers call back hundreds of defective cars, we are rightly scandalized. When a large percentage of high school graduates and job applicants cannot write a literate letter, we should be equally scandalized.

Writing is an especially accurate index of education. Whereas reading can be considered a passive skill, writing forces one to formulate one's own thoughts, organize them in a coherent way, and put them on paper in a form that communicates a message to others. It requires familiarity with vocabulary, syntax, and sentence structure, and a thought process that puts it all together. President John H. Bunzel of San Jose State University summed it up very well when he said: "I agree with George Orwell, 'If people cannot write well, they cannot think well; and if they cannot think well, others can do their thinking for them.'"

Even in the colleges themselves, the evidence is mounting that eighteen-, nineteen-, and twenty-year-olds cannot read and write the English language as well as students a generation ago, or even a decade ago. In the last four years, the number of college freshmen at many state universities who must take remedial English courses, known as "bonehead English," has doubled. At some state universities, the figure is as high as 80 percent.

Textbook publishers are finding that their books are too hard for today's students and must be rewritten in simplified language. After the Association of American Publishers published a pamphlet to tell incoming college freshmen how to make the best use of their textbooks, it had to be rewritten on the ninth grade level. Oral expression by today's students reveals similar disabilities. Anyone who does much talking with teenagers knows that they can hardly utter a single sentence without saying "you know" or "I mean."

There are many constructive organizations, groups, and individuals working today toward the goal that our children be taught basic skills in the schools rather than experimented upon.[16] These efforts promote the use of phonics to teach reading, the reading of the classics rather than a monotonous diet of fifth-rate contemporary materials, the acquisition of skills in useful math, the teaching of history and geography instead of the nebulous social studies, the elimination of undisciplined and "open" classrooms, and the substitution of real learning rather than "social adjustment" and "group dynamics."

Some Positive Women will find it worthwhile to work with these groups. Others will find their mission in educating their own children. When I tell friends that I taught all my children at home to read and write, add and subtract, and did not enter them in school until the second grade where they promptly proved themselves to be good readers and excellent students, the usual reaction is to assume that there was something special about my abilities or my children that made this a practical and successful venture.

Not so. Any mother can teach her child to read. Take, for

example, the case of a Positive Woman and a friend of mine named Willie Bea Reed, who wanted her daughter to have the very best education she could possibly give her. She didn't want her daughter to be handicapped like other children by inferior schools, or busing, or wasted time spent on frills and field trips instead of on the essential task of learning.

Mrs. Reed isn't well to do, or well educated, or specially talented. She is black and has had to support herself all her life as a cook and a housekeeper. She never went to college and would never qualify for a teacher's certificate.

But she had the vision to set a goal for herself and the perseverance to pursue it despite all obstacles. That goal was to teach her child to read at home. Mrs. Reed was smart enough to know that reading is the key to all learning and that being a good reader would open more doors for her daughter than any other skill. So she acquired the necessary books and successfully taught her child to read, using a 100 percent phonics method— the only sure method by which a child can learn to read and spell.

It was tough going for the first few weeks as mother and daughter tackled a new experience. But as the child learned the basic phonetic sounds of the English language and began to unlock the words on her own, learning became an exciting challenge. Next to learning to walk and talk, learning to read is the most thrilling of all childhood achievements.

The moment of truth came when Mrs. Reed entered her child in school and sought admission—not to the first, but to the second grade. The daughter passed the test with flying colors and was rated as reading two years above her age level.

Another Positive Woman was Mrs. Daniel James, a black with only a high school education and thirteen children. Living in a Pensacola, Florida, ghetto, she was not satisfied with the kind of schooling her children were getting in the segregated schools of the 1940s. So she took her children out of school and taught them at home until they entered high school. She gave them not only the tools of learning, but moral training and motivation. One of them rose to become the first black four-star general in United States history. Air Force General Daniel James, Jr., credits his mother with giving him not only his knowledge, but his patriotism and desire to achieve and to serve his country, which persisted through 101 combat missions in the Korean War and 78 combat missions over North

Vietnam. General James now commands the North American Air Defense Command.

The Positive Woman refuses to permit the schools to corrupt the religious faith, the morals, or the intellectual potential of her children. She adopts a plan of action that meets the problem as her circumstances permit.

The Moral Climate of the Community

Mark Twain is usually credited with the expression, "Everybody talks about the weather but nobody does anything about it." The same complaint might be voiced about the subject of violence on television. For years, newspapers, magazines, speakers, and scientific studies have piled up data setting forth the staggering statistics of crimes portrayed on the tube and the way they stimulate aggressive and brutal behavior among our youth. Many children spend as many hours in front of television as at school. Many preschoolers average eight hours a day. Malcolm Muggeridge pointed up the problem:

> The corruption of our children is absolutely appalling. On television they see the family ridiculed, marital fidelity ridiculed, and a crass materialism constantly being preached. . . . Parents would do well to never let their children watch television.

Dr. Michael B. Rothenberg, a child psychiatrist, writing in the American Medical Association *Journal,* said that the time is long past due for a "major, organized cry of protest from the medical profession . . . to what I consider a national scandal." He cited studies showing that the average American child, by the time he finishes school,

> will have witnessed 18,000 murders and countless highly detailed incidents of robbery, arson, bombing, forgery, smuggling, beating and torture averaging approximately one per minute in the standard television cartoon for children under the age of 10.

TV Guide corroborated this statistic, estimating that the average child by the age of fifteen will have witnessed 13,400 television killings. Dr. Rothenberg pointed out that: "There is an average of six times more violence during one hour of chil-

dren's television than there is in one hour of adult television."
He added that the negative effect of such violence on children
and the young can no longer be questioned. This concentrated
viewing of violence produces increased aggressive behavior in
the young and a decreased emotional sensitivity to media violence. Classical desensitization takes place. There is an increased ability to be violent with others. Dr. Rothenberg called
for immediate remedial action in TV programming, putting the
responsibility directly on parents: "To be silent is to acquiesce,
and it is clear that if we truly care about our children, we
cannot be silent."[17]

Professor Anne R. Somers, writing in the *New England Journal of Medicine,* was correct when she said television is a
molder, not a mirror, of social values. She concluded:

> For a considerable proportion of American children and
> youth, violence has become a major health problem. For an
> alarming number it is a way of life. One contributing factor is
> television's massive daily diet of symbolic crime and viol-
> ence in "entertainment" programs.[18]

The reason for the failure to come to grips with the problem
may have been unearthed by Donald T. Lunde, professor of
law and psychiatry at Stanford University. He made a five-year
study of the increasing real-life murder rate and came to the
conclusion that the principal cause of the crime rise is that the
whole generation of Americans who grew to adulthood since
World War II has been trained to blame its troubles on "society" and to look to the government for the solution to all
problems. The permissive child rearing, the decline in self-
discipline, and the diminishing influence of religion have all
had their impact on a generation that has abdicated responsibility for individual actions.

While Dr. Lunde did not apply his findings to TV violence, it
is obvious that parents have abdicated their moral responsibility to supervise the entertainment of their young children.
Thus, the average citizen may bemoan the prevalence of television violence, but he confines himself to saying, "Isn't it terrible," "There ought to be a law," or "It's up to the FCC to stop
it."

What is the matter with the parents who permit their children to watch thousands of televised murders? What is the
matter with parents who continue to patronize the advertisers

154

whose commercials are sandwiched in between the murders and the robberies, and whose advertising budgets have purchased the high-priced prime time? What is the matter with the parents who fail to protest bad programs to their local television stations and to the sponsors?

If parents really want to get rid of TV violence, nobody is restraining them from using the telephone, the mails, and the switch on the tube.

The late mayor of Chicago, Richard Daley, gave a good demonstration of leadership by coming to grips with the fact that violence in the movies and television is to the urban concentration of teenagers, minorities, and unemployed what a lighted cigarette is to a parched forest. Just as safety of the people allows us to prohibit a smoker from tossing his lighted cigarette butt out of a car window, the safety of city dwellers requires that we stop the movie violence that panders to impressionable teenagers with sadism and senseless brutality.

Mayor Daley lashed out at "the national disgrace of TV violence" and called for mass public organization to get "pornography, crime, and violence off the public airwaves." "It is a well known fact," he said, "that criminals watch these TV programs for every little detail of what they can do. Details about kidnappings are shown, and the criminal picks them up." Daley appealed to women to write to television directors and producers to protest such programs.[19]

Mayor Daley then persuaded the Chicago City Council to pass an ordinance (by a vote of forty-five to two) prohibiting the admission of anyone under the age of eighteen to movies that are obscene or extremely violent, including such acts as "cuttings, stabbings, floggings, eye-gouging, brutal kicking, and dismemberment."

Alderman Adeline P. Keane, a Positive Woman, effectively supported Mayor Daley when, in urging passage of the ordinance, she said: "Kids are mimics, and they mimic whatever they see . . . when they see this violence, they are liable to act it out."

One of the specious arguments made against such city ordinances is that we should leave it to the movie industry to police itself. At the 1976 film festival in Cannes, France, films of violence received all the prizes, despite a strong condemnation from the American playwright Tennessee Williams who was president of the jury. Williams condemned films that "take a voluptuous pleasure in spilling blood and in lingering on terrible cruelties as though one were at a Roman circus." He said that "watching violence on the screen is a brutalizing experience for the spectator."[20]

The movie selected for the top trophy at the 1976 Cannes Film Festival was *Taxi Driver.* After a Chicago youth saw this very movie, he went out and shot up a northwest Chicago convent.

The same rights that permit us to restrict teenage drinking, drug use, driving, and marriage permit us to prohibit movies that incite teenagers to criminal violence.

The First Amendment right to freedom of speech and press is not, was never intended to be, and should not be an absolute right to say or print anything one wants. You have no right to utter obscenities, blasphemies, profanities, libels, or slanders, because those acts interfere with the rights of others. You have no right to commit a public nuisance, a public indecency, or a public disturbing of the peace. In Oliver Wendell Holmes' famous phrase, you have no right to cry fire in a crowded theater.

One of the unfortunate legacies of the Earl Warren Supreme Court was the overturning of the law on obscenity that Americans had respected for 178 years. By ruling for obscenity dealers in thirty-six out of thirty-eight cases in 1967, 1968, and 1969, the Warren Court enshrined the pornographer's right to commit his public nuisance above the right of all the rest of the people to live in an orderly and decent community.

In many of these cases, the Supreme Court did not issue any opinion supporting its decision or even reveal which of the Justices approved the decision. The court just handed down anonymous decisions that reversed the convictions of smut peddlers found guilty by local juries, and thereby stripped the communities of all legal power to defend themselves against obscenity. The result of permitting the smut peddlers to clothe themselves in radical new interpretations of the First Amendment has been the pornography explosion of the 1970s.

The week before Senator Everett Dirksen died, he completed an article for the November, 1969, *Reader's Digest* called "A New Plan to Fight Pornography." Calling attention to "the mounting flow of obscene books, films and magazines threatening our national health," he identified the principal cause of the smut epidemic as the shocking series of pro-obscenity decisions handed down by the United States Supreme Court.

Senator Dirksen then presented his own solution for the pornography problem: a bill to remove jurisdiction from the Supreme Court in accordance with the powers granted Congress in Article III of the United States Constitution. Article III gives Congress the power to limit the jurisdiction of the federal courts, a handy means of cutting off the power to persist in their hurtful decisions. During the 1930s, Congress used this constitutional provision several times, depriving the federal courts of jurisdiction to enjoin state tax collections, state-fixed utility rates, and picketing by labor unions. The purpose of the Dirksen bill was to return to state courts and juries their right to make the final determination as to whether a book, magazine, or movie is obscene.

Although Senator Dirksen's bill did not pass, it may be that the Supreme Court got the message that it should stop turning smut peddlers loose or the court might find that it had lost part of its jurisdiction. On June 21, 1973, the Supreme Court ruled against smut peddlers in five cases, thus calling a halt to the long series of pro-obscenity decisions. While the court did not restore full rights to local juries to make the final determination as to what is obscene, it did take two constructive steps in that direction.

First, the court threw out the false principle that a slick lawyer had conned Justice William J. Brennan, Jr., into adopting in the *Fanny Hill* case. This phony standard asserted that no book or movie is indecent unless it is proved that it is "utterly without redeeming social value." This ridiculous rule blocked obscenity convictions for seven years.

Secondly, the Court rejected a *national* standard of obscenity, saying that, in judging whether a book or movie is obscene, a jury should use the view of "the average person, applying contemporary community standards."

What if juries decide differently in various parts of the country? Chief Justice Warren Burger dismissed this problem by saying: "It is neither realistic nor constitutionally sound to read the First Amendment as requiring that the people of Maine or Mississippi accept public depiction of conduct found tolerable in Las Vegas or New York City."[21]

In July, 1976, in *Young v. American Mini Theatres*,[22] the Su-

157

preme Court went a step farther and upheld zoning laws which either geographically disperse X-rated movie theaters and so-called adult bookstores, as Detroit does, or concentrate such objectional businesses in one area, as Boston does, in what is called its "combat zone." The Supreme Court at last realizes that civilized cities must have additional means of protecting their citizens against the public display of moral garbage. The Supreme Court recognizes that pornography is an "admittedly serious problem," that cities must be permitted to try "to preserve the quality of urban life," and therefore must be allowed "a reasonable opportunity to experiment with solutions."

Although the Supreme Court has retreated from its former total license for depraved pornography pushers, a casual look at the newsstands and the movies will quickly show that recent court decisions have done nothing to stem the tide of filth unleashed in earlier indefensible decisions. The latest rage at New York's Times Square pornographic bookstores is films featuring eight- and ten-year-old children performing sexual acts. The Postal Service has granted Second Class mail privileges to at least a dozen outrageously obscene magazines, and a dozen more have their applications for Second Class permits pending. The field is wide open for the energies and indignation of the Positive Woman.

Pornography can best be defined as the degradation of woman. It exploits women individually and as a group in the most offensive, degrading, and cruel way. In the modern jargon, pornography is the most "sexist" activity of all.

The women's liberationists prove their hypocrisy by their nonattitude toward pornography. They profess outrage at the role-concept fostered by school textbooks that include pictures of women in the home as wives and mothers, but they raise no protest about the role-concept fostered by obscene pictures of women as playthings for male lust and sadism in obscene and "bondage" books, magazines, and movies. The women's liberationists are indignant at the use of the four-letter word *lady* and "sexist" words such as *chairman* and *forefathers,* but raise no voice against the verbal obscenities in pornographic books, magazines, and movies.

This double standard may result from the women's liberationists' philosophical compatibility with any attack on moral standards or the homemaker's role and status. Or perhaps the double standard can be explained by the women's liberationists' own financial stake in the profits to be made by appealing to prurient interests. *Playboy* helped to finance the campaign for the Equal Rights Amendment in Illinois,[23] and the editor of *Penthouse* revealed on CBS television in February, 1977, that he was an early financial backer of ERA.

The Integrity of the Family

The energies and dedication of the Positive Woman are needed as never before to fend off the attacks on the moral, the social, and the economic integrity of the family.

Take, for example, the tremendous drive to set up child-care centers—taxpayer-financed, government-managed, "universally" available for "all socioeconomic groups" regardless of means. This adds up to an attempt to make it public policy to remove babies from the family unit and place them in an institutional environment.

Several groups see it as in their self-interest to promote a policy to replace mother care with government care. The women's liberationists are persistent pushers for this objective, based on their dogma that children are a burden from which women must be liberated.

Certain branches of the teachers' lobby also share this goal because they see it as the solution to the growing problem of empty classrooms and teacher unemployment caused by the severe decline in the American birth rate. Obviously, if our society can be induced to accept and finance the notion that every child should be put in school or a school substitute at age two or three instead of at age five or six, this would eliminate teacher unemployment.[24]

The third force working resourcefully and effectively to move babies out of the home into government kiddy-care centers and mothers out of the home into the job market is the consortium of vested interests that always works toward more government (especially federal) spending and control. It is obvious that the American people are now paying all the taxes they are willing to pay; they vote against higher taxes every chance they get.

Where, then, can the bureaucrats, the planners, the government spenders, find new sources of revenue to expand their staffs, increase their budgets, and consolidate their control over

159

our activities? The 40 million homemakers in the United States offer a tempting source of new tax revenues. When they stay in their homes, care for their own babies, and cook their own meals, no money changes hands. If these homemakers can be induced to leave their homes and take jobs, thereby having to purchase child care and other domestic services (such as packaged foods), the tax collector gets his share and more and bigger government is required.[25]

Finally, there are the self-appointed planners, convinced that they are better able to mold a child's mind than are his parents and that the earlier they get the child under their supervision, the more thorough the indoctrination can be. The behaviorists and humanists assume that parents are incapable of properly raising their own children and that children's development will be enhanced if they are turned over at an early age to government and welfare workers or to academic and psychological experts.

All these groups backed the Brademas-Mondale Child and Family Services Bill as the centerpiece of their effort to put government in the business of child-rearing. This is a proposal to spend nearly $2 billion of the taxpayers' money to set up a new bureau in charge of babysitting and child development facilities to be operated by the Department of Health, Education and Welfare. A new federal Office of Child and Family Services would supervise a network of federal day-care centers for children.

With all the other mischief HEW has been getting into, such as forced busing of students and worrying about whether schools are committing sex discrimination by allowing a mother-daughter fashion show or a father-son baseball game, it is hard to see why anyone would want to give HEW new jurisdiction over the lives of preschool children, too.

The scope of the Brademas-Mondale Bill is vast. By no means is it limited merely to custodial care. It covers the physical, educational, nutritional, social, recreational, psychological, and emotional development of the child, as well as "other such services and activities as the HEW Secretary deems appropriate." The bill makes child rearing a "partnership" between parents, HEW, and other state and local bureaucrats and organizations that claim they are "interested" in your child.

The dictionary defines *parent* as a "father" or a "mother." The Brademas-Mondale Bill, however, defines *parent* as "any

160

person who has primary day-to-day responsibility for any child." This could transfer your rights as parents of your own children into the hands of HEW bureaucrats, social workers, or teachers who have supervision over the children put into their care.

Nor is the Brademas-Mondale Bill a measure primarily designed to help the poor and needy. It clearly states that the program "shall include children from a range of socio-economic backgrounds." The taxpayers will thus be forced to pay the costs of caring for the preschool children of middle-class and even wealthy mothers who choose to evade the so-called burden of caring for their babies.

There are moral, social, and financial issues involved in the Brademas-Mondale Bill. Do we want to transfer the responsibility for the care of preschool children from the family to the federal government? Do taxpayers want to pay the cost of a giant federal babysitting service for all mothers regardless of means? Is it a social good to offer financial inducements to promote an exodus of mothers and babies from the home? Can we afford to give HEW billions of dollars to create a giant laboratory to tinker with the minds of very young children?

During 1975 and 1976, Positive Women answered no to all these questions so emphatically that the Brademas-Mondale Bill generated more mail to Capitol Hill than any other bill in many years. According to then Senator Walter Mondale, it "started down in Oklahoma and Texas, then it came north like the hoof-and-mouth disease."

The powerful forces lobbying for the concept of government child care rather than mother care will not go away. They will be back again with even more resourceful and well-financed techniques.

The Positive Woman starts from the premise—which is self-evident to most people but which can also be scientifically demonstrated[26]—that babies grow and develop better in a family with a mother's loving care than in an institution. The Positive Woman, therefore, will work tirelessly to safeguard the mother-care concept and to defeat government-care proposals.

Based on the dogma that a woman's susceptibility to becoming pregnant is the most oppressive inequality that women suffer, the women's liberation movement is compulsively oriented toward abortion on demand, financed by the govern-

161

ment and made socially acceptable any time, any place. For the abortionists, their claimed right to kill an unborn child must take precedence over every other moral, marital, family, social, or legal value.

The Supreme Court abortion decision of January 22, 1973, was just the beginning. Since then, the court has held that a father has no right to protect his unborn child from abortion. Although a young girl cannot get her ears pierced or go on a school field trip to the zoo without parental permission, she can have an abortion without parental knowledge or consent. Many kinds of state laws designed to put reasonable limits on the abortion business have been invalidated by the courts. The Department of Health, Education and Welfare has been spending large federal sums to finance abortions.

Until January 22, 1973, the worst decision of the United States Supreme Court was that in the Dred Scott case, which legalized slavery. But the Supreme Court decisions that legalized abortion are even worse. The United States Supreme Court in effect espoused the view that human life does not begin until live birth. No medical evidence whatsoever was presented in the Supreme Court cases to support this most unscientific conclusion. None of the Supreme Court justices is a doctor of medicine.

Every advance in medical knowledge and science proves further that the unborn infant is a separate human life, with separate unique fingerprints, a separate heart that starts beating at twenty-four days, and separate brainwaves that can be detected at forty-three days. No one could look at a photograph of any of the 4 million babies who have been aborted in the United States and conclude it was anything other than human.

The abortionists argue that a woman has a right to do what she wants with her own body. All medical textbooks and professors of embryology and obstetrics are witnesses to the fact that an unborn infant is not a mere extension of the mother's body, like an appendix or tonsils. Abortion involves the destruction of somebody else's body—which is living within the life-support system of the mother, as the astronauts lived within their life-support systems on the moon.

The abortionists argue that unwanted babies should be eliminated. There are no unwanted babies in the United States. The demand for babies far exceeds the supply. Couples are now paying up to $24,000 for a baby they can adopt.

A few decades ago, the famous physician, Sir William Osler, said that most people over sixty are unproductive and should be chloroformed. After he reached sixty, he changed his views, but his antilife suggestion has lingered on. In recent years, there has been an ominous acceptance of the idea of terminating the lives of senior citizens because they are useless or unwanted. This is the same as Hitler's philosophy of eliminating people whom he judged unwanted or mentally or physically defective. Unfortunately, Hitler's idea has survived his death.

All human life, whether young or old, productive or dependent, is sacred. Positive Women should renew their efforts for a constitutional amendment to protect our very young and our very old from the Supreme Court and from Hitler's philosophy.

The various state legislatures are being flooded with proposed legislation that, in sum, constitutes an attack on the moral, social, and economic integrity of the family and on the legal rights of homemakers. The ingenuity of the antifamily forces seems endless, but here is a checklist of laws that the Positive Woman should be alert to defeat:

(1) Changes in the state support laws to eliminate the legal right of the wife and mother to be supported by her husband, to reduce it to a minimal, reciprocal sex-neutral obligation of each spouse to support the other spouse only if he or she is incapacitated.

(2) Changes in the state alimony laws to make wives liable to court orders for the financial support of their ex-husbands.

(3) No-fault divorce—a concept that encourages the easy dissolution of marriage by one spouse without adequate compensation to the innocent or injured spouse. It promotes "serial marriages," which is destructive to moral standards, a stable society, the rights of the innocent or injured spouse, and the well-being of the children. *Slaughtered* is the word most customarily used to describe what happens to wives in states that have adopted no-fault divorce. It has created a new class of women who are financially impoverished and emotionally devastated.

(4) Laws to deprive husbands of the right to establish the family domicile and the surname of their children.

(5) The neuterization of all state legislation to replace all such words as *man, woman, husband, wife, male, female,* with

such sex-neutral words as *person, spouse,* and *taxpayer.* This omnibus approach affects hundreds of laws pertaining to marriage, property, inheritance, divorce, public and private schools, insurance, prisons, reform schools, hospitals, and public accommodations. It is just as nonsensical to legislate in such an irresponsible blunderbuss fashion as it would be to pass or defeat a package of 500 to 1,000 bills without evaluating them on their individual merits or defects.

(6) Laws to give homosexuals the rights to get marriage licenses, adopt children, or teach in the schools.

(7) Laws to change *rape* to *sexual assault.* There is nothing sex-neutral about rape. The punishment for this terrible crime against women should not be diminished to the punishment for the much lesser crime of assault.

(8) Laws to create and finance feminist commissions which function as a lobby to promote women's lib goals at the taxpayers' expense. These are usually called state, county, or city commissions or councils on the "status of women."

At the federal level, the women's liberationist "congresspersons" have been introducing many bills to achieve their goals, including:

(1) Federal child-care centers, "universally available."

(2) The Percy-Ribicoff bill that would set up a Cabinet-status women's lib lobby at taxpayers' expense. This "National Center for Women" would be a new federal super agency of massive proportions. It would give federal administrative, compliance, and subpoena power to a narrow special-interest group to promote women's lib objectives.

(3) Double Social Security taxes on every husband whose wife is in the home. This would have the result of imposing a federal financial penalty on wives and mothers who choose to be full-time homemakers.[27]

(4) Displaced housewives bills. The problem of, "displaced housewives" has been largely created by no-fault divorce and the elimination of alimony. We don't need any "solutions" that come from the same sources. The financial support of wives is the responsibility of their husbands, not of the taxpayers.

The economic integrity of the family depends on a wage earner who "brings home the bacon." The women's liberation movement constitutes an attack on this economic integrity by its insistence on reverse discrimination for women, enforced with the power of the federal government.

The Equal Employment Opportunity Act of 1972 prohibits discrimination in employment on the basis of race, religion, or sex. In the hands of federal bureaucrats, however, this has been interpreted to require job preference for employed women in order to achieve arbitrary race and sex quotas. The federal government has thus been requiring job discrimination on the basis of sex. The consent decree forced on the telephone company by the federal courts in the AT&T case established "goals," "intermediate targets," and "timetables" under which the employer is forced to override every other value (including qualifications, seniority, and number of dependents) in order to achieve its "affirmative-action" quota for women.[28] This reverse discrimination is now being enforced on employers by the federal bureaus and the federal courts.

The result of such antifamily objectives and practices is that there will be more and more two-income families and more and more husbands and fathers unemployed.

The economic hardship of unemployment, however, does not fall equally on everyone out of a job. Those with children to support are hurt the most. Reverse discrimination unjustly discriminates against the person who is trying to support a family. When the principal wage earner of a family unit is denied a job or a promotion, the end result is that many more persons are hurt, especially children. More people go on welfare, which in turn increases the taxes that all of us must pay.

The question is, if there are not enough jobs to go around, who should get the job preference when qualifications are roughly equal? Should preference be given on the basis of race or sex? Or should it not rather be given to that person, regardless of race, religion, or sex, who is supporting a family?

Congress should amend the Equal Employment Opportunity Act of 1972 to authorize employers to give job preference in hiring and promotions and retentions during layoffs to the spouse designated as the "principal wage earner" in each family. Each married couple could itself decide which spouse is to be designated as the principal wage earner, and this decision would be registered with the Social Security Administration for employers to verify. Where there is only one parent, he or she would be the principal wage earner.

This plan would be wholly voluntary, and it has the logic of simple justice. It would distribute the available jobs in the most equitable manner. It would be fair to all races and both sexes. It would reduce the welfare burden and save taxes. It

165

would safeguard the dignity and economic independence of the family and give needed help to widowed or divorced parents trying to support their children.

This plan would even be of great economic benefit to the single person, man or woman. Nothing could be more in the self-interest of the single wage earner than to have a public policy of encouraging homemakers to stay in the home, rather than competing in the labor market for the scarce available jobs. Some 2 million homemakers went into the job market for the first time in 1976, and unemployment rose to a level approximately 2 million higher than at any time since the Great Depression of the 1930s. The single wage earner will be the big loser if women's liberation compels or encourages any significant percentage of America's 40 million homemakers to enter the job market.

To reject the obligation to take whatever action is necessary to safeguard the moral, social, and economic integrity of the family is to abandon the future to a bunch of marital misfits who are seeking their identity as *Ms*, mistaken about morals, misinformed about history, motivated by the axiom "Misery loves company," and who want to remake our laws, revise the marriage contract, restructure society, remold our children to conform to lib values instead of God's values, and replace the image of woman as virtue and mother with the image of prostitute, swinger, and lesbian.

The Positive Woman will never acquiesce in the face of this attack. She accepts and meets the challenge. She knows the essential truth of the conclusion of the great French commentator Alexis de Tocqueville:

> I sought for the greatness and genius of America in her commodious harbors and ample rivers, and it was not there. I sought in her fertile lands and boundless prairies, and it was not there. Not until I went into the churches of America and heard her pulpits aflame with righteousness did I understand the secret of her genius and her power. America is great because she is good, and if America ceases to be good, America will cease to be great.

It is the task of the Positive Woman to keep America good.

Vision for America

The Bible tells us, "Where there is no vision, the people

perish." The Positive Woman must have a vision for America that gives perspective to her goals, her hopes for the future, and her commitment to her country. The Positive Woman starts with the knowledge that America is the greatest country in the world and that it is her task to do her part to keep it that way.

By common consent over nearly two centuries, the day Americans celebrate as our most important national patriotic anniversary is the Fourth of July. The bicentennial of our nation, July 4, 1976, was not the anniversary of the signing of the United States Constitution, or the ratification of the Bill of Rights, or the start or finish of the Revolutionary War—important as all these events were. The Fourth of July is the anniversary of the adoption of the Declaration of Independence on July 4, 1776.

This basic document of our national existence is the most perfect orientation of man to God and government outside of Holy Scripture. It is the most important document in American history and the most inspired writing in world history that ever flowed from the hand of man alone. Here is why:

(1) The Declaration of Independence is the official and unequivocal recognition by the American people of their belief and faith in God. It is a religious document from its first sentence to its last. It affirms God's existence as a "self-evident" truth that requires no further discussion or debate. The nation it creates is God's country. The rights it defends are God given. The actions of its signers are God inspired. There are four references to God—God as Creator of all men, God as the Supreme Judge, God as the source of all rights, God as our patron and protector.

(2) The Declaration of Independence declares that each of us is created equal. This means equal before God. It does not mean that all men are born with equal abilities, and so on, as some try to claim. Nor does it mean that all men can be made equal, as Communist dogma alleges. Obviously and realistically, and as your own individuating fingerprints prove, each of God's creatures is unequal and different from every other person who has ever lived or ever will live on this earth.

(3) The Declaration of Independence proclaims that life and liberty are unalienable gifts of God—natural rights—which no person or government can rightfully take away.

(4) The Declaration of Independence proclaims that the purpose of government is to secure these unalienable individual rights and that government derives its powers from the consent

of the governed. For the first time in history, government was reduced from master to servant.

The Declaration of Independence comes to us after 200 years in all its pristine purity. Whereas the United States Constitution has had to suffer the slings and arrows of some outrageous federal court interpretations and judicial distortions, neither the meddling judges nor the bungling bureaucrats have confused or distorted the Declaration of Independence. As the Declaration was in the beginning, it is now and ever shall be because it proclaims truth and facts that are not subject to change or amendment.

The Supreme Court that banned God from the public schools has not been able to censor Him out of the Declaration of Independence. The Supreme Court has forbidden public school children to declare their dependence upon God, but the Declaration of Independence pledges the firm reliance of the American people forever on the continued protection of God's Divine Providence.

After thus orienting our nation toward God's law, the Founding Fathers then gave us the United States Constitution —"the most wonderful work ever struck off at a given time by the brain and purpose of man." It provides the foundation for a political system that restrains the power of government through the separation of powers between the federal government and the separate states, and then among the three branches of the federal government, and also for an economic system based on private property, individual enterprise, and the use of government to maintain a free competitive system. The result has been that America has enjoyed more freedom and more material benefits than any nation in history.[29]

There are those today who espouse the notion that government can solve all problems by allowing bureaucratic experts to spend more and more of our money. There is no evidence to justify this policy. Progress has been the least in those areas where government has traditionally undertaken the job, namely, the postal service, public schools, and garbage collection. Progress has been the greatest in those areas where there has been private enterprise without government interference, such as automobiles, airplanes, and computers. There is no ceiling on man's ingenuity and resourcefulness to cope with problems—so long as we operate in the American climate of freedom. The "can do" philosophy that carved our great nation out of the wilderness can build a future brighter than any of us could ever dream.

Those who are inclined to go the route of the welfare state rather than private enterprise should take a good look at what has happened to Great Britain. For the last thirty years, Britain has had nationalized electricity, gas, water, coal, steel, railroads, and long-distance trucks and buses. Because of the absence of competition, prices in nationalized industries increased much faster than those in private industries. "Bringing coals to Newcastle" used to be an expression that described England's unlimited abundance of that essential national resource. Yet after the coal mines were nationalized, the inefficiency was so great that England had to import coal.

In housing, the social planners argued that tenants should be protected from greedy landlords and that rent control would fix a "just price" for all. The result of artificially low rents is the virtual elimination of privately owned apartments or rooms to rent. Landlords sell their property whenever tenants leave because the rent does not cover the costs, and the law makes it difficult if not impossible to remove even the most objectionable tenants. Those who cannot afford to own their own homes, or whom circumstances compel to take temporary housing, must resort to public housing, which is plagued with muggings, vandalism, noise, and inconvenience.

Socialized medicine has resulted in long queues for medical care, long waiting lists to get into hospital beds (the waiting list for an operation to have eye cataracts removed is two years), and the emigration of many experienced doctors and specialists, while more and more money each year is spent on administration.

About 64 percent of the gross national product is taken by the British government. The progressive income tax rate goes up to 98 percent. The average British worker pays one-third of his wages for the welfare state. British socialism is a spectacular economic failure, and the proof is in the pound. Since 1971 when the pound was allowed to "float" against other currencies, it has suffered an effective devaluation of 45 percent.

England has been a model for America in many ways. The Positive Woman will do all she can to make sure that we do not follow England's leadership into socialism and bankruptcy. Yet, in the United States, government is taking more and more of our personal income. In 1930, government on all levels took 15 percent of the personal income of Americans. By 1950, the government bite of our personal income had risen to 32 percent. By 1976, the government's hand in our pocketbook was taking 44 percent. At the current rate of increase, by the mid-1980s, government will be taking 54 percent of our personal income.

The Positive Woman will also reject socialism because of its effect on the family through its pursuit of the destructive goal of equality. The connection was explained in a book edited by Aleksandr Solzhenitsyn:

> The basic propositions of the socialist world view have often been proclaimed: the abolition of private property, religion and the family. One of the principles which is not so often represented as fundamental, though it is no less widespread, is the demand for *equality, the destruction of the hierarchy into which society has arranged itself.* The idea of equality in socialist ideology has a special character, which is particularly important for an understanding of socialism. In the more consistent socialist systems equality is understood in so radical a way that it leads to a negation of the existence of any genuine differences between individuals: "equality" is turned into "equivalence."[30]

It will do no good, however, to have the greatest material prosperity in the world if we do not meet the challenge of the nuclear age posed by the tremendous buildup of military power by the Soviet Union. Since 1962, the year of the Cuban Missile Crisis, the Soviets have built the mightiest arsenal of weapons of destruction the world has ever known—weapons that have only one utility, the destruction or blackmail of the United States.[31]

The paramount question confronting America is: What is our national response to this challenge? Are we building the nuclear weapons we need to enable us to live in freedom and independence in the face of the Soviet threat? Make no mistake about it, our freedom of religion, speech, and press, our independence as a nation, and our entire Judeo-Christian civilization are possible only in a world defended by America's armed forces with their nuclear weapons. Without the superiority of American defenses over every potential aggressor, there can be no freedom, independence, or civilization as we know it.

If we want to hang on to the precious vitality that built our great nation, we must teach our young people that the password of freedom is Patrick Henry's eloquent "Give me liberty or give me death"—not the plea of the handout hunter, "Gimme, gimme, gimme." If we want our independence to endure, we must teach our young people to reject the lure of the Soviet appeasers who cry, "Better Red than dead"—and instead to kindle the patriotic fervor of Nathan Hale, the young teacher who said, "I regret that I have but one life to give for my country."

The Positive Woman must be a patriot and a defender of our Judeo-Christian civilization. She, therefore, must support the legislation, the legislators, and the funding necessary to defend the values of home and country against attack by aggressors who respect neither.

The reason why the pressure groups pushing women's lib, more federal control, and a weakening of American military defenses have had significant successes is not that they have more persuasive arguments, not that they have history on their side, and not even that they have the support of the majority of voters. Indeed, they have none of these. The reason they have been winning is that they have developed skills in the techniques of: (1) the legislative and election process, (2) the litigating of social change through the courts by the use of lawyer specialists, (3) the placing of their agents and sympathizers in the media and the educational system, and (4) the use of *other people's money* through tax funds, tax-exempt foundations, and other tax-exempt organizations.

The Positive Woman accepts her obligation, insofar as she is able, to develop the skills and the techniques to safeguard the values of God, family, and country. In the words of Saint James, she becomes a doer of the word, and not merely a hearer:

> Be ye doers of the word, and not hearers only, deceiving your own selves.
> For if any be a hearer of the word, and not a doer, he is like unto a man beholding his natural face in a glass; for he beholdeth himself, and goeth his way, and straightway forgetteth what manner of man he was.
> But who so looketh unto the perfect law of liberty, and continueth therein, he being not a forgetful hearer, but a doer of the word, this man shall be blessed in his deed.[32]

Is a national vision too broad in scope for the average American woman? Are the problems of our military defense and private enterprise economics too complex or too controversial? Time and again, God has given women the mission to save their country.

Saint Brigitte was a Positive Woman who met the challenge of her day and station in life. A queen in fourteenth century Scandinavia, she started her public career as a widow with eight children. She accepted the call of Christ to be His vehicle to preach moral renewal and Christian unity in a period when men in power were characterized by failure of nerve and principle. She spoke to kings and popes all over Europe with the courage and confidence of a woman who knew that her revelations and her prophecies were the truth. She built hospitals, schools, and convents; she founded religious orders; she turned the hearts and minds of all those whose lives she touched to Christian charity.

Saint Brigitte preached a personal ennoblement through devotion and obedience to Christ, an ennoblement of the human heart through Christian education and culture, and an ennoblement of human existence through service to God and our fellow man. She spoke out against adultery, abortion, and the worldly corruption of the priestly ministry. In her battle for spiritual renewal and ecumenism, she was a Viking warrior who became a Christian heroine.

Saint Margaret was a Positive Woman of the eleventh century who met the challenge that fate served up to her. Raised in the Christian court of Saint Stephen of Hungary, as a young woman she was shipwrecked on the rocky coast of Scotland. In romantic fairy-tale fashion, the king of Scotland discovered her, fell in love with her, and made her his queen. In her short life before she died at the age of forty-seven, she not only bore him six sons, but she exerted an influence on Scotland that will never end. Because her husband's love and faith in Margaret were so total, she was able to use the royal power to bring Christianity, civilization, and education to Scotland.

A woman certainly does not have to be a queen to save her nation. No woman was ever more humbly born than Joan of Arc, a teenager of peasant parentage who overcame every handicap of social custom, military practice, and religious bigotry to snatch victory from the jaws of defeat and drive the British invaders from her native France. She was one of the great military strategists of all history.

172

Does a woman have to hear actual voices from heaven in order to save her country from aggression? Are all such examples of women saving their country merely tales from the distant past?

On the contrary, the Positive Woman of the modern age has been served the same challenge—and some have accepted it. Brazil offers an outstanding example of how women can save a nation from Communist takeover.

In 1964 the power of the Brazilian government had been assumed by a crypto-Communist named Goulart. He was in the process of rapidly consolidating his control, taking over the radio stations, the press, the police, and the unions. People were afraid to resist because of the customary Communist tactics and retaliations.

Goulart's speech on March 13, 1964, made it clear to anyone who cared to look that he was rapidly taking Brazil into the Communist camp, from which there would be no return. The following day, one woman made up her mind that this was not going to happen. Dulce Salles Cunha Braga called a meeting of fifteen of her key friends, and together they planned a big demonstration in the streets of Sao Paulo for March 19 at 2:00 P.M. They called it the March of the Family with God for Freedom. They telephoned for days, printed fliers, and passed the word in every way they could.

When the demonstration took place on March 19, one million people crowded into the streets of Sao Paulo. This fantastic demonstration of grassroots opposition to communism was what gave the men the backbone they needed to act. When the military leaders saw that the people would support decisive and timely anti-Communist action, they moved swiftly, and on March 31 they threw out Goulart and his Communist lieutenants. Brazil was saved from the disaster of a Communist government.

And this was due to the inspired leadership of one Positive Woman, Dulce Salles Cunha Braga (later elected a Brazilian congresswoman), and the other Positive Women who rallied to the banner she raised.

It is primarily the women who deserve the credit for the overthrow of the Communist Allende in Chile. After he was elected as a minority president, he consolidated his control in typical Communist fashion. He took over most of the banks and the large, rich farms. His comrades encouraged factory

173

workers to strike, and then they used the strikes as a pretext for the government to take over the factories. Industrial and agricultural production fell off substantially as the Allende government channeled the energies of the workers into political rallies and preparations for civil war. Newspapers that published the truth were closed for weeks and their reporters jailed.

Allende's policies caused severe food shortages for the first time in Chile's history. The shelves of the stores were empty, and many items could not be bought at any price. Housewives had to spend up to six hours a day standing in line for food and other essentials.

When Fidel Castro came to Chile for a three-week visit in 1973, Chilean women decided they had had enough. On December 3, the night before Castro left Chile, the women staged an impressive demonstration called the March of the Empty Pots. Thousands of women marched through the streets of Santiago beating with spoons on their empty pots and pans. That first demonstration was followed by several other such marches, during which the women were harassed by tear gas thrown by Allende's police and potatoes embedded with razor blades burled by the Communists.

After it became too dangerous to march in public, the women retaliated by leaning out of their windows at ten o'clock every evening and beating on their pots and pans to make a deafening clatter. When, later, truckers and copper miners staged strikes, the women encouraged them and brought them food. The women kept up their demonstrations until, finally, the men had the courage to save Chile and, in a nearly bloodless coup, took control away from Allende, who committed suicide. The coup came just in time to prevent Allende from sending all anti-Communists "to the wall" as his buddy Castro had done.

Anything that Brazilian and Chilean women can do, positive American women can do. No national problem is too immense for American women. Our religion teaches that we must avoid the sins of both presumption and despair. Presumption is the sin of believing that God will take care of everything, so there is no need for the individual to do anything. Despair is the sin of believing that all is lost, that nothing we can do will make any difference. The Positive Woman accepts the message of hope and treads that narrow line of faith and action that succumbs neither to presumption nor to despair.

Here is a starting checklist of goals that can be restored to America if Positive Women will apply their dedicated efforts:

(1) The right of a woman to be a full-time wife and mother and to have this right recognized by laws that obligate her husband to provide the primary financial support and a home for her and their children.

(2) The responsibility of parents (not the government) for the care of preschool children.

(3) The right of parents to insist that the schools:
   a. permit voluntary prayer,
   b. teach the "fourth R," right and wrong, according to the precepts of Holy Scriptures,
   c. use textbooks that do not offend the religious and moral values of the parents,
   d. use textbooks that honor the family, monogamous marriage, woman's role as wife and mother, and man's role as provider and protector,
   e. teach such basic educational skills as reading and arithmetic before time and money are spent on frills,
   f. permit children to attend school in their own neighborhood, and
   g. separate the sexes for gym classes, athletic practice and competition, and academic and vocational classes, if so desired.

(4) The right of employers to give job preference (where qualifications are equal) to a wage earner supporting dependents.

(5) The right of a woman engaged in physical-labor employment to be protected by laws and regulations that respect the physical differences and different family obligations of men and women.

(6) The right to equal opportunity in employment and education for all persons regardless of race, creed, sex, or national origin.

(7) The right to have local governments prevent the display of printed or pictorial materials that degrade women in a pornographic, perverted, or sadistic manner.

(8) The right to defend the institution of the family by according certain rights to husbands and wives that are not given to those choosing immoral lifestyles.

175

(9) The right to life of all innocent persons from conception to natural death.

(10) The right of citizens to live in a community where state and local government and judges maintain law and order by a system of justice under due process and punishment that is swift and certain.

(11) The right of society to protect itself by designating different roles for men and women in the armed forces and police and fire departments, where necessary.

(12) The right of citizens to have the federal government adequately provide for the common defense against aggression by any other nation.

All things are possible to those who take as their text:

> They that wait upon the Lord shall renew their strength; they shall mount up with wings as eagles; they shall run, and not be weary; and they shall walk, and not faint.[33]

Appendix One

The Pictures the Press Didn't Print

On Sunday, May 16, 1976, the proponents of the Equal Rights Amendment held their biggest demonstration in history. They brought in persons from at least thirty-one states to stage a big rally on the steps of the State Capitol in Springfield, Illinois, for the announced purpose of pressuring the Illinois legislature to ratify ERA. Some of the media reported a crowd of 12,000 persons, others reported 6,000. It wasn't that large—probably closer to 3,500. But it was a sizable crowd. They came on some fifty buses and on a train from the East Coast that made special stops along the way.

Participants in the rally were solicited in many ways: (1) by a $10,000 ad in the *New York Times* and other eastern newspapers, (2) by fliers on college campuses advertising trips to Springfield at bargain-basement prices (e.g., twenty dollars round-trip from Detroit, twenty-five dollars from Atlanta—and if you couldn't afford that, you could apply for a "scholarship"), (3) free "public service announcements" provided by some television stations giving the phone number one could call to join the demonstration, and (4) free editorials and "news" articles in some metropolitan newspapers drumming up attendance.

The free media coverage given to this rally was so tremendous that one would think it was the most important national event since an American walked on the moon. The day after the demonstration, the *New York Times* gave it a front-page picture plus a large inside story. There was extensive coverage all across the country, and newspapers whose readers never heard of Springfield, Illinois, published large pictures of the rally. Some papers printed a full page of pictures. Of course, there was network television coverage.

177

179

At the demonstration, greetings were read from President and Mrs. Gerald Ford, presidential candidate Jimmy Carter, Senator Hubert Humphrey, Congressman Morris Udall, and Illinois Senators Charles Percy and Adlai Stevenson. Illinois Governor Dan Walker and Illinois Senate President Cecil Partee attended and spoke to the demonstrators.

On the preceding pages are authentic pictures of the May 16, 1976, ERA rally that the press failed to print. They show the unkempt, the lesbians, the radicals, the socialists, and the government employees who are trying to amend the United States Constitution to force us to conform to their demands. Even these pictures don't tell it all, because they don't reveal the obscene language and foul four-letter words that are part of the everyday language of the women's lib movement.

The May 16 demonstration was planned, organized, and led by the National Organization for Women. NOW ran newspaper ads to raise money and spent $40,000 on the rally. NOW distributed the fliers. NOW members all over the country were ordered to attend. The principal speakers at the rally were Betty Friedan, founder of NOW, and Karen DeCrow, president of NOW.

The radical and antifamily tactics and objectives of NOW are clearly spelled out in its *Revolution: Tomorrow Is NOW* (see appendix two). This pamphlet shows that NOW is for abortion mandated in all hospitals, financed by the government, and taught in all schools as though it were just another routine operation. NOW is for taxpayer-financed state kiddy-care centers for all children. NOW is for prolesbian legislation giving perverts the same legal rights as husbands and wives—such as the rights to get marriage licenses, to file joint income tax returns, and to adopt children.

NOW's primary legislative goal is ratification of the Equal Rights Amendment, which is basically an attack on the legal and financial rights of the homemaker. NOW is even trying to change school textbooks so as to promote a "gender-free," unisex society.

But there is much, much more. *Revolution: Tomorrow Is NOW* spells out NOW's efforts to force the churches to ordain women and to recruit them actively into seminaries. It describes how NOW is even working to deprive the churches of their tax exemption. It also shows how the NOW women hate veterans and are working actively to eliminate all veterans' preferences.

Appendix Two

Revolution: Tomorrow Is Now

In this appendix you will find a *verbatim* reproduction of the original twenty-one-page *Revolution: Tomorrow Is NOW,* published in 1973 by the National Organization for Women, the leading women's liberationist group. The subject index below is provided for easy reference to NOW's goals and proposals as set forth in its official manifesto.

Index

REVOLUTION: tomorrow is

This is a summary of NOW's existing resolutions and policies by issue. It can be used to acquaint Chapter members with NOW's policies prior to the National Conference. Use this in conjunction with the workbook for action you received earlier to hold pre-Conference discussions with your Chapter. Only if all members are well acquainted with existing policies can we move forward at the 1973 Conference to devise strategy to implement these policies, as well as making any new policy we might need.

I EQUALITY UNDER THE LAW

A. Equal Rights Amendment

Passage and ratification of the Equal Rights Amendment to the U. S. Constitution *without amendment:*

"Equality of rights under the law shall not be denied or abridged by the United States or by any State on account of sex."

B. Civil Rights

1. Add sex discrimination prohibitions to Titles II (public accomodations [*sic*]), III, IV (public education), VI (federal funding) of the Civil Rights Act of 1964. (Oct., 1966)
2. Legislation to include women on all commissions, boards and other appointive bodies. (Oct., 1966)
3. Broaden Civil Rights Commission mandate to include sex discrimination in its studies. (Oct., 1966)
4. Inclusion of sex in all new Civil Rights legislation, where relevant. (Oct., 1966)
5. Broaden Civil Rights Commission mandate to include study and reports on sex discrimination. (Dec., 1968)
6. 1968 Housing Law should be added to include prohibition of sex discrimination as well as race, religion, national origin based discrimination. Sex discrimination prohibitions should also be added to all state and local housing laws. (Dec., 1968)
7. State legislation establishing Commissions on the Status of Women. (March, 1970)
8. Study and initiate positive changes in action policies and hiring practices of all human and civil rights agencies as they relate to women. (Sept., 1971)
9. Equalizing social security and other social benefits laws eliminating distinctions based on sex. (Oct., 1966)

II ECONOMIC EQUALITY

A. Report of the Compliance Task Force. September, 1971—September, 1972

At the September, 1971, National Conference, the following resolutions were adopted:

1. That NOW rename its *Task Force on Federal Compliance* to the *Task Force on Compliance* and that part of the work of that task force be to study and initiate positive changes in the action policies and hiring practices of all human and civil rights agencies as they relate to women; and that NOW establish a caucus of its members employed by or members of civil and human rights agencies in order to combat blatant sex discrimination and the indifference towards women's rights that exists within these agencies; and that NOW urge NOW chapters to establish similar caucuses at state and local levels to work with state and local agencies.
2. The [*sic*] NOW urge the House Government Operations Committee to hold hearings to evaluate federal enforcement against sex discrimination in its internal and public programs, covering all agencies and executive departments, including evaluation of their in-house programs, enforcement programs and procedures, enforcement records and allocation of resources, and that the Conference direct the Compliance Task Force to adopt the securing of these hearings as its immediate priority.
3. That NOW request a meeting with the U.S. Civil Rights Commission to inform them of our program to secure extension of their mandate to include jurisdiction over sex discrimination with the necessary increase in appropriations, and NOW offer information and assistance

183

to the CRC in developing relevant policies and programs to protect and secure women's rights.

4. That NOW call upon the Office of Federal Contract Compliance (OFCC) to amend its rules and regulations to require Federal Contractors to issue a semiannual progress report on their Affirmative Action plans to all affected classes in their employment and to the public whose taxes finance their contracts.

5. That NOW support passage of the Equal Employment Opportunity Enforcement Act without weakening amendments, to grant cease and desist enforcement authority to the Equal Employment Opportunity Commission (EEOC), and to cover teachers and federal, state and local employees.

6. That NOW demand that the Department of Labor adopt the provision of childcare facilities as a work place standard, and that OFCC incude the requirement to provide child care as an ingredient of Affirmative Action Programs.

7. That NOW oppose any state, federal, county or municipal employment law or program giving special preference to veterans.

8. That NOW demand of General Services Administration (GSA), Small Business Administration (SBA), and the Department of Commerce that the advantages of the Minority Business Enterprise Program be extended to women of all races and that all such federal programs, now or in the future, define the word "minority" to include women of all races.

9. That NOW demand that the Department of Labor drop the term "Manpower" and substitute a non-sexist term like "Workpower."

10. That NOW insist the following federally required form—EEO-1, breakout of the workforce, which shows the pattern of employment in a company with relation to race, ethnic group and sex, EEO-2, union membership, EEO-3, participants of Joint Apprenticeship Committee-sponsored apprenticeship programs—be made public documents. Such public reporting may be made on the basis of a percentage of the total workforce.

11. That NOW call on the EEOC to issue an immediate ruling prohibiting applications that require information on sex, including given name of the applicant, and that NOW demand that the EEOC prohibit questions concerning marital or parental plans or status and other such invasions of privacy from pre-employment inquiries of any sort.

12. That NOW urge the EEOC, OFCC, and CSC sponsor conferences or educational forums on discrimination against women for employers, public and private employment agencies, college and university placement offices, labor unions and government agencies.

13. That NOW call upon the EEOC to withdraw from circulation its publication "Equal Job Opportunities—A National Goal" until it is revised to eliminate such sexist phrases as "appoint a man" and until it includes guides for affirmative action for equal opportunities for women, and to review all publications and to withdraw all other such sexist publications.

14. That NOW demand that the OFCC, EEOC, and the Wage and Hour Division prohibit employers from discriminating against women by issuing immediate rulings requiring employers to provide equal contributions and equal benefits in all fringe benefit programs, including retirement programs.

15. That NOW calls upon that Office of Management and Budget immediately to issue Form A as proposed by OFCC with the inclusion of women in items concerning promotions.

184

16. That NOW calls upon the Office of Management and Budget to evaluate Equal Opportunity Enforcement Programs for women as they are now so doing for the other minorities.

Since the September, 1971 Conference, letters, phone calls, and/or personal visits from members of the Task Force, from NOW National Officers, and/or from others, have brought the following successes in the above areas: (coupled with the efforts of others)

1. Representative Edith Green has convened a Federal panel to hear testimony in cities around the country on discrimination against women in the federal government.
2. An act granting jurisdiction over sex to the U.S. Civil Rights Commission is before Congress with reasonable certainty of passage.
3. Although OFCC has not yet amended its rules and regulations to require that affirmative action programs be made public, some compliance agencies (e. g. HEW) have taken this position.
4. The Equal Employment Opportunity Enforcement Act of 1972 passed Congress and was signed into law in March, granting EEOC the right to go to court for enforcement, and extending the coverage of Title VII to state and local government employees. The law also allows individuals and groups to file on behalf of others, extends the period of filing from 90 to 180 days, and grants coverage (although not under EEOC jurisdiction) to federal employees. NOW has been credited by many, including EEOC officials, with primary credit for the passage of this law.
5. The Department of Labor adopted the provision of childcare facilities as a work place standard.
6. NOW has continually opposed law giving preference to Veterans, its most recent efforts being directed against the Emergency Employment Act of 1971. These laws continue on the books, largely because of the strong influence of Veterans organizations.
7. We have demanded of the Office of Minority Business Enterprise of the Department of Commerce that they include women of all races in their definition of minority. In recent weeks this office compounded the problem by including veterans among the groups to be given preference for SBA loans and set-asides. They have not yet included women of all races, but it appears from their responses to our letters that we have raised the consciousness of this office.
8. President Heide has been doing a most effective job of convincing people to use non-sexist terms such as "human-power" and "work-power." Department of Labor, unfortunately, has not yet seen the light.
9. EEOC has begun to revise some of its literature per our requests. Just recently, in response to a direct request by letter, they altered one of the tables in a statistical report to show breakdowns for white women.
10. The new EEOC sex discrimination guidelines specifically forbid sex discrimination in fringe benefit and retrement programs.
11. The Higher Education Act of 1972 was passed, prohibiting sex discrimination in admissions and financial aid in colleges and universities receiving federal funds.
12. Amendments to the Fair Labor Standards Act were passed, extending equal pay coverage to 15 million professional, executive, and technical workers, and bringing household workers under the minimum wage.

185

13. Revised Order No. 4 was issued by the OFCC in December, 1971, extending the provisions of Order No. 4 to women.

Recommendations:

A specific policy is needed regarding the amount of individual mail a task force coordinator can reasonably be expected to answer, and what to do about NOW's image should coordinators simply stop answering their mail. At the rate mail comes in now, there is no time left to coordinate task force actions and advise chapters.

This task force could easily get by with *no* further resolutions for at least a couple of years. Our lines of responsibility and policy statements in the area of compliance are quite clearly drawn. I do not feel further clarification is needed at this time.

Resolutions should not be quite so specific. The Coordinator should be left free to design and modify actions based on current progress, agency awareness, and chapter feedback. Having specific actions so elaborately spelled out leaves the coordinator with no room for flexibility or new actions which might be more profitable.

Conference resolutions should state broad policy within which the most effective action can be determined by the coordinator and the task force members.

MARY LYNN MYERS

II ECONOMIC EQUALITY (Cont'd)
B. Labor Standards
1. Extension of Fair Labor Standards Acts and Equal Pay Acts to cover all workers (Dec., 1968) including all public and private employment. (Oct., 1966)
2. Support the amendment of the Federal Fair Labor Standards Act to require equal pay for equal work for female professional, executive or administrative positions. (Mar., 1970)
3. Extension of the minimum wage act to cover all workers. (Mar., 1970)
4. Extend the protections that are granted under state "Protective" labor laws that are genuinely needed to men; abolish the obsolete restrictions that today operate to the economic disadvantages of women by depriving them of equal opportunity. (Oct., 1966, Nov., 1967, Dec., 1968, Mar., 1970)
   Ask Women's Bureau, Department of Labor, to conduct educational program on how state "protective" laws are now discriminatory and used against women and to promote the policy that "protective" laws, where necessary, must apply equally to men and women. (Dec., 1968)
5. Department of Labor substitute a non-sexist term like "Workpower" for Manpower.
C. Employment and the Family
1. There be an end to discrimination in employment against those who choose to participate fully in family life; and that employers may neither require unpaid services from an employee's spouse nor discriminate against an unmarried person. (Sept., 1971)
2. Campaign to eliminate, by federal and state law, discrimination on the basis of maternity. Provide paid maternity leave as a form of social security for all working mothers, with the right to return to her job. (Oct., 1966) Help stop discrimination against teachers for pregnancy. (Nov., 1967)
3. That present employee benefits, including maternity leave and child

care facilities, be extended to both men and women and that NOW work for such non-sexist goals as "parent leave" instead of maternity leave. (Sept., 1971)
   4. Child care facilities for working parents. (Oct., 1966, Dec., 1968) Full deduction of child care expenses from income tax, (Oct., 1966) whether listed as dependent or not. (Dec., 1968)

D. Help-Wanted Ads
   1. Demand replacement of the EEOC guidelines on employment advertisements. (Oct., 1966; it was replaced.) Set a date for national action on segregated help-wanted ads, picketing or asking the President to intervene. (Nov., 1967) Pressure local newspapers to develop or expand joint male/female columns. (Dec., 1968) Take every means possible to press for prompt enactment and enforcement to the EEOC guidelines for desegregating the help wanted ads and that NOW shall combat the American Newspaper Publishers Association suit against the EEOC with every means at our disposal. (Dec., 1968) Continue confrontations with publishers, picketing, filing complaints with local civil rights commissions. We would like to see a NOW chapter or member prove that a newspaper does exercise judgment in accepting and printing classified ads by trying to place a racist and sexist help wanted ad. (Mar., 1970)

E. Conferences, Coalitions & Training
   1. Assistance to women in any industry or profession in the organization of conferences or demonstrations to protest policies or conditions which discriminate against them; to open avenues of advancement to the decision-making power structure from which they are now barred, whether it be from executive training courses, the main line of promotion that leads to corporate presidencies or full professorships, or the road to union leadership. (Oct., 1966)
   2. Campaign to open new avenues of upgrading and on-the-job training for women now segregated in dead-end clerical, secretarial, and menial jobs in government, industry, hospitals, factories and offices— providing them training in new technological skills, equally with men and new means of access to administrative and professional levels. (Oct., 1966) See also Women in Poverty.
   3. All chapters develop employment conferences on employment problems to implement NOW policy on equal opportunity in employment and disseminate information on problems in opportunity for employment and promotions, wages, hours, working conditions, protective laws, fringe benefits. (Pension, leave, etc.) (Dec., 1968)
   4. Chapters should work with local labor unions, particularly when many union members are women, to get ideas and enlist support for joint action. Chapters should also contact other women's organizations (BPW, National Council of Women, Negro Women's groups) to attempt to use group pressure to combat sex discrimination in employment. (Dec., 1968)
   5. Urge expansion of service occupations such as shopper service, wardrobe tenders, development of "practical mothers" (like practical nurses) etc. (Oct., 1966)
   6. Offer career counseling to all women. (Mar., 1970)

F. Talent Banks
   Develop Executive banks of able women so when employers indicate willingness to hire women, but claim they can't find qualified women, NOW can supply them with names. (Dec., 1968)

G. Women in Business
   1. Encourage and support the formation of businesses for women and women in business. (Mar., 1970)
   2. Provide information on securing Small Business Administration loans

187

and obtaining government contracts available to minority business. (Mar., 1970)

3. Encourage and suggest procedures for women who wish to pool money to form economic co-ops for businesses, etc. (Mar., 1970)
4. Urge repeal of state and local laws which deny women the same freedoms, conditions and privileges as men have for borrowing money, owning real estate, and operating businesses. (Mar., 1970)
5. That NOW develop lists of business and professional women and businesses owned by women on national and local levels and disseminate them for the purpose of encouraging support of the businesses or practices of such women. (Sept., 1971)

H. Age Discrimination

Campaign against age discrimination, which operates as a particularly serious handicap for women re-entering the labor market after rearing children, and which is imbued with the denigrating image of women viewed solely as sex objects in instances such as the forcing of airlines stewardesses to resign before the age of 32. (Oct., 1966)

I. Veteran's preference

That NOW oppose any state, federal, county, or municipal employment law or program giving special preference to veterans. (Sept. 1971)

J. Income Tax, Social Security and Retirement

1. Eliminate tax provisions which discriminate against single persons;
2. Child care deductions, as above.
3. Revise social security laws to eliminate discrimination against divorced women and working wives. (See also Marriage and the Family)
4. Revise retirement and pension plans to eliminate sex discrimination. (Dec., 1968)
5. Demand that OFCC, EEOC and Wage and Hour Division prohibit employers from discriminating against women by issuing immediate rulings requiring employers to provide equal contributions and equal benefits in all fringe programs, including retirement. (Sept., 1971)
6. Amend the Social Security Act to provide benefits to husbands and widowers of deceased and disabled women workers under the same conditions as they are provided to wives and widows, and to provide more equitable retirement benefits for families with working wives. Guarantee husbands and children of women employees of the Federal Government the same fringe benefits provided for wives and children of male employees. Provide tax deductions for child-care expenses incurred in the home. (April, 1971 board meeting)

K. Report of the Women and Volunteerism Task Force, October, 1972

1. NOW's standpoint on volunteerism.

The 1971 NOW Conference passed the following resolution:

that NOW distinguish between (1) voluntary activities which serve to maintain woman's dependent and secondary status on the one hand, and (2) change-directed activities which lead to more active participation in the decision making process;

that NOW seek to raise the consciousness of women engaged in these volunteer activities, so that they use their "volunteer power" in an effort to change policies detrimental to the interests of women.

NOW thus makes a rough dicotomy between *service volunteering* and volunteering for change. NOW encourages the latter kind which is in essence citizens' participation in the democratic process.

The first kind, which is the kind women usually do, is simply public services which are performed by non-paid personnel. Or it is charity which is dispensed as a supplement to the public service sector. For women it is also often memberships in auxiliaries or clubs which serve to aid their husband's careers.

Service-volunteering has been surrounded by an ideology which asserts that women's superior morality and aptitude for service make them particularly suited to serve as the unpaid conscience of the nation. Community service is in essence housekeeping on a large scale, and has been considered a fitting occupation for the nation's housekeepers.

NOW's position may be summarized as follows:

"Volunteering for women is yet another form of activity
   which serves to reinforce the second-class status of women;
   which is one more instance of the ongoing exploitation of
      women;
   which takes jobs from the labor market, and therefore divides
      middle class from poor and working women
   which buttresses the structures which are keeping women in a
      subordinate role;
   which is antithetical to the goals of the feminist movement
      and thus detrimental to the liberation of women."

2. Implementation

As a first step, a pamphlet which contained the resolution, position-paper and other pertinent material was prepared and circulated among the NOW membership. It has also received a great deal of attention outside of membership ranks.

A plan to implement the second point—"that NOW seek to raise the consciousness of women engaged in these volunteer activities, so that they use their 'volunteer power' in an effort to change policies detrimental to the interests of women"—is presently in progress. A new pamphlet has been prepared which is directed especially to the volunteer, and chapter task-force coordinators are asked to distribute the pamphlet as widely as possible within the volunteer world. This should have the effect of stimulating discussion on the local level, where each task-force coordinator may plan her campaign in whatever way is most suitable for that local area; she may engage speakers, arrange discussion-meeting with volunteer leaders, solicit articles for publication, etc.

3. Goals for 1973 conference

The above-mentioned campaign should be well underway at the time of the 1973 conference. A workshop on Women and Volunteerism should at that point decide whether NOW's position needs to be augmented by further resolutions. It may be expected that NOW should take an official standpoint on the effort to give certain kinds of volunteering tax-deductible status. Three bills to this effect are presently pending in Washington. All three limit tax-deductions to service-volunteering, *calculated at* minimum wage.

L. Women in Poverty

1. NOW will work to insure that all federal poverty-related programs, including the JOB CORPS and MDTA, shall be administered without discrimination on the basis of sex and shall provide serious training for disadvantaged girls and women, as well as boys and men, in order

189

that they may take a rewarding and productive role in society. We will fight the current practice of ignoring women and girls in such government programs; of providing them with training, under the MDTA, of only the beauty care or unskilled clerical sort that is not geared to the future or even to the hope of adequate pay. (Oct., 1966) See Emp.

2. Recommendation for a conference on "Women in Poverty" (Nov., 1967)

3. Since it is the right of all to employment and there are not enough jobs, we support a shortened work week which will open more jobs to women and allow more men to spend more time in the home. (Mar., 1970) We support full employment and when the private economy cannot provide decent jobs, the public economy must. We look to the future by supporting in principle a guaranteed income. (Mar., 1970)

4. NOW demand the removal of such derogatory terms as bastard, illegitimate, and unwed mother from national, state, and local statutes dealing with welfare and other concerns of women in poverty. (Sept., 1971)

5. NOW insists that no woman be denied public assistance or services for refusal to identify the father of her child. (Sept., 1971)

6. NOW will actively work to oppose efforts such as bills to force women to accept involuntary sterilization which take away a woman's right to control her own reproductive life. (Sept., 1971)

7. NOW demand equal participation in planning and implementation of voluntary job training programs and equal opportunity for placement of all job training programs. (Sept., 1971) That NOW chapters be encouraged to investigate fraud perpetrated on women by programs such as WIN, Manpower (MDTA), On Job Training and Job Corps. (Sept., 1971)

8. NOW demand the government at all levels take immediate and effective action to end the exploitation of women by organized crime. (Sept., 1971)

9. NOW actively opposes the current proposed Family Assistance Plan because it guarantees an income below the poverty level as set by the Bureau of Labor Statistics, it would deprive a woman of freedom of choice by forcing her to accept menial employment and a wage below the federally set minimum wage rather than staying home caring for her children. (Sept., 1971)

10. Whereas, U.S. Census figures show that 10% of all families & 20% of all households are headed by women and the great majority of such families is near or below the poverty line and that poverty among such families increased throughout the 1960's while poverty among males declined sharply, and whereas, this poverty is frequently caused by the double burden imposed on the person who must both care for and financially support children, and whereas, court awarded child support is very often not enforced or inadequately enforced (as documented for example by the Task Force on Absent Parent Child Support of the Ca. Social Welfare Comm.) and whereas, a parent in poverty bearing the double burden of care and support, deprived of adequate enforcement of support orders often has no other recourse than to apply for welfare.

THEREFORE BE IT RESOLVED: that NOW press for legislation and establishment of procedures which will alleviate this double burden and afford those so burdened a means whereby they may avoid having to apply for welfare, including the following:

  a. Equitable sharing of child support by parents who are financially able.

190

b. Genuine enforcement of child support laws and orders.

c. Establishment and maintenance of enforcing agencies adequately staffed by trained and motivated personnel and sufficiently funded.

d. Immediate payment of support directly to the parent.

e. Where support is not immediately forthcoming from the assessed spouse, that courts order such payments be paid immediately from public funds, with appropriate means taken to recover such payments from the assessed.

f. Complete deductibility from all income taxes of all payments for child care.

g. Prevention of similar poverty in the future by providing education for all persons that enables them to be economically independent and encourages them to achieve full human potential. (Sept., 1971)

11. Because 2/3 of the American people over 16 who live in poverty are women and because the impact of inflation on women in this country is particularly severe and because NOW is opposed to a wage-price freeze without controls on profit and interest while the government continues to hand out tax rebates to big business, NOW resolves to call on women and the labor movement to take the initiative in formulating a more effective and equitable program for combatting inflation than that which is embodied in the administration's economic stabilization package; specifically, a more equitable program should rectify the two major weaknesses of the existing government policy:

a. that it favors the interests of profit receivers over those of wage earners,

b. that it freezed [sic] the existing wage structure with its many inequities and in particular those which discriminate against women;

and we also resolve that any structure set up to deal with this problem should reflect the sex compositions of the population as well as consumers, labor, etc. (Sept., 1971)

M. Minority Women

1. That NOW supports all women in their struggle for equal rights and recognizes the double oppression of minority women and so adds a national task force on minority women for the purpose of making coalitions with organizations of minority women to support them on common issues. (Sept., 1971)

2. NOW recognizes the right of all to employment and also that there are not enough jobs currently in this country so that minority men and women and white women are forced to struggle for the limited number of jobs available. We also recognize that minority women are often particularly discriminated against on account of both race and sex. We therefore go on record as supporting minority women where there is common ground and abhor all efforts to divide us as disadvantaged groups. (Sept., 1971)

3. Government Services Administration, Small Business Administration and the Department of Commerce extend the advantages of the Minority Business Enterprise Program to women of all races and that all such federal programs, now or in the future, define "minority" to include women of all races. (Sept., 1971)

N. Report of the Taxes and Credit Task Force—October, 1972
Summary of the Problem and NOW's Position

Under the present state of law, women effectively have no credit rights in

191

this country, and are viewed by lending, financial and retailing institutions as mere wards or appendages of the husband. Regardless of how creditworthy a woman is and even if she is the chief family wage earner, creditors generally will issue credit only in the husband's name. It is very difficult for a woman to get a loan without a male signature and then the male signer is considered to be the "principal borrower" with his credit rating the basis for qualifying the loan. Even single women are not granted credit on the same terms as men. It has been documented that a single man has a much better chance of receiving a loan or higher credit line than a single woman of the same means and circumstances, including identical income and occupation. Thus, all women are detrimentally affected: widowed and divorced women in particular have great difficulty since the credit follows the former husband and they are left with no credit rating or economic viability so necessary in this credit-oriented economy.

As for taxes, women are expected to *pay* equally but when it comes to the benefits women receive less. For example, female employees covered by pension and social security plans often find that though they contributed at the same rate as their male counterparts, they receive smaller pension checks for equal contributions than the male employee receives, and moreover that they are denied spouse's survivor benefits for their husbands which male employees are guaranteed for their wives. Additionally, present income tax law works to penalize married women who work by punitively taxing a two income family at a higher rate than two single individuals making the same income. The penalty for a two job marriage becomes increasingly severe as the two incomes become higher and more equal.

NOW believes that there should be equal credit access and financial opportunity for all persons without regard to sex or marital status, and that tax systems and laws should not maintain sex-based differences in application. NOW seeks to eliminate all discriminatory and punitive tax and social security retirement plan provisions which presume women to be dependent adjuncts of male workers.

Major Activities of the Task Force to October 1, 1972
(1) Development of credit committees and task forces within chapters. These committees are surveying practices of local creditors, lenders, and financial institutions and are organizing actions.
(2) Presentation of testimony before the National Commission on Consumer Finance in Washington, D.C. May 22-23, 1972 documenting the refusal of major creditors and lenders to grant credit or loans to women.
(3) Widespread distribution of documentative and consciousness-raising information to national media, organizations and individuals.

Evaluation of Activities
(1) The activities of chapters and individual women in resisting discriminatory credit and loan policies and the National Commission on Consumer Finance hearings has given the problem a national focus generating long overdue public exposure to these unfair practices. This exposure seems to be succeeding in raising the awareness of women to their real lack of rights and freedom to transact business on the same basis as men do.
(2) Legislation is being drafted and introduced at local, state and federal levels. Nationally, Representative Bella Abzug has introduced House Bills No. HR15546, HR15547 and HR15548 which would prohibit discrimination on the basis of sex or marital status in credit and lending

192

practices. These bills presently sit in Wright Patman's House Banking and Currency Committee.

(3) At least one government agency, the Federal Deposit Insurance Corporation, which was maintaining a sex discriminatory guideline to banks (calling for exclusion of one half the wife's income in determining effective income for a mortgage), has revised its discriminatory guideline.

Suggested Goals for 1973

(1) Support and passage of the Abzug bills and passage of similar legislation on local and state levels.

(2) The filing of charges by individuals with the Federal Trade Commission offices throughout the country on every instance of sex discrimination by creditors and lending institutions. Although the Federal Trade Commission in the past has largely ignored the problems of women in obtaining credit, women should press for relief with this government agency in 1973 as this agency appears to already have sufficient authority to remedy unfair credit restraint.

(3) A major national action against a large chain retailer or bank card system whose sex discriminatory practices have been documented.

(4) The filing of a legal action. One chapter of NOW is currently considering the feasibility of such a suit on a class action basis.

Lynne C. Litwiller, Coordinator

O. Report of the Federal Communications Commission (FCC) Task Force—October, 1972

At its fifth annual conference held in Los Angeles, NOW resolved "that the NOW FCC Committee be expanded to be able to provide assistance to local chapters" in gathering evidence, filing petitions to deny licenses of broadcasters and "to insure that the FCC guarantee fair treatment of women (image, programming, and employment) in the broadcasting industry."

In the fall of 1971 and early spring of 1972, the task force concerned itself primarily with developing a workable national strategy, based on the legal arguments delineated by former FCC Committee Chair-One, Nancy Stanley in the November 1971 *Hastings Law Review.* (Essentially, there are 3 basic arguments, which we refer to as (1) Ascertainment,[1] (2) Fairness,[2] and (3) Employment.[3]) In developing the national strategy, we consulted with Citizens Communications Center, which had had experience in filing legal challenges on behalf of minority and other groups. It became apparent that the most effective, it not only, time a group could take action was during the license renewal period or at the time of a transfer (when a licenses sells its station to another company and the buyer must seek FCC approval). We then developed an information kit which included an outline of women's basic legal arguments against broadcasters and a simplified explanation of the legal and non-

[1] In ascertaining the problems, needs, and interests of the community, the broadcaster must meet with representatives of women, and it must air programming to meet the needs, etc. of the women's community.

[2] Under the Fairness Doctrine, the station must balance the traditional view of women (in the home, etc.) with portrayals of women outside the home, performing as independent, rational humans.

[3] Under FCC rules, as well as Federal law, the station must afford equal employment opportunity for women. These three arguments are explained in more detail in the FCC Task Force Kit.

193

legal strategies chapters might employ—during both the renewal and interim time periods.

(Report of actions taken relative to FCC are available from National Office. Length prevents its inclusion here.)

In summary, I feel at this time that we have taken significant steps toward the goals of providing assistance to chapters in filing petitions to deny and taking other actions and in working with the FCC. The annual conference resoltuion "to insure that the FCC guarantee fair treatment of women . . ." is unrealistic at present—the FCC doesn't guarantee fair treatment to anyone but broadcasters. Nevertheless, broadcasters themselves are highly reluctant to tie themselves up with legal challenges and are beginning to respond, sometimes substantively, to our pressure.

Since NOW is getting to be rather well-known among broadcasters, they are increasingly contacting local NOW chapters in ascertainment interviews. This development raises some strategic problems: broadcasters can thus claim they *have* consulted with women's rights groups and hence put serious holes into or complicate our ascertainment argument. Our next immediate objective is to put together information for chapters on what to do when contacted for an ascertainment interview and how to negotiate. A newsletter will be going out shortly.

One final note: I have become increasingly aware of the importance of public pressure on the FCC as a necessary complement to our legal actions. For example, the FCC is beginning to take some affirmative steps regarding children's programming because it received over 100,-000 letters regarding its children's programming rule-making. Neither the FCC nor the U.S. Court of Appeals is going to understand nor deal with adequately our fairness arguments (in the long run the most important) unless the image of women really becomes a hot issue. I am most in need of advice and assistance on this problem. I have thought about the possibility of NOW's convincing the Women's Bureau, the Women's Action Program of HEW, and congresswomen to hold a large conference—or something—to draw together sociologists, psychologists, feminists, etc. to make a public to-do about the problem. One goal (and there is precedent in children's programming and violence) might be to get the Surgeon General to do a study on the impact of the broadcasting media on the public health problem of sexism.

Whitney Adams

III EQUALITY OF EDUCATION
A. Report of Task Force on Education

Our society has encouraged females to pursue an ultimately self-defeating course in school. During the elementary and junior high school years, when girls are generally not offered the scouting and athletic outlets that most communities provide for boys, girls tend to concentrate on their school work. But upon reaching puberty, girls frequently begin to underachieve. This underachievement has been linked by researchers to the passive adult female role which is promoted and popularized by our society.

Not only have the schools failed to challenge this pattern, but they have institutionalized sex discrimination within their own structures, barring females from many of the more technical courses of instruction. If our

194

schools are to take seriously their responsibility to teach children justice, which is basic to democracy, and logic, which is fundamental to classical education, then they can no longer permit the institutionalized discrimination and the sentiments of prejudice now directed against girls and women at every level of public and private education.

Our schools must be held accountable for the effective motivation and education of all students. Therefore, NOW urges educators and legislators to work with us toward the following goals:

• an end to all distinctions based on sex, whether made by the board of education (in declaring sexually exclusive schools, shops, or special programs), by administrators (in hiring and promotion of personnel or in treatment of students), by instructors (in setting classroom procedures or in defining work areas for students), by guidance counselors (in college and career counseling), or by students (in limiting the membership of school-sponsored clubs);
• the integration of all physical education courses from kindergarten through high school with athletic standards set by the entire school population, not separately by males and females, allowing all students the dignity of competing against the same standard (which will protect many males from the emotional tension and physical stress of having to perform up to an unnecessarily high male norm, but will not prevent high athletic achievers from setting new records).
• in extra-curricular sports, the establishment of female teams in every sport for which there are male teams, and vice versa, with equal funding for both, *except* in cases where a school can demonstrate that its single varsity team has an equal representation of both sexes.
• the provision of self-defense courses for all students;
• the upgrading of sex education courses to include factual information on contraception and on the ecological crisis of overpopulation, and to remove all references to "ideal" or "normal" "masculine" or "feminine" etiquette, social behavior and vocations;
• the provision of contraceptive and abortion counseling in the same way that drug and draft counseling are now a part of many school programs;
• the guarantee of continued education for the pregnant student, in her own school or in another if she prefers, during and after her pregnancy;
• the provision of daycare facilities to enable the student mother to continue her education (the same facilities should also be available, with preference based on need, to the children of secretaries, paraprofessionals and related staff, teachers, and administrators);
• the establishment of accredited inservice courses for teachers to study and discuss the attitudes and issues underlying sexism;
• the distribution of bibliographies and resource manuals on women's studies to school librarians and teachers, and the supplementation of current social studies texts with women's studies materials; the establishment of female studies courses.
• the notification of publishers that linguistic sexism and other images of girls and women presented in books for all courses and libraries will be taken into consideration on any future purchases;
• the requirement of all companies doing business with the public schools to show employment and salary figures proving their status as equal opportunity employers for women as well as for minority racial and ethnic groups.
• the provision of after-school supervision for children of working parents.
• the inclusion of questions of sex discrimination on local, state, and

national surveys to determine the extent of sexually exclusive schools, courses, and requirements, the comparative budgets spent on male and female instructional and athletic programs, the comparative salaries paid to male and female teachers, etc.
• the publication of annual reports showing the number of men and the number of women holding school-related jobs at each level of rank and salary (including fellowship, loan and scholarship recipients as well as paraprofessionals, cafeteria, custodial, secretarial, and any other workers);
• the establishment of standing committees to detect and correct all sex discrimination in the schools;
• in early childhood education, an end to militarism, narcissism, and sexually stereotyped advertising and packaging in children's toys;
• an end to sexist children's television programming, and the inclusion of as many positive, self-reliant female role models as there are male.

Proposed Goals, 1973
1. Publicize the Educational Amendments Act of 1972, Title IX, concentrating our efforts on it as our primary tool against educational sex discrimination, and specifically urging chapters to
   a. locate educational institutions in their area which are receiving federal funds and determine the specific uses of these funds (e. g. textbook purchase).
   b. determine whether these uses are sexist (if it's textbooks you can bet it is).
   c. inform the local institution ("You must not use this textbook one more day!"), OCR's Education Division ("Withhold funds from MCP Institute because . . .") and the task force (our specialist on textbooks is Joan Bartl, Central NJ NOW).
2. Investigate the possibility of establishing an Experimental School Program to Eradicate Educational Sexism through the National Institute of Education, OE.
3. Continue 1972 goals:
   a. have every chapter actively represented on the task force.
   b. seek funding to produce non-sexist materials.

Anne Grant, Coordinator

B. Higher Education
1. Eliminate discrimination on college and university faculties. Encouragement of any action to require universities and colleges that are federal contractors to end discrimination against women in conformity with the guidelines of the Office of Federal Contract Compliance under Executive Orders 11246 and 11375 or to extend Title VI of the 1964 Civil Rights Act to cover sex discrimination in educational institutions and force compliance with its provisions. (Oct., 1966, Dec., 1968, Mar., 1970)
2. Establish contact with the "catalysts on campus". Establishment of female studies which we envision as interdisciplinary courses, both curricular and for credit, and extracurricular, designed to raise consciousness about and expose the biases against and ignorance on women, especially in the fields of history, literature, psychology, sociology, and marriage and family courses. (Oct., 1966, Mar., 1970)
3. Eliminate sex segregation in schools. The mobilization of, support for, erasing sex discrimination whereever it exists in education as in admissions, scholarships, fellowships, loans, textbooks, guidance

196

counseling, division of students by sex in home economics, shop, sports and vocational training. We also urge the erasing of sex discrimination in policies on marriage, pregnancy or parenthood as related to students, faculty and staff, stocking of libraries with appropriate books, day care for all students, faculty and staff, in hiring, salaries, tenure and nepotism, in appointments such as college presidencies, in teacher training, curricula, in provision of role models outside the traditional sex role to reflect a society where women have status equal to men. We suggest studies of hiring and other forms of discrimination against women faculty on the model of the analysis at Columbia University. (Oct., 1966, Nov., 1967, Dec., 1968, Mar., 1970)

4. The seeking of funding for female studies, scholarships, fellowships, loans, and research, from foundations, corporations, alumni and alumnae groups, and such organizations as the BPW, AAUW and NOW itself and from bequests and donations from individuals. (Mar., 1970)

IV POLITICAL EQUALITY
A. Resolutions passed in conferences

1. NOW recognizes the need to act politically to achieve equal rights for women. We are non-partisan; we owe allegiance only to the cause of women's liberation, not to any political party, but we will work through existing political institutions to achieve our aims. We urge women to run for office from any political party and we will work for candidates who support and campaign for our goals. (Mar., 1970)
Resolved that NOW set up a political promotion fund which will be used to support the candidacy and election for public office of qualified persons sympathetic to and advocating NOW's purposes. (Dec., 1968)
NOTE: NOW CANNOT ENDORSE CANDIDATES.

2. We support the formation of women's rights caucuses within existing political parties and organizations and the establishment of independent women's political caucuses. These groups would seek out candidates for office in support of women's issues and would seek passage of legislation to further the cause of women's rights.

3. Even when election appears unlikely, NOW members should run for office to educate the public about our concerns. Local chapters should encourage women already active in politics to run on women's issues. Local chapters should set up committee to seek out candidates. Regional conferences should include workshops to train prospective candidates and campaign workers. (Mar., 1970)

4. NOW urges all political parties to dissolve their women's divisions which have relegated women to servant roles in political life. Women should be included on all levels of party activity on an equal basis with men. In view of the fact that only 2% of all elected officials are women, we call on political parties to seek out and run women candidates who represent women's rights and needs. (Mar., 1970) We urge women working in political parties to refuse to lick stamps and give teas unless men do their share and women are elected to policy making positions. (Nov. 1969)

5. Women must be given proportionate representation on all policy making boards, commissions and committees to reflect the number of women in the area that said commission represents. (Nov., 1967)

6. That NOW request that national and state Commissions on the Status

of Women be renamed Commissions on Sex Role Policy to formulate policy that promotes equality between the sexes and to begin requesting government sponsored Commissions on Sex Role Policy. (Sept., 1971)

7. That NOW insist on the inclusion of a women's rights plank in all party platforms and recommends that the NOW national board present our demands to the Platform Committees at the parties' national conventions. (Sept., 1971)

8. That NOW urge the FCC to require stations to allot prime time as "people's time" so that all candidates may be heard equally and that NOW demand legislation that would compel all stations to furnish free and equal time in the public interest. (Sept., 1971)

9. That NOW endorse the National Women's Political Caucus in our joint effort toward the following goals: forming women's caucuses within every party and every state; forming a caucus within every county in every party; forming a caucus within every congressional district in every party; ensuring that 50% of delegates to national conventions are women; raising funds to send a woman delegate to challenge the seating of state delegations of the national political parties if they are not proportionately representative of women; ensuring that women delegates are not "Aunt Toms" chosen to support the status quo; teaching women through schools for political candidates and otherwise how to get candidates not only on the party ticket but elected in the primaries and later elected against the opposition candidates from major parties. Be it understood that NOW's support for the NWPC does not preclude similar activities by NOW or its chapters. (Sept., 1971)

10. That NOW urges its members to support the NWPC by helping to organize women's political caucuses at the state level and that NOW educate its members to work effectively in political parties with the object of educating citizens about women's rights and with the object of persuading them to nominate feminist candidates for party and public offices, and that NOW shall inform women immediately as to methods of delegate selection in each state and give top priority to organizing support for female candidates to ensure that 50% of each delegation to national political conventions shall be women. (Sept., 1971)

11. Include women on all commissions, boards, and other appointive bodies at all governmental levels. (Dec., '68)

B. Report of Politics Task Force—October, 1972

The title of the NOW National Conference, *September, 1971, in Los Angeles,* was *"From the Doll's House to the White House."* This shows our obvious heavy focus on politics, as a key means for getting women into the "mainstream of American life," and more important, for changing the mainstream of American life.

During the last two years, the Politics Task Force has worked with hundreds of NOW members who have run for office. Many have been elected. I have conducted *Schools for Candidates*—at which women are taught, in a crash-Head-Start manner, some of the skills necessary for running for office—in a dozen states.

Prior to the *Democratic National Convention,* members of the Politics Task Force worked with the Clearinghouse (of women's groups, minority groups, and youth caucuses) to coordinate efforts of challenges to the Credentials committee, challenges to the Rules committee, and submissions to the Platform committee. Politics Task Force members testified at the ten pre-convention hearings on platform, which were held all around the country. We were also present at the convention, primarily in an educational role, but also did our share of power-brokering.

Prior to the *Republican National Convention,* three NOW members testified at the Platform hearings in Miami Beach; each made much news and influenced to a great extent the tone of the GOP convention. For example, the *only* plank in the final Republican platform which differed from that submitted by Richard Nixon was the plank on child care.

The major thing which we have done, and which we will continue to do, is *to change the consciousness* of political leaders, and of the women and men of this country, *as to the proper and just role women must play in American political life.*

At the Los Angeles conference, the following resolutions were passed by the Task Force:

Be it resolved that NOW endorse the National Women's Political Caucus in our joint goals toward the following:
1. Form women's caucuses within every party and every state.
2. Form a caucus within every county in every party.
3. Form a caucus within every congressional district in every party.
4. Raise funds to send a woman delegate to challenge the seating of state delegations of the national political parties if they are not proportionately representative of women.
5. Ensure that women delegates are not "Aunt Toms" chosen to support the status quo.
6. Teach women how to get women candidates on the party ticket and elected in primaries against opposition candidates from major parties.
7. Run Schools for Candidates.

Be it resolved that NOW insist on the inclusion of a women's rights plank in all party platforms, and recommends that the NOW National Board present our demands to the Platform Committees at the parties' national conventions.

At the *Second National Conference* of NOW, held in *November, 1967, in Washington, D.C.,* we had resolved:

To urge women in political parties to refuse to lick stamps and envelopes and give teaparties [*sic*] unless men do their share, and women are elected to policy-making positions. (A short editorial: what was wild, revolutionary dreaming in 1967 became standard rhetoric in 1972.)

Women must be given proportionate representation on all policy-making boards, commissions, and committees, to reflect the number of women in the population.

NOW supports the adoption of federal legislation to make unlawful any distinction on account of race, color, religion, sex, national origin, or economic status in the qualifications for service, and in the selection of any person to serve, on grand or petit juries in any federal or state court.

At the *Third National Conference, in December, 1968, in Atlanta, Georgia,* it was resolved that NOW set up a political promotion fund which will be used to support the candidacy and election to public office of qualified persons sympathetic to and advocating NOW's purposes. (There is more . . .)

Karen DeCrow, Politics Task Force

V LEGISLATIVE GOALS

A. Report of Task Force on National Legislation—October, 1972

Full report of actions of Legislative Task Force available from National Office. Length prevents its inclusion here)

The primary concern has been development of the task force and establishment of state coordination this year to facilitate state lobbying for the ERA. Materials have been developed for Task Force members:

A *NOW Lobbying Kit,* available free to members of the Task Force, and $1 to other members of NOW.

A position sheet, which is a description of Task Force activities

A solicitation letter to chapters not represented in the Task Force

Legislative alerts

An ERA ratification kit

A kit on the EEOC bill

A legislative Program sheet for the Marriage and Divorce Task Force

A Directory of NOW chapters and some individual members has been compiled by Congressional District.

Equal Rights Amendment

NOW has put together materials to aid in the ratificaiion effort. We have devised a three-step ratification strategy including what is to happen *after* the state legislature ratifies the Amendment, and have put together a kit for the state legislative coordinators.

Future direction of the Task Force

The Task Force on Legislation is a sort of service task force for the members of NOW and the other task forces. The next goal of the task force should be to work with the other task forces in developing legislative programs for the year, and for encouraging those task forces to work together on the chapter level.

A second goal should be to encourage the State Legislative Coordinators, along with the chapters in their states and the task forces, to develop state legislative programs, including drafting their own legislation.

Finally, lobbying should be considered as all the kinds of pressure we bring to bear on the institution of American society. We should consider national actions as part of our function, including demonstration and confrontation.

Ann Scott, Legislative Task Force

B. Report of Task Force on State Legislation—October, 1972

The Task Force on State Legislation, like the National Legislation Task Force, is principally a service task force. The actual expertise in areas comes from the other task forces—e.g. the Compliance Task Force supplies the experts of State Fair Employment Practices Acts, the population control task force supplies the experts on abortion law. The State Legislative Coordinators and the members of their task forces organize the people with the expertise, supply them with information on the mechanics of getting legislation enacted and coordinate the legislative efforts throughout their state.

The National Task Force on State Legislation provides a mechanism for sharing information from state to state. Generally, the exact wording of bills, the needs for specific types of legislation, etc. will vary from state to state. But a clearing house *is* needed for ideas for bills, for testimony that has taken days to prepare and may be helpful to people in other states, and for hints that have worked in your state.

The National Task Force on State Legislation would also provide a measure of what is happening to the laws of the 50 states because of NOW. This information has been a well kept secret up to now.

The Goals for State and Local Action in 1970 were:
1. Repeal of abortion laws
2. Repeal of restrictive and discriminatory state protective legislation for women only and extension of valid labor protection to men
3. Establishment of (or pressuring for action) states' commissions on the status of women.

The Goals for State and Local Action in 1971 were:
1. Repeal of restrictive state protective legislation for women (and extension of valid protective laws to men)
2. Repeal of abortion laws
3. Legislation establishing Commissions on the Status of Women
4. Repeal of all married women's statutes which prevent married women in some states from contracting or going into business in their own name or from changing their names without the consent of their husbands, etc.
5. Repeal of all laws which discriminate against women by granting men privileges which are withheld from women (e.g. husbands may sue for loss of consortium, wives may not; husbands are allowed an occasional unfaithfulness, wives are not; husbands are not punished for killing a man found in the act of sexual intercourse with their wives, but a wife killing her husband under the same condition would be guilty of murder)
6. Repeal of all property laws which deny women the same rights to property as are afforded men.

The Goals for State and Local Action for 1972 were:
1. Passage of State Equal Rights Amendments and resolutions asking Congress to enact the Federal Equal Rights Amendment. This is now—Ratification of the Equal Rights Amendment
2. Repeal of abortion laws
3. Repeal of discriminatory state protective legislation and extension of valid labor protection to men, including the extension of maximum hours of work or voluntary overtime provisions to all workers so that an employee may refuse to work excessive overtime without penalty.
4. Establishment of (or pressing for action of) state Commissions on the Status of Women.
5. Amendment or repeal of laws penalizing women because of pregnancy: enactment of laws establishing job security during maternity leave and establishment of a general system of basic protection for men and women against wage loss due to temporary disability, including illness, pregnancy and maternity, to be provided in one insurance program.
6. Extension of unemployment insurance to employees forced to seek a change of employment because of a move to another city with their spouses.
7. Passage of laws to change marriage to an equal partnership.
8. Elimination of inequities in state tax laws.
9. Provision for full deduction of child care expenses on state income taxes.
10. Amendment or enactment of state laws to provide loans or credit on an equal basis regardless of sex.
11. Extension of state Civil Rights and Fair Employment Practices Acts

201

to outlaw discrimination by sex and provisions for sufficient funding for these agencies to perform their responsibilities.

12. Extension of jurisdiction of state and local human relations commissions to include the elimination of sex discrimination.

13. Enactment of laws providing for comprehensive child care and the funding necessary for its implementation.

14. Passage of laws guaranteeing women equal educational opportunity or amendments to existing laws prohibiting discrimination in education on other bases to include sex.

It is impossible to give the status of these resolutions in the 50 states.

We would, however, like to have available summaries of laws which discriminate against women, differentiate between men and women, cover sex discrimination in employment, education, restrict abortion, etc. in the 50 states.

We are asking State Legislative Coordinators to work with Task Force members in their states in compiling legislation presently in force in their states, both restrictive to women and helpful in eliminating sex discrimination. Many states now have lists of codes which differentiate between men and women and which may violate the Equal Rights Amendment. We would like copies of these when they are available. We would also like summaries of laws which forbid sex discrimination in employment, housing, educational opportunities, etc. and laws which restrict abortion and provide for child care facilities and tax deductions for child care expenses by working parents. We would also like lists of well-prepared testimony on bills by subject area, so that an interested person might obtain a copy of testimony someone prepared in one state and use those parts which might apply in another state (such as the status of laws of this type in other states or the federal government, statistics, etc.)

Mary Samis, Task Force Coordinator

VI CHILD CARE
A. Resolutions passed at national conferences
(See also Marriage and the Family and Employment)

1. Campaign to permit the deduction of full child care expenses in income taxes of working parents. (Oct., '66)

2. Resolved that NOW actively work to have federal and state government set up child care centers for children of all ages and that immediate consideration be given to the subject of tax deduction for child care. Second, employers and educators should be encouraged to establish such centers for employees and students to facilitate work and study opportunities for men and women. Use of child care centers optional. (Dec., '68)
NOW establishes a Task Force on Child Care to implement above.

3. Child care must become a political priority. We therefore propose a coalition of organizations representing all socioeconomic, professional, educational, philanthropic organizations, etc., interested in the establishment of child care facilities in keeping with NOW's goals. The purpose of this coalition would be to join together to exert pressure on the power structure in labor, industry and government to immediately make available facilities, funds, etc. and to grant tax deductions for quality child care. (Mar., 1970)

4. We propose to send the following telegram to Congressman John

Brademus; The 4th annual conference of the National Organization for Women supports the philosophy behind the Brademus Bill HR 13520 which addresses itself to child care facilities for children of all economic and social groups. (Mar., 1970)

5. Child care facilities for working parents (facilities adequate to needs of all children from pre-school through adolescense as a community resource available to all citizens from all income levels). (Dec., 1968)

B. Resolutions passed at western regional conferences—April, 1971, March, 1972

1. The father has equal responsibility with the mother for the child care role. Society has a supplementary role in assisting families to provide quality care for all children. The child care crisis involves every segment of our society and the total community must participate in finding acceptable solutions.

2. NOW endorses the ideal goal of free child care facilities, available as a community service as are libraries, schools, playgrounds, and public parks. As interim steps, we support flexible fees, if any, to reflect the more urgent needs and limited resources of some families now.

3. NOW endorses the goal of child care available 24-hours per day to meet the various needs of parents who, for example, work shifts, who might become ill, or who might need child care outside of the regular working day.

4. NOW endorses the goal of developmental care based on the child's needs at various ages rather than mere custodial care. Crucial to a developmental program are nutritional, medical, physical, emotional and educational components.

5. Due to the diversity of child care needs and the desirability of maintaining a variety of options to meet these needs, child care must encompass a multiplicity of types of care, including:
   infant care (birth to 1 year old)
   toddler care (1 to 2-1/2 years old)
   preschool care (2-1/2 to 5 years old)
   extended care for children in school
   drop-in care for emergencies such as out-of-town visitors, conventions, etc.
   sick care, both contagious and recuperating
   care during school vacations
   week-end care
   help after a baby is born
   care for exceptional children such as those with learning disabilities or physical handicaps

6. Child care facilities should be conveniently located throughout the community and readily accessible, as determined by community needs and priorities, including:
   neighborhodd centers
   centers at places of employment, e.g. union negotiated
   hospitals
   existing educational facilities—public and private, elementary, colleges, and universities

7. Child care facilities should be parent and community controlled wth the assistance of trained professionals. Both women and men should be represented at all levels of responsibility and participation.

8. Quality care must provide:
   a. A safe, wholesome, comfortable, secure "home away from home".

b. Warm, sensitive adults who are continuously responsive to each child's physical, emotional, and intellectual needs, and who understand that "children's play is their work". In-service training should be provided so that lack of professional training does not preclude participation by adults with these qualities.

c. Educational and enrichment experiences with an opportunity for social interaction with children of varying social and economic backgrounds.

9. Realizing that each individual child has the capacity for the full range of human characteristics, the child should not be channeled into a role based on sexual stereotypes. Further research must be undertaken to discover ways to prevent sex-role channeling.

10. To affirm that profit should not be made from children and to ensure uniform standards for both public and private child care centers, we must reorder our priorities for the use of national resources and reallocate our tax money to support child care facilities. In the interim national and state legislation should be enacted to allow parents to deduct child care on their income-tax forms as a business expense. Child care should be recognized as being as legitimate an expense as luxury items like business lunches, drinks, entertainment and travel which can presently be deducted.

11. Recognizing that legislation and programs concerning child care are a bureaucratic maze and piece-meal at best, we should strive for a uniform child care program.

VII REPRODUCTION

A. The basic human right to limit one's own reproduction includes the right to all forms of birth control (contraception, including sterilization, and abortion), recognizing the dual responsibility of both sexes. We therefore oppose all legislation and practices that restrict access to any of these means of birth control and advocate positive measures requiring:

— that all public hospitals offer contraception, sterilization and abortion to anyone requesting these services;

— that these services be made accessible to as many people as possible by the establihsment of a network of local public clinics;

— that the availability of these services be widely and continuously publicized;

— that public funds be allocated for research into new methods of contraception, sterilization and abortion which would increase their safety and availability. (Mar., 1970, Dec., 1968 for individual's control, Nov., 1967, Oct., 1966)

B. Repeal of all abortion laws. (Oct., 1966, Nov., 1967) Women should be guaranteed their civil right to an abortion performed by an qualified person in any suitable setting. Urge regional conferences on abortion law repeal. (Mar., 1970)

VIII EQUALITY IN FAMILY RELATIONS

A. **Report of the Task Force on Marriage, Divorce and Family Relations—October, 1972**

The basis of the present guidelines for the Task Force are largely action resolutions adopted at the *December, 1968, Atlanta Conference,* the *March, 1970 Chicago Conference* and resolutions passed in *1971* at the *Los Angeles Conference* by the Women in Poverty Task Force, which dealt with child support.

The Goals of the Task Force as stated in the resolutions are:

204

1. We demand that women be protected by law to ensure their rights to return to their jobs within a reasonable time after childbirth without loss of seniority or other accrued benefits, and be paid maternity leave as a form of social security and/or benefit. (1967)
2. We demand immediate revision of tax laws to permit the deduction of home and child care expenses for working parents. (1967)
3. Resolved that all states adopt the U.S. Standard Certificate of Divorce of the U.S. Government. (This refers to reporting divorces by state) (1968)
4. Resolved that the Social Security Act be amended to reduce from 20 to 10 the number of years a divorced woman must have been married to her former husband in order to be treated as his wife or widow for purposes of eligibility for wife's or widow's insurance benefits. (1968)
5. Resolved that the Social Security Act be amended to insure the housewife as an individual and not as her husband's dependent.
6. Amend the Internal Revenue Code of 1954 "to extend the head of household benefits to all un-remarried widows and widowers and to all individuals who have attained age 21 and who have never been married or who have been separated or divorced for one year or more." (1968)
7. Review income tax laws to allow deductions for child care, whether or not child may be listed as dependent. (1969)
8. Revise Social Security laws to eliminate discrimination against working wives. (1969)
9. Revise Social Security laws to eliminate discrimination against divorced women. (1969)
10. Resolved that marriage should be an equal partnership with shared economic and household responsibility and shared care of the children. (1970)
11. Resolved that the economic responsibility for the family should be shared proportionately according to income, if both partners work outside the home. (1970)
12. Resolved that if only one partner works outside the home, half the income should by law belong to the other partner. (1970)
13. Resolved that all institutions should acknowledge that parenthood is a necessary social service by granting maternal and paternal leaves of absence without prejudice and without loss of job security or seniority. (1970)
14. Resolved that a pamphlet on the legal rights of both partners as well as divorce and population statistics should be issued with the marriage license. (1970)
15. Resolved that the Social Security law should be amended to provide: a) separate Social Security deductions for employed persons and their dependent spouses in acknowledgment of the fact that the employer is receiving the services of the household spouse as well as the employed person, b) full Social Security payments should continue to children regardless of the remarriage of their parents, c) as long as the present Social Security law is in effect, a dependent spouse should be guaranteed continued coverage regardless of the years of marriage or the financial arrangments of the divorce. (1970)
16. Resolved that upon dissolution of a marriage, the dependent spouse be guaranteed health and accident insurance by the government. (1970)
17. Resolved that government-sponsored child care centers should be available to all in acknowledgment of the responsibility of society toward children. (1970)

18. The dependent spouse should be guaranteed government-sponsored retraining for re-entry into the job market. (1970)
19. Company pension plans should be expanded to include coverage for the widow, if she so desires. (1970)
20. We encourage insurance companies to issue "end of marriage" insurance. This could be a form of term insurance to be paid to the economically dependent spouse as a form of pension. The sum paid would depend upon the years of service. (1970)
21. Resolved that the wife should be able to keep her own name or the husband to take his wife's name, and/or there should be the option of both partners choosing a neutral second name to be used also by the children, or the children should use both the wife's and husband's name. (1970)
22. A woman's title should be "MS" without differentiation as to marriage, and a woman should use her given first name. (1970)
23. Amend the Social Security Act to (1) provide benefits to husbands and widowers of disabled and deceased women workers, and (2) provide more equitable retirement benefits for families with working wives. (1971)
24. Pass legislation to guarantee husbands and children of women employees of the Federal Government the same fringe benefits for families with working wives. (1971)

And from the Task Force of Women in Poverty, 1971 resolutions passed: resolved the NOW press for legislation and establishment of procedures which will:

25. Provide for equitable sharing of child support by parents who are financially able.
26. Provide for genuine enforcement of child support laws and orders.
27. Provide for establishment and maintenance of enforcing agencies adequately staffed by trained and motivated personnel and sufficiently funded.
28. Provide for immediate payment of support directly to the parent.
29. Where support is not immediately forthcoming from the assessed spouse the court should order such payment be paid immediately from public funds, with appropriate means taken to recover such payments from the assessed spouse.

ACCOMPLISHMENTS

Our most outstanding success was our support and publicity of the Elizabeth Barrett case against Internal Revenue for child care tax deductions in May, 1971; subsequently the Internal Revenue Act of 1971 substantially liberalized employment related expenses for child care. Other minor, or smaller scale accomplishments are: divorce statstics are now being reported by almost all states instead of the 22 that prompted our resoltuion. Every year, Federal legislation revising Social Security has been introduced at our request—it is still pending. New York State in 1971 passed a bill making it mandatory to offer to convert group health and medical insurance to the divorced spouse. The increasing adoption of the title "MS" and the liberalization of maternity and paternity benefit leaves reinforce our goals. Increasingly insurance companies and other groups are studying divorce insurance. We are beginning to assemble literature on marriage contracts.

As more focus is placed on divorce, chapter committees have testified and met with government and bar association officials to work with enforcement, legal and financial problems and grievances. Efforts to obtain statistical data to back up our claims are underway in both Chicago and New York. NOW members in Los Angeles, under other auspices, pioneered in reports on lack of child enforcement orders. The N. Y. C. Chapter's Marriage and Divorce Committee, under the leadership of Mildred Chatzinoff, saw its recommendations translated into a pilot divorce bill which was introduced in the New York State legislature in 1972.

FUTURE DIRECTIONS

Established policy goals cover most of the areas the Task Force works in. However, more clearly defined policy is needed in the area of divorce and as we work toward the 1973 Conference we will need resolutions on:

1. Ownership of marital property
2. Alimony and child support
3. Child custody rights
4. No fault grounds for divorce

Betty Berry, Task Force Chair-One

IX RELIGION

A. Religion Resolutions

1. Discrimination on the basis of sex is contrary to assumptions of Church teaching and laws, and that it is in the very best interests of humanity to oppose such discrimination. (Nov., 1967)
2. Because the wearing of a head covering by women at religious services is a symbol of subjection within many churches, NOW recommends that all chapters undertake an effort to have all women participate in a "national unveiling" by sending their headcoverings to the task force chairman. At the Spring meeting of the task force of women and religion, these veils will be publicly burned to protest the second class status of women in all churches. (Dec., 1968)
3. Since church bodies have contributed to the development of concepts which encourage discrimination against women and have faithfully reflected these ideas in their own practices, and since the National Council of Churches represents such a large coalition of churches, we urge the NCC to:
   a. Challenge and assist church bodies to rethink and restate theological concepts which contribute to a false view of women.
   b. Give stronger leadership to efforts to eliminate discrimination against women in society and in the life of the church.
   c. Take the lead in uniting women of all denominations and religious groups to work together to support efforts to recognize the right of women to be ordained in religious bodies where that right is still denied.
   d. Place the issue of discrimination against women and its relationship to the work of the NCC on the agenda of its general board, its divisions and their departments.
   e. Develop personnel policies and practices that will achieve a more adequate representation of women at all levels of the executive staff of the National Council of Churches and its affiliated churches.
   f. Ensure that women are included in significant numbers among the planners, leaders, speakers and participants in all NCC-sponsored conferences. (Mar., 1970)
4. We decry the outdated, blatant discrimination displayed by the Ro-

207

man Catholic Church recently in refusing to accept the credentials of the woman appointed to represent the West German government at the Vatican. (Mar., 1970)

5. In light of the enslavement of body and mind which the church historically has imposed on women, we demand that the seminaries:
   a. immediately stop and repudiate their propagation of sexist, male supremacist doctrine,
   b. initiate women's studies courses which cut through the traditional male, religious mythology to expose church and other social forces denying women their basic human dignity,
   c. actively recruit, employ and justly promote women theologians and other staff in all departments,
   d. actively recruit, enroll, financially aid and seek equal placement for women theological students. (Mar., 1970)

6. We demand that the churches desexigrate help-wanted ads in their own publications.

7. We demand that Title VII of the 1964 Civil Rights Act be amended so that religious groups no longer have legal sanction to discriminate on the basis of sex. (Mar., 1970)

8. NOW will challenge the tax exempt status of the Catholic Church since it is lobbying against abortion law repeal. (Apr., 1971)

B. Report: NOW Ecumenical Task Force on Women and Religion—October, 1972

At the beginning of this year, January, 1972, I was appointed Chair-One for this Task Force, replacing Elizabeth Farians.

The Packet—In May I edited a packet of materials, *"Women and Religion"* and have since then received requests for over 340 copies; the registrar at The Yale Divinity School requested 56 of these and 40 more were sent by request to The Religion Advisory Committee of The National Planned Parenthood Association. The other packets were requested by various educational institutions and individuals, and about 40 went to our local Religion Task Forces.

Publication—I wrote a Task Force statement which was printed in the Sept.-Oct. edition of *"Church and Society,"* a publication of the United Presbyterian Church U. S. A. and the Presbyterian Church U. S.

Advisory Committee—Because of my concern and discomfort with making unilateral decisions about Task Force statements, I set up an advisory committee consisting of seven NOW members from around the country.

Future Projects—Projects in the works include a newsletter for our local NOW chapters with information about the programs which the chapters have been working on. Joyce Slayton Mitchell of Wolcott, Vermont, is preparing that. I am now, by request, writing a statement for a McGraw-Hill Publishing House one-volume *Encyclopedia of the American Woman.* The statement will describe our Task Force work and goals.

Implementing a Resolution—The work for implementing Resolution No. 104, passed by the NOW National Conference, 9/3/71, is being done by Mary Jo Smith of Detroit. She has drawn up the corporation papers, and they are almost completed. The Women Tithe for Women board presently consists of Mary Jo Smith, Elizabeth Farians and myself. This board is temporary, as we want to have members who are on the NOW National Board, and also want to structure a more complete separation between Women Tithe for Women and the NOW Ecumenical Task Force on Women and Religion.

A Task Force Position—A formal Task Force position regarding women and religion is, at this time, difficult to formulate from the few resolutions which have been passed at the national conferences. The few resolutions which were passed generally were directed at sexist policies within individual groups (The Roman Catholic Church and the Salvation Army) or requested specific action from an individual group (The National Council of Churches). But there has been no inclusive resolution by a national conference condemning sexism in ALL religious groups.

Suggestion for a Resolution—For the 1973 conference, I recommend some kind of an inclusive resolution. I hope that our local chapters will discuss this, and send in suggestions. I will soon be getting material out to them to encourage this local chapter participation in the formulation of resolutions.

Emily A. Champagne, Task Force Chair-One

X WAR AND VIOLENCE

1. Whereas, war is the expression of the masculine mystique that historically has used violence as a solution to problems—not only international and political ones, but those relating to personal and social relations as well, and whereas, war and violence are logical extensions of a system that sees the use of power, dominance and coercion as an accepted way of life, and whereas, for centuries women have been victimized by this tyrrany [*sic*], for centuries wars have taken the lives of men and women, for centuries human values of compassion, equality and cooperation have been sacrificed to the military system;—*Be it resolved:* That as feminists, we seek to bring a universal end to war and to create a society in which feminist, humanist values will prevail, and—*Be it further resolved:* that NOW oppose the further pursuit of a military solution to the conflict in Indochina and call for an immediate end to all American military activity there. (Sept., 1971)

2. Whereas, women are victims of the military in war, through rape and forced prostitution, and
   Whereas, military training relies upon sexual slurs against women to inflame soldiers into aggression, and
   Whereas, military decisions are exclusively made by male supremists, and
   Whereas, men themselves are subject to loss of life and personhood by being subject to compulsory military service from which women are exempt, and
   Whereas, women in the military are restricted on the basis of sex in job training, education, area of service and are confined to low level, non-policy positions,
   Therefore be it resolved: That NOW condemns the degradation of women by sexist practices within the military and the sexist basis for compulsory military service. (Sept. 1971)

XI CRIMINAL JUSTICE
A. Rape

Whereas, rape victims meet with disbelief and/or derision when attempting to report a rape to police, and
Whereas, the conventional method of investigation is to pry into the private life of the rape victim in order to excuse the act committed, and
Whereas, when the case is brought to court, the victim's personal life style is on trial with attendent publicity, and
Whereas, the crime of rape as legally defined treats women as a separate class,

Therefore be it resolved: That NOW take a strong position that the crime of rape be redefined as felonious assault,
Further: That we work against humiliating treatment of rape victims by police officers, judges, District Attorneys, probation officers and other legal personnel as well as, by society generally, and
Further: We recommend that the investigation of these cases be done by women. (Sept., 1971)

XII FEMININE AND MASCULINE MYSTIQUES
A. Masculine Mystique
Whereas, the ideal of NOW is truly equal partnership for men and women and the reality is that many women continue to find men a stumbling block to their own development, and many men are not free to develop in ways other than those considered typically male; and the pervasive effects of privileges for women and perogatives for men are equally injurious to their mutual growth; and human liberation necessarily involves the critical examination, vigorous analysis and daily reacceptance of themselves as men and women, and consciousness raising groups of a continuing nature provide both the time and framework within which such an examination can occur; *Therefore we resolve to* create a task force on the Masculine Mystique charged with suggesting the best methods in which women and men can successfully raise their consciousness to make truly equal partnership a reality. (Sept., 1971)

B. Women's Self-Image
We must develop a better means of reaching the many women who are victims of self-hatred. Our anger, so often directed at ourselves, must be focused where it belongs, on the discriminatory laws, policies, and attitudes of our society. We can help women to become aware of the need for feminism by approaching the factors that divide and immobilize women:
1. Failure to recognize our sisterhood.
2. Overcoming stereotypes and labels which have socialized us in a male-chauvinist society.
3. Consciousness of the common oppression that affects all women regardless of age, economic status, race or religion.
4. Fear of the feminist movement because of the "sex object" image we have been socialized to believe.

We resolve that:
1. Every chapter and each member of NOW develop skills of communication to large and small groups and on an individual basis. Sensitivity groups could be used to develop support for one another.
2. Training programs be provided to educate women in public speaking, organizing, sensitivity and desexigration techniques.
3. We must trust ourselves and other women approaching new situations. United we stand and progress. (Mar., 1970)
4. Local chapters encourage the development of programs which bring women together in situations of crisis such as divorce, aging and the "empty nest" syndrone. (Sept., 1971)

C. Media Image of Women
1. Elimination of separate "women's pages" in newspapers. (Oct., 1968)
2. Implement Creative Complaining Project by sending information or copies of all offensive advertising to Claudia Lipschultz. (Dec., 1968)
3. Citizen's suit for equal time for feminist views on TV, radio. (Mar., 1970)

210

4. FCC complaints against unfair representations about women. (Mar., 1970)
5. NOW Legal Defense and Education Fund will seek grant for commercials for a positive image of women. (Mar., 1970)
6. We decry sex role stereotypes on educational TV and call for meeting between producers of Sesame Street and feminist psychologists and writers. (Mar., 1970)
7. Establish a committee for awards to movies, etc. for honest portrayal of women as human beings and for progress toward eliminating sex stereotypes. (Mar., 1970)
8. Call for more women media executives.
9. Organize and educate women already in media. Work toward getting them in NOW.
10. Call for more women on news and substantive programs on TV networks.
11. At chapter meetings, conduct letter-writing campaigns to companies with particularly obnoxious commercials.
12. Stickers on ads—"this ad is offensive to women."
13. Every member should write to commend fair coverage of the women's movement.
14. We can now complain to newspapers about unfair, dishonest or snickering treatment, and the reporter (Male or Female) who writes such an article should receive no further cooperation. The committee unanimously adopted a motion to urge cooperation with any honest reporter, male or female.
15. To improve coverage in the media, we can: picket newsstands urging boycotts of particularly obnoxious newspapers, NOW news conferences should be scheduled at 9 a.m., if possible, and scheduling of other NOW events should take competing news into consideration.
16. Investigate the power of sit-ins to encourage the media to be fairer to women. Ladies Home Journal sit-in produced a number of desirable changes. (Mar., 1970)
17. The FCC be expanded to provide assistance to local chapters to collect evidence documenting discrimination by offending radio and TV stations, to file necessary petitions to deny licenses to offending stations, and to insure that the FCC guarantee fair treatment of women (image, program, employment) in the broadcasting industry. (Sept., 1971) (See also FCC—II O)

A critique of resolutions passed on the subject of the image of women has been prepared by Anne Hall, Chair-One, Image of Women Task Force, and is available at the national office.

XII HUMAN SEXUALITY
A. Lesbianism
1. Amend NOW's policy statement to read:
   . . . NOW endorses the principle that it is a basic right of every woman to control her reproductive life and therefore NOW supports the furthering of the sexual revolution of our century by pressing for widespread sex education, provision of birth control information and contraceptives, and the repeal of all laws restricting abortion, contraception and sexual activity between consenting adults in private. (Sept., '71) (Parts as above, Dec., 1967)
2. *Whereas,* the first wave of feminist anger in this country recognized the fundamental issue of women's liberation as "the most sacred right of all—a woman's right to her own person." This is the right that

NOW reaffirmed a century later when it took up the banner and dedicated itself to changing those conditions in society, the laws, the practices, the attitudes—that prevented women from realizing their full human potential. Recognizing that a woman cannot reach this potential if she is denied the basic right to control of her own body, NOW has demanded the dissemination of birth control information and contraceptives and the repeal of all laws against abortion. It has stopped short, however, af clarifying its position of every woman's right to define—and express—her own sexuality; to choose her own lifestyle. Specifically, NOW has been silent on the issue of lesbianism. Yet no other woman suffers more abuse and discrimination for the right to be her own person than does the lesbian, and

Whereas, the lesbian is doubly oppressed, both as a woman and as a homosexual, she must face the injustices and degradation common to all women, plus endure additional social, economic, legal, and psychological abuses as well. In education and employment, the lesbian confronts more than discrimination or tokenism. She can be arbitrarily rejected or dismissed from many professions, even those—including teaching—traditionally relegated to women. Married women are denied equality under the laws that decree men as head of the household, but a wife is nonetheless allowed some legal protection. A lesbian, however, who shares her home with another woman—regardless of her income or responsibilities—foregoes all the economic and legal compensations granted, [*sic*] to the married woman, including tax deductions, insurance benefits, inheritance rights, etc. and

Whereas, this prejudice against the lesbian is manifested in the courts as well, and

Whereas, most divorced women are conceded the right to their children, a lesbian is automatically presumed unfit for motherhood and can have her children taken from her, and

Whereas, these are but a few of the laws and practices in our society that reflect irrational assumptions about lesbians. Just as the false and demeaning image of all women provides the rationale to keep them subjugated, so does the distorted stereotype of the lesbian sanction her persecution. Not only is she assumed to be unstable or sick or immoral; but because she defines herself independently of men, the lesbian is considered unnatural, incomplete, not quite a woman—as though the essence of womanhood were to be identified with men. Obviously, this Playboy image of the lesbian reduces her to an abject sexual object, deprived of the most basic civil and human rights due every person, and

Whereas, because she is so oppressed and so exploited, the lesbian has been referred to as "the rage of all women condensed to the point of explosion." This rage found a natural outlet in the women's liberation movement that seemed to view women in a new way and promised a new pride and sisterhood for every woman in search of equality and independence. Lesbians became active in NOW and in other groups fighting for all the feminist goals, including child care centers and abortion repeal. As a result of their activism in the movement, lesbians—as did all feminists—reached a new consciousness, a new sense of their worth and dignity as women and human beings. They began to rebel against the intolerance of a society that condemned their life style. But instead of finding support from their sisters, lesbians discovered that NOW and other liberation groups reflected some of the same prejudices and policies of the sexist society they were striving to change, and

212

Whereas, lesbians were never excluded from NOW, but we have been evasive or apologetic about their presence within the organization. Afraid of alienating public support, we have often treated lesbians as the step-sisters of the movement, allowed to work with us, but then expected to hide in the upstairs closet when company comes. Lesbians are now telling us that this attitude is no longer acceptable. Asking women to disguise their identities so they will not "embarrass" the group is an intolerable form of oppression, like asking black women to join us in white face. Furthermore, this discrimination is inconsistent with NOW's stated goal to "recognize our sisterhood" and to help women "overcome self-degradation." If this pledge is to be anything more than idle rhetoric, NOW must reassess the priorities that sacrifice principles to image, and

Whereas, some members of NOW object that the lesbian question is too controversial to confront right now, that we will weaken the movement by alienating potential and current members who are comfortable with NOW's "respectable" image. The same argument, that women would be frightened away, was raised a few years ago when NOW took a bold stand on the controversial abortion issue. The argument did not prove prophetic then, and we do not believe it is valid now. We are, after all, a reform movement, with revolutionary goals. The DAR can be "respectable", but as Susan B. Anthony pointed out: "Cautious, careful people always casting about to preserve their reputation or social standards, can never bring about a reform . . ."

Whereas, it is encouraging to note that feminists are not so easily frightened. Since the resolution supporting lesbians was passed in Los Angeles two months ago, the chapter has increased, not decreased, in membership. If a few cautious, careful people scurried away, the loss was imperceptible. And we are stronger now because many women feel more relaxed and are freer to work with us towards NOW goals, and

Whereas, another objection to the resolution contends that lesbian oppression is simply not relevant to the concerns of NOW; the movement will be weakened or even destroyed if we diffuse our energies on non-feminist issues. This is a curious argument, since all one has to do is read the NOW Bill of Rights to find that we have pledged support to the cause of "equal rights for all those who suffer discrimination and deprivation;" further, we have recognized a "common oppression that affects all women." If lesbians are women, and if lesbians suffer discrimination and deprivation, then the conclusion is inescapable: their oppression is not only relevant, but an integral part of the women's liberation movement; and

Whereas, we are affected by society's prejudices against the lesbian, whether we acknowledge it or not; as feminists we are all subject to lesbian-baiting by opponents who use the tactic of labelling us the worst thing they can think of, "lesbians", in order to divide and discredit the movement and bring women to heel. Even within NOW, regrettably, this tactic is employed by some members who conjure up the sexist-image of lesbians and shout "lavender menace" at anyone who opposes their views. NOW is inevitably weakened by these attempts to undermine the spirit and efforts of its members; we can no longer afford to ignore the problem; and

Whereas, the resolution does not mean that we are changing our emphasis and concentrating on specific lesbian issues, however. We have not been asked, nor do we intend, to diffuse our energies in any way. The resolution, in itself, is an action—the first step towards breaking down the barriers between women that have kept them weak

213

and suppressed. We are giving notice that we recognize our sisterhood with all women and that we are fighting for every woman's
"sacred right to her own person." As feminists, we can do no less;
THEREFORE, BE IT RESOLVED: That NOW recognizes the double
oppression of women who are lesbians, and
Be it further resolved: That a woman's right to her own person includes the right to define and express her own sexuality and to choose
her own lifestyle; and
Be it further resolved: That NOW acknowledge the oppression of
lesbians as a legitimate concern of feminism. (Sept., 1971)

Compiled by: Mary Samis, Tish Sommers, Marjorie Suelzle and Nan Wood

Notes

Chapter One

1. Babe Didrikson, a beautifully coordinated woman who excelled at every sport she tried, is considered by some to be the greatest all-around American athlete. Starting in track and field events, she won two gold medals in the 1932 Olympics. Turning to tennis, she gave champion Bill Tilden a good match. She would have won the big women's tennis tournaments such as Forest Hills, but in those days professionals were excluded. She was a star baseball and basketball player who once struck out the great Joe DiMaggio in Yankee Stadium.

Having conquered most other sports, the last one she learned was golf. Miss Didrikson quickly mastered this difficult game and won seventeen tournaments in a row. When she played in a charity exhibition golf match with the famous Babe Ruth, she bet him $50 a hole that she could outdrive him. Ruth, who could hit a golf ball much farther than his baseball home runs, quickly accepted. After four drives, Babe Ruth had lost $200 and he refused to bet any more. In 1943, Miss Didrikson entered the Phoenix Open Golf Tournament and won the qualifying medal with a sixty-seven, beating such great golfers as Ben Hogan, Sam Sneed, and Byron Nelson. Then the powers that ran the men's professional golf tournaments barred her from further play.

The dean of sportswriters, Grantland Rice, frequently said that Miss Didrikson could beat any man in the world in multisport competition that included such events as running, the high jump, the long jump, baseball, tennis, and golf.

Miss Didrikson was also an inspiration by the brave way she cheerfully accepted terminal cancer at age forty. Most people never knew that she won a dozen golf tournaments while playing with a colostomy.

2. Arianna Stassinopoulos, *The Female Woman* (New York: Random House, 1973), p. 30–31.

3. *Chicago Tribune,* August 17, 1975.

4. HEW Regulation on Sex Discrimination in Schools and Colleges, effective July 18, 1975, # 86.21(c)(4).

215

5. Amaury de Riencourt, *Sex and Power in History* (New York: David McKay Co., Inc., 1974), p. 56.

6. The Minnesota Sex Bias Report was sent for comment to Dr. Rhoda L. Lorand, a nationally respected clinical psychologist and psychoanalyst in New York City. She stated bluntly that, if the program was adopted, the result would be "the promotion of lesbianism, the downgrading of the institution of marriage, of motherhood, childrearing, the nuclear family, the advocacy of single parenthood and communal living, as well as contempt for all occupations and qualities traditionally recognized as feminine." She added:

> Putting pressure on boys and girls to behave like the opposite sex is placing them under a great strain because these pressures are at odds with biological endowment. Therapists have begun to note the confusion and unhappiness resulting from the blurring of gender-identity. Conflicting pressures between environmental and instinctual drives hinder the development of a firm sense of identity as a male or female (an intended goal of Women's Lib), lacking which the individual cannot acquire stability, self-esteem, or clear-cut goals.
>
> Moreover, it is taking all the joy and excitement out of life. Girls are made to feel ashamed of their longings to be courted and cherished, to be sexually attractive, to look forward to marriage, motherhood, and homemaking. Boys are made to feel ashamed of their chivalrous impulses. Feelings of protectiveness toward a girl and of manliness cause them to feel guilty and foolish, resulting in a retreat into passivity, while the girls end up unhappily trying to be sexual buddies of the boys. This unisex drive had its beginnings in the hippie movement and has been greatly intensified by all the publicity given by the communications media to the demands and accusations of the femininists (who really should be called masculinists, since they despise everything feminine).

7. *Kahn* v. *Shevin,* 416 U.S. 351 (1974) upheld Florida's property tax exemption for widows only. *Schlesinger* v. *Ballard,* 419 U.S. 498 (1975) upheld a United States Navy rule that permitted female officers to remain four years longer than male officers in a given rank before being subject to mandatory discharge.

8. The largest antidiscrimination settlement in history *(Equal Employment Opportunity Commission* v. *American Telephone and Telegraph Company,* 365 F. Supp. 1105, E.D. Pa. 1973) required back pay of $38 million (mostly to women) and the signing of a consent decree that mandates the telephone companies to give preferential treatment (reverse discrimination) to females over better-qualified males in order to achieve "goals," "intermediate targets," and "timeframes" for the "full utilization" of women "at a pace beyond that which would occur normally." 1 CCH Emp. Prac. # 1860 at 1553. (See also chapter four, note 28.)

9. *Federal Register,* vol. 40, no. 108, pp. 24137–145, sections 86.40, 86.57, and 86.21.

10. Alexis de Tocqueville, *Democracy in America,* 1840 (New York: Alfred Knopf, 1945), vol. II, pp. 211–14. De Tocqueville continued:

In no country has such constant care been taken as in America to trace two clearly distinct lines of action for the two sexes and to make them keep pace one with the other, but in two pathways that are always different. American women never manage the outward concerns of the family or conduct a business or take part in political life; nor are they, on the other hand, ever compelled to perform the rough labor of the fields or to make any of those laborious efforts which demand the exertion of physical strength. No families are so poor as to form an exception to this rule. If, on the one hand, an American woman cannot escape from the quiet circle of domestic employments, she is never forced, on the other, to go beyond it. Hence it is that the women of America, who often exhibit a masculine strength of understanding and a manly energy, generally preserve great delicacy of personal appearance and always retain the manners of women although they sometimes show that they have the hearts and minds of men.

Nor have the Americans ever supposed that one consequence of democratic principles is the subversion of marital power or the confusion of the natural authorities in families. They hold that every association must have a head in order to accomplish its object, and that the natural head of the conjugal association is man. They do not therefore deny him the right of directing his partner, and they maintain that in the smaller association of husband and wife as well as in the great social community the object of democracy is to regulate and legalize the powers that are necessary, and not to subvert all power. . . .

Thus the Americans do not think that man and woman have either the duty or the right to perform the same offices, but they show an equal regard for both their respective parts; and though their lot is different, they consider both of them as beings of equal value. They do not give to the courage of woman the same form or the same direction as to that of man, but they never doubt her courage; and if they hold that man and his partner ought not always to exercise their intellect and understanding in the same manner, they at least believe the understanding of the one to be as sound as that of the other, and her intellect to be as clear. Thus, then, while they have allowed the social inferiority of woman to continue, they have done all they could to raise her morally and intellectually to the level of man; and in this respect they appear to me to have excellently understood the true principle of democratic improvement.

Chapter Two

1. Hedrick Smith, *The Russians,* as condensed in the *Reader's Digest,* August, 1976, pp. 124–25.

2. *Los Angeles Times,* April 16, 1975.

3. The Virginia Slims American Women's Opinion Poll, vol. III, p. 33.

4. Interview in *Chicago Tribune,* August 17, 1975.

5. Ralph G. Martin, "Kate Hepburn: My Life & Loves," *Ladies' Home Journal,* August, 1975, pp. 102–103.

6. Jean Curtis, *Working Mothers* (New York: Doubleday, 1975).

7. *Radcliffe Quarterly,* September, 1975, p. 1.

8. Midge Decter, *The New Chastity and Other Arguments Against Women's Liberation* (New York: Coward, McCann and Geoghegan, 1972).

9. Harriet Belin, "Dropping Out of Motherhood," *Radcliffe Quarterly,* June, 1976, p. 4.

10. Samuel L. Blumenfeld, *The Retreat from Motherhood* (New Rochelle, N.Y.: Arlington House, 1975), p. 15.

11. Charles Higham, *Kate—The Life of Katharine Hepburn* (New York: Norton, 1975).

12. Albert Martin, *One Man, Hurt* (New York: Macmillan, 1975).

13. Rachel Carson, *Silent Spring* (Cambridge, Mass.: Houghton Mifflin, 1962), pp. 2–3.

14. *Parade,* November 28, 1976.

Chapter Three

1. *Minor* v. *Happersett,* 21 Wall. 162 (1875).

2. *Ohio Revised Code Annotated,* 3103.03.

3. Internal Revenue Service, Rev. Rul. 68-379, 1968-2, CB414.

4. *American Jurisprudence, 2d,* vol. 41, "Husband and Wife," sections 329, 330, 331, 332, 334.

5. Ch. 160, Section 1. 43–1–1, Colorado Revised Statutes 1963 was amended as follows:

Nonsupport of spouse and children—penalty—bond. (1) Any ~~man~~ PERSON who shall willfully neglect, fail, or refuse to provide reasonable support and maintenance of his ~~wife,~~ SPOUSE, or for his legitimate or illegitimate child or children, under sixteen years of age, or who willfully fails, refuses, or neglects to provide proper care, food, and clothing in case of sickness for his ~~wife~~ SPOUSE or such legitimate or illegitimate child or children, ~~or the mother of his illegitimate child during childbirth and attendant illness,~~ or any such child or children being legally the inmates of a state or county home, or school for children in this state, or who shall willfully fail or refuse to pay to a trustee, who may be appointed by the court to receive such payment, or to the board of control of such home or school the reasonable cost of keeping such child or children in said home, or any ~~man~~ PERSON being the father OR MOTHER of a child or children, under sixteen years of age, who shall leave such child or children, ~~or his wife~~ with intent to abandon such ~~wife or~~ child or children, OR ANY MAN WHO SHALL WILLFULLY NEGLECT, FAIL, OR REFUSE TO PROVIDE PROPER CARE, FOOD, AND CLOTHING TO THE MOTHER OF HIS ILLEGITIMATE CHILD DURING CHILDBIRTH AND ATTENDANT ILLNESS, shall be deemed guilty of a ~~felony, and upon conviction thereof shall be punished by imprisonment in the penitentiary for a term of not more than five years unless it shall appear~~ CLASS 5 FELONY. IT SHALL BE AN AFFIRMATIVE DEFENSE, AS DEFINED IN SECTION 40-1-507, C.R.S. 1963, TO A PROSECUTION UNDER THIS SECTION that owing to physical incapacity or other good cause ~~he~~ THE DEFENDANT is unable to furnish the support, care, and maintenance ~~herein~~ required ~~provided, that~~ BY THIS SECTION.

6. Professor Paul A. Freund, "The Equal Rights Amendment is Not the Way," *Harvard Civil Rights-Civil Liberties Law Review,* March, 1971, p. 240.

7. Among the many cases in which the courts upheld the wife's obligation to support in an ongoing marriage where there was no divorce or even separate maintenance, is *Carson, Pirie Scott Co.* v. *Stanwood,* 228 Ill. App. 281 (1923).

8. Joint Privileges and Elections Committee, Virginia Legislature, January 15, 1974.

9. *Congressional Record,* October 12, 1971, p. H9385.

10. *American Jurisprudence 2d,* vol. 41, "Husband and Wife," Section 331.

11. *Wall Street Journal,* May 29, 1974.

12. Arkansas Legislative Council for the Joint Judiciary Committee, Arkansas General Assembly, July 19, 1974.

13. *Arkansas Gazette,* August 25, 1974.

14. *Kahn* v. *Shevin*, 416 U.S. 351 (1974).

15. A famous example was the denial of custody of her child to Mrs. Nelson Rockefeller after she abandoned her first husband and children to marry the governor of New York.

16. *Conway* v. *Dana*, 456 Pa. 536 (1974). "We hold that insofar as [former] decisions suggest a presumption that the father, solely because of his sex and without regard to the actual circumstances of the parties, must accept the principal burden of financial support of minor children, they may no longer be followed. Such a presumption is clearly a vestige of the past and incompatible with the present recognition of equality of the sexes. The law must not be reluctant to remain abreast with the developments of society and should unhesitatingly disregard former doctrines that embody concepts that have since been discredited."

17. U.S. House Judiciary Committee, "Equal Rights for Men and Women," Report No. 92–359, July 14, 1971, p. 3.

18. Professor Arthur E. Ryman, Jr., "A Comment on Family Property Rights and the Proposed 27th Amendment," *Drake Law Review,* June, 1973.

19. Syndicated column, April 9, 1975.

20. A Report by the Ohio Task Force for the Implementation of the Equal Rights Amendment, July, 1975. (Columbus, Ohio, Attorney General, 1975.) The section on child-care centers is the most sensational part of the Ohio Report, but it also makes clear that ERA will mandate the following other mischief: (1) The establishment of a 50 percent female quota for "all agencies, commissions, boards, etc., appointed by an officer or arm of government." (2) The establishment of a permanent "lobby for women" with "adequate funding" from state tax funds. (3) The abolition of "the husband's primary duty to support his family" and the placing of "liability for household and family expenses on both spouses equally." (4) Changing the child-support law to make the mother equally obligated with the father for the financial support of their children. (5) Eliminating the law that the husband establishes the family domicile, and recognizing the wife's right "to determine her own domicile apart from" her husband; (6) Eliminating any requirement that a child take its father's name or that a wife take her husband's name. (7) Reducing the age at which boys can marry with parental consent from eighteen to sixteen (so they will be equal with girls). (8) Making women workers subject to compulsory overtime just like men. (9) Making coed the juvenile delinquent correction facilities which use "a cottage system of living." (10) Legalizing prostitution.

21. *Federal Register*, vol. 40, no. 108, pp. 24137–145.

22. *Congressional Record,* March 22, 1972, p. S4578.

23. Samuel T. Perkins and Arthur J. Silverstein, "The Legality of Homosexual Marriage," *Yale Law Journal,* January, 1973.

24. United States Senate, Committee on the Judiciary, Report No. 92–689, March 14, 1972, pp. 47–48.

25. *Forbush* v. *Wallace,* 405 U.S. 970 (1972) upheld an Alabama regulation requiring that a married woman seeking a driver's license use her husband's surname. On December 13, 1976, the United States Supreme Court refused to hear a challenge to a Kentucky requirement that a married woman use her husband's surname when she applies for a driver's license.

26. See appendix two, p. 184.

27. Agreement signed by WXYZ-TV and NOW, Detroit, August 7, 1973.

28. HEW Regulation on Sex Discrimination in Schools and Colleges, # 86.57(2).

29. See appendix two, pp. 184, 185, 188.

30. George F. Gilder, *Sexual Suicide* (New York: Quadrangle, The New York Times Book Co., 1973).

31. United States House of Representatives, Committee on the Judiciary, "Equal Rights for Men and Women," Report No. 92–359, p. 3.

32. "The Equal Rights Amendment: A Constitutional Basis for Equal Rights for Women," *Yale Law Journal,* April, 1971, pp. 969–78.

33. *Schlesinger* v. *Ballard,* 419 U.S. 498 (1975).

34. Curtis W. Tair, *Selective Service Bulletin,* July 31, 1972, p. 37.

35. "Israeli Women Trade Their Rifles for Aprons," *Philadelphia Evening Bulletin,* February 8, 1973.

36. "Seagoing Women Add Salt to the New Navy," *Chicago Tribune,* February 18, 1973.

37. Here is the text of a letter sent to the North Dakota state legislature during the 1973 debate on ERA by Betty Horner, age twenty, a student at Bismarck Junior College:

> The whole nation is rejoicing about the return of our prisoners of war, who have endured prison in North Vietnam for so many heart-

breaking years. Those years of prison were mighty hard on those young men. They suffered so much at the mercy of cruel Communist captors.

But I am glad about one thing. I am glad that not one of our POWs was a girl. If the Equal Rights Amendment had been ratified ten years ago, probably half the Americans taken prisoner would have been girls. But when the release date came, half would not have been girls, because they probably would not have lasted that long. In addition to the fact that girls have not the strength of men, there is the horrible fact that the fate of a girl in the hands of vicious men is a hundred times worse than that of a man.

We are all so relieved that the Vietnam War is over, and we weep for those 50,000 men who died there. But I am glad that 25,000 were not girls as they would have been if the Equal Rights Amendment had been ratified ten years ago. Everyone admits that the Equal Rights Amendment will make girls subject to the draft on an equal basis with men. There is no dispute about this. The Equal Rights Amendment proponents say that this is what they want.

I hope we do not have any more wars. But no one thought we would have the Vietnam War. I remember all those years our leaders promised peace, peace, peace. Still we had wars, and jungle fighting, and battle deaths, and prisoners of war.

I am not the kind who would be a conscientious objector or run off to Canada. If the law said I would have to be drafted, I would obey the law. I am willing to make sacrifices and serve my country in whatever way girls can help in any national emergency. But I do not believe that coed armies or coed navies ever won any wars, and I cannot believe that you can close your eyes to the reality of what the Equal Rights Amendment really means. Vietnam is proof that wars do happen even when no one wants them.

Please do not vote me any equal rights to be a POW. This is really what the Equal Rights Amendment is all about. I am pleading with you not to do this to me, and my sisters, and your daughters, and all the girls who are at the mercy of your vote. Thank you.

38. U.S. District Court, Eastern District of Michigan, Southern Division, Preliminary Injunction, Civil Action No. 39943, May 13, 1974.

39. *Detroit News,* June 20, 1974.

40. *Detroit Free Press,* May 15, 1974; Associated Press dispatch, June 14, 1973.

41. *Baltimore Sun,* June 13, 1973.

42. *New York Times,* July 15, 1974.

43. Myra K. Wolfgang, testimony before the Michigan Senate Committee on the Judiciary, April 18, 1972. She continued:

The person who glibly states that no one has to work overtime, if they don't want to, does not understand that, when there are not enough jobs to go around, people fight to keep those that are available. Thousands of women, because of economic necessity, will submit to excessive hours in order to obtain or hold a job. Thousands will work excessive hours out of fear of discharge, particularly when they see some of their Legislators calling for the nullification of protective legislation by urging ratification of the Equal Rights Amendment—and in the name of "equality" yet! . . .

The reason for protective legislation for women is not mysterious, nor is it founded entirely in male chauvinism or sexist attitudes. Women, despite all the denials of the obvious, have different bodies and different social roles than do men.

Is a man who works 60–72 hours a week confronted with the same problems that, say, the mother of three children working 60–72 hours a week is? Don't talk theory to me, tell me the practice. In the first place, men are better able to work overtime than women. Repeated studies have shown that women's accident proneness and efficiency drop substantially, after long hours of work, more than men doing the same job.

In the second place, who of the two is held responsible by society for the health, care and safety of children? Let the kids answer as they bob into the back door after school with a "Where's Mom?"

And while you're at it, ask the average woman about the "shared roles" ideology that is so popular with the neo-feminists. She'll tell you that she still bears the primary responsibility for her home and children. She may not phrase her reply so politely, at that. For let's face it—the "shared roles" ideology is just an ideology as far as most women are concerned. The average working mother and homemaker is going to be doing her outside job as well as meeting her family responsibilities. She will have little or no help at her second job at home. If she has a husband at home—and is not widowed, divorced, separated or unmarried, as many working women are—she will probably not find him very eager to put on an apron and do dishes, or to bathe the children, or to cook dinner, or to do the laundry. Unjust as this may well be, it's the way things are. If you think you're going to "enable" women to share their roles by an Equal Rights Amendment, better ask the average husband how he feels about housework. All the Equal Rights Amendment will do, in most cases, is make the role of the working women harder, by removing the legislation that protects her in outside employment, and sending her home to her second job exhausted.

Unless we are foolish enough to imagine we can re-structure in one broad sweep our entire society, we will realize no Equal Rights Amendment can alter the traditional role of women, not only as the bearer of children, but also as the one responsible for their care, their growth and development. This being the case, "sameness" of treatment will never result in true equality. The Equal Rights Amendment, however, prohibits any legal differentiation between the sexes and compresses all relationships into one tight formula. This can't be done. There are many laws that now differentiate between men and women, and indeed, they should. . . .

It's one thing for a professional woman to talk about fulfillment, through her job. It's another story for a woman who supports her family by scrubbing out other people's bathrooms.

It's one thing for a professional woman who can hire domestic help to talk about the "right" to work overtime. It's another story for the average working mother who cannot work overtime. . . .

It is your duty to refuse to accept the simplistic, spurious solution to sex discrimination proffered by the proponents of the Equal

Rights Amendment and to work instead for specific bills for specific ills. . . .

The Equal Rights Amendment, pushed through Congress by a vocal, if relatively small group of misguided middle-class feminists, will, if ratified by the States, wreak untold havoc in the lives of the great majority of American working women.

44. *Time,* March 26, 1973, p. 64.

45. Mrs. Naomi McDaniel, a member of the United Rubber Workers, testified at ERA legislative hearings in Illinois, Colorado, Pennsylvania, Texas, West Virginia, Kentucky, Missouri, Indiana, Louisiana, and Ohio. In responding to questions about the belated switch of the AFL-CIO from anti-ERA (the AFL-CIO testified against ERA when it was considered by Congress) to pro-ERA, she said: "May I point out to you what is behind the much-heralded reversal and recent endorsement of the Equal Rights Amendment by the National AFL-CIO Convention? This resolution was introduced by the Newspaper Guild, seconded by the Teachers Union—and passed with no debate."

46. United States House of Representatives, Committee on the Judiciary, Report No. 92–359, June 14, 1971, p. 11.

47. In 1975, the Committee on the Status of Women made a survey of women's colleges that showed their commitment to retain their single-sex status. Here typical responses from women's colleges. Rhoda M. Dorsey, president of Goucher College in Baltimore, Maryland, wrote:

> If there is a way for women to transcend the stereotypes, to realize their full potential, I believe it is in women's colleges. . . . They are the most likely places for women to begin to believe in themselves, to speak out for themselves without fear of being labeled pushy or aggressive. They are the most likely places for women to learn how to excel. In women's colleges, students can see women being successful. . . .
>
> Two recent studies bear out these claims, indicating that women achievers—that is, those who do more than the traditional female role prescribes—tend to have been graduated from women's colleges. Last year Kenneth Hardy published research in *Science* Magazine which indicated that during the first decades of this century, a group of women's colleges were clustered at the top of a list of colleges rated according to their productivity of scientists and scholars.
>
> Two years ago, in her study of "career-successful" women, Elizabeth Tidball discovered that not only high achievers tend to have been graduates of women's colleges, but also that the number of women's college faculties—as role models—has a positive effect on the number of achievers produced by the institution.
>
> The Tidball and Hardy studies are very important to us, because they reveal what these illustrious graduates have shown us all along that, given a chance, women can excel in all areas of human en-

224

deavor. Knowing as we do the encouraging results produced by women's colleges, and given statistics which show that the drop-out rate for women in coeducational institutions is higher than that for women's colleges, it would be a tragic mistake to close or make coed these institutions which are dedicated to women.

David B. Truman, president of Mount Holyoke College, wrote:

Women's colleges . . . serve a highly important need and have a strong future. What is more, the response to women's colleges within the last two or three years demonstrates pretty clearly that the college-bound young woman looks with even stronger favor on the women's college than was the case a few years ago. Coeducation is neither an inevitable nor better status. It would be a disaster for this country if every institution were coeducational, because it would be one more step toward destroying the diversity which is essential to educational strength and therefore toward reducing the entire enterprise to a dead mediocrity. . . .

I would regard as a very real danger that a foolish and uncritical conformity with fashion may have very real social losses. . . .

Women on their own campus . . . are first class citizens, thoroughly able to gain the experience and the confidence that comes from successful leadership.

Gwyneth Murphy, president of Barnard College Undergraduates, wrote:

Each student has the right to choose a college which is coed, single-sexed, or a college such as Barnard or Columbia. . . . We, the students of both Barnard and Columbia, hold unique places in higher education, being able to attend a small, single-sexed, liberal arts college, and at the same time live, take courses and interact on a daily basis with members of the opposite sex, taking advantage of what both schools have to offer.

We do not have true coeducation. No student is forced to live in coed housing, to take a class at the sister or brother school, or to participate in an activity with members of the opposite sex. Each of us has a right to choose the degree to which we wish to make our college career a coeducational one. . . .

During her four years at Barnard, a woman can never say she was treated a certain way or denied anything because of her sex. She is forced to develop to her full potential and cannot use her womanhood as an excuse for failure. This results in self-confidence in herself as a person, an awareness of who she is, and an honest self-appraisal of her limitations and capabilities.

48. A typical memorandum alert sent to fraternity and sorority members was one from the international president of Alpha Phi, dated September 9, 1974:

The proposed regulation . . . reaches into the rights of organizations in the schools. A recipient educational institution would be prohibited from providing financial support for a single-sex honorary society, such as Mortar Board or Alpha Lambda Delta, or a single-sex organization such as the Association of Women Students or Campus Panhellenic.

And, most vital to sororities is the provision that institutions may permit single-sex organizations, such as fraternities and sororities, to operate on campus only if they "receive no support or housing from the university and did not operate in connection with the university's education program or activity."

Officials of HEW do not define "support." Does this mean fraternities may not use meeting rooms in a college building? What about chapters which have built houses on land leased from the schools, or who have houses or lodges which are owned by the schools? Does "support" mean recognition? And what is an education "activity"? . . .

The ramifications are threatening. . . . All of us could be in litigation for years over housing and special services. What happens to Panhellenic Houses and sorority suites in dormitories? How much does Panhellenic "operate in connection with the university's education programs or activity," and how is this defined? Does this mean that faculty members cannot be advisors to sororities as part of their academic duties? . . .

49. *Commonwealth of Pennsylvania* v. *Pennsylvania Interscholastic Athletic Association,* Commonwealth Court of Pennsylvania, March 19, 1975. The opinion concluded:

> Although the Commonwealth in its complaint seeks no relief from discrimination against female athletes who may wish to participate in football and wrestling, it is apparent that there can be no valid reason for excepting those two sports from our order in this case. . . .
>
> Article XIX, Section 3B of the Pennsylvania Interscholastic Athletic Association is hereby declared unconstitutional, and the Pennsylvania Interscholastic Association is hereby ordered to permit girls to practice and compete with boys in interscholastic athletics, this order to be effective for the school year beginning in the fall of 1975 and thereafter.

50. June, 1974.

51. The HEW regulation specifies that schools and colleges may not "provide any course or otherwise carry out any of its education program or activity separately on the basis of sex . . . including health, physical education, industrial, business, vocational, technical, home economics, music, and adult education courses" (sec. 86.34). Although the HEW regulation in one section appears to permit grouping of students in physical education classes and activities by "ability as assessed by objective standards . . . without regard to sex," this is promptly negated two paragraphs later by the provision that "where use of a single standard of measuring skill or progress in a physical education class has an adverse effect on members of one sex, the [school or college] shall use appropriate standards which do not have such effect" (sec. 86.34[d]). This can only mean that, if applying a standard of ability and performance results in a disproportionate number of boys in a physical education class, then the school must

find some other standard by which a proportional balance of girls can be achieved, regardless.

Such a rule is lacking in common sense, it does nothing positive for girls or boys, and it is clearly not the purpose of the Education Amendments of 1972. No "appropriate standards" have yet been devised that can honestly enable girls to perform equally with boys in push-ups, weight lifting, tennis, or many, many other noncontact sports.

The HEW regulation does not use the expression fifty-fifty coed. But when it bars "limited participation" of one sex in any program or activity, then that is the same thing as requiring "full participation," which must mean fifty-fifty or roughly fifty-fifty, since there are only two sexes. When the HEW regulation speaks contemptuously of letting any class contain "a substantially disproportionate number of individuals of one sex," schools and colleges will get the message that they had better not let this happen or they will face a cutoff of federal funds.

The HEW regulation contains an open-ended requirement that specifies "affirmative action" even if there is no past or present discrimination. It specifies affirmative action in order to "overcome the effects of conditions which resulted in limited participation" of one sex—even if that limited participation was not due to discrimination (sec. 86.3[b]). This is a blank check, not only for arbitrary control over our schools and colleges, but a blank check for the militant radicals to promote a "gender-free" society with every aspect of our school system forced into a fifty-fifty coed ratio, whether we want it or not, and whether those participating want it or not.

Thus, even if there is no discrimination whatsoever in class assignment or counseling, it is probable that there will still be "limited participation" of high school girls in shop classes and of high school boys in cooking classes. Under the HEW regulation, affirmative action can be used to change this imbalance to conform to the gender-free schooling mandated by HEW and demanded by the women's lib movement. The schools will thus be under pressure to induce role-reversals of boys and girls through counseling in order to prevent any possibility of a sex discrimination charge that might result in a cutoff of federal funds.

The author of the Education Amendments of 1972, Congresswoman Edith Green, in a 1977 speech at Brigham Young University, expressed her sad disillusionment with the way the law has been distorted by HEW bureaucrats. Calling attention to the fact that Title IX was designed to give women equal opportunity in education and to end discrimination in pay, she said:

> Title IX was not designed to force integration by sex of every physical education class in the country. Title IX was not designed to do away with all male choirs, father-son or mother-daughter banquets, or to require the integration by sex of Boy Scouts, Girl Scouts, Campfire Girls, YMCAs, YWCAs, sororities, fraternities. In each one of these instances, the regulation grew out of the fertile imaginative brain of someone in the administrative branch of the government.

52. New Orleans *Times-Picayune,* November 27, 1974.

53. *Federal Register,* vol. 40, no. 108, pp. 24137–145, sections 86.40, 86.57, 86.21.

54. The Education Amendments clearly state that the ban on sex discrimination applies to "any education program or activity receiving federal financial assistance." Without any statutory authority, the HEW regulation expands federal control to an enormous additional area not contemplated by the law. The HEW regulation applies "to each education program or activity *operated by such recipient [school or college]* which receives *or benefits from* federal financial assistance." (Emphasis added.)

The italicized words show how HEW changed the meaning of the law in two ways. First, it extended the long arm of federal control past every "education program or activity receiving federal financial assistance" to encompass every education program or activity operated by a school or college that receives federal assistance—whether or not that program or activity itself receives federal assistance.

Second, HEW extended the long arm of federal control past programs "receiving" federal money to encompass programs that "benefit from" federal money—a much, much broader definition.

Together, these changes in wording have the result of extending HEW control over every detail of the day-to-day functioning of our schools and colleges.

55. See appendix two, pp. 207–8

56. Internal Revenue Service, Rev. Rul. 71–447, 1971–2, CB230.

57. *Bob Jones University* v. *Simon,* 40 L. Ed. 2d 496 (1974).

58. *Runyon* v. *McCrary,* 49 L. Ed. 2d 415 (1976).

59. U.S. Senate Judiciary Committee, "Equal Rights for Men and Women," Report No. 92–689, p. 34.

60. *Katzenbach* v. *Morgan,* 384 U.S. 641 (1966).

61. *Jones* v. *Alfred H. Mayer Co.,* 392 U.S. 409 (1968); *Sullivan* v. *Little Hunting Park,* 396 U.S. 229 (1969); *Tillman* v. *Wheaton-Haven Recreation Assn.,* 410 U.S. 431 (1973); *Johnson* v. *Railway Express,* 421 U.S. 454 (1975); *Runyon* v. *McCrary* (1976); *McDonald* v. *Santa Fe Transportation Co.* (1976).

62. U.S. Senate Subcommittee on Constitutional Amendments, *Women and the Equal Rights Amendment,* edited by Catharine Stimson in conjunction with the Congressional Information Service (New York: R. R. Bowker Co., 1972), p. 245.

63. *Newsweek,* December 29, 1975.

64. *". . . To Form a More Perfect Union . . ."*, Report of the National Commission on the Observance of International Women's Year, June, 1976, p. 219.

65. Betty Friedan, *It Changed My Life,* (New York: Random House, 1976), p. 77.

66. The following monies were diverted to the IWY Commission: $50,000 from the State Department, $125,000 from HEW, $35,000 from the Department of Transportation, $20,000 from the Interior Department, $10,000 from the Justice Department, the service of one $35,000 executive each from the Defense Department and the Labor Department, and the services of two executives from the United States Information Agency. In January, 1977, the General Accounting Office reported that $266,234 of this money was diverted to the IWY Commission without any legal authority.

67. A compilation of eminent legal opinion in support of the legality of rescission is available in a booklet published by Michigan Stop ERA, *Yes . . . We Can Rescind* (P.O. Box 19161, Detroit, MI 48219; $2.50). For example, Professor Charles L. Black, Jr., of Yale University Law School, states:

> I warmly favor the Equal Rights Amendment. I'm strongly for it. But I'm opposed to such "Mickey Mouse" tactics as claiming that, once a state has ratified the amendment, it's locked in forever, as in a lobster trap. Clearly, a state can change its mind either way before the amendment is officially declared to be ratified.
>
> You can't tell me that it would be sound policy to tell those states, "You're trapped. You can't get out." You could then have a situation where a majority of states had turned against an amendment but were still counted as voting for it, and it could even be declared officially "ratified."
>
> The crucial question is whether or not three-fourths of the states favor the amendment at the same time.
>
> Parading precedents is a fallacy. The Supreme Court has reversed itself, sometimes, and it is Congress' responsibility to do the rational thing. The states may freely withdraw their ratification at any time before an amendment is officially declared a part of the Constitution. It would be very dangerous to have any states corralled into approving it.

68. Among the hundreds of organizations opposing the Equal Rights Amendment at this writing are:

Eighteen state legislatures
Three state referendums
Veterans of Foreign Wars
American Legion (many states)
Farm Bureau (many states)
National Council of Catholic Women

Catholic Daughters of America
Knights of Columbus
Lutheran Church, Missouri Synod (Commission on Theology
  and Church Relations)
General Association of Regular Baptist Churches
Mormon Church
Church of Christ, dozens of congregations
Union of Orthodox Jewish Congregations
Union of Orthodox Rabbis
Yeshiva University Alumni Association
Texas PTA
Illinois Federation of Women's Clubs
Michigan Federation of Women's Clubs
Florida Federation of Women's Clubs
Arkansas Federation of Women's Clubs
New York City Federation of Women's Clubs
Virginia Federation of Women's Clubs
Conservative Party of New York
Young Americans for Freedom
Young Republican National Federation
Woman's Christian Temperance Union
Daughters of the American Revolution
Women for Responsible Legislation
Women in Industry
American Legislative Exchange Council

Chapter Four

1. There is much, much more to "Of Women and Men." It was a professional presentation of women's lib dogma, attitudes, lifestyles, values, and demands, given with unabashed approval by Barbara Walters and Tom Snyder. Walters assured us that women will not be "drones" any more, thus mouthing the basic women's lib doctrine that the role of wife and mother is menial and degrading, and that the home is a prison from which women must be liberated. The program portrayed the women's lib demands on schools, school textbooks, family relationships, religious literature, television programming, sexual mores, the Constitution, government programs, politics, and athletics. (One sequence showed a pitiful little girl boxing with a boy in a regular boxing ring and a woman "liberated" to break her nose playing ice hockey with men.) The show even featured an interview with the godmother of women's lib, Betty Friedan, boasting that "it's revolution and it's marvelous." Not one critic of any of the women's lib proposals was given a moment on the three-hour show.

The windup pitch for the Equal Rights Amendment was given by Walters, along with the bandwagon propaganda that ERA chances were much improved by the 1974 elections.

230

Here is NBC's prediction for the future relationship "of women and men," as narrated by Walters and Snyder:

WALTERS: I think also there will be a difference in the openness between two people and that there will be an easier sexuality, a franker relationship, again, men and women as people. We see this especially with the young people. They don't have the fears. They don't have the hangups. And there is the honesty in all aspects of their relationship.

SNYDER: And there's going to be some change in the way men and women live together. Do you not think that we aren't simply going to have, for better or for worse, till death do us part, from this day forward, that sort of thing, where a marriage was for a lifetime and you are my one-and-only and it's going to continue for a long time? We've all heard about these contract marriages, serial marriages; is that not the term? Where there's a series of relationships, of a man and a woman for a time and then going on to something else? But I think there'll still be marriage, and I think that men and women will grow old together, and I think that they will have children and watch their children have other children, and it's going to be a little bit different and, hopefully, everybody will be ready for it. . . .

WALTERS: Well, it may be that women are playing the parts of husbands. They may be earning more of the income. They may be on the executive level. And it won't just be the man up there on the executive level with the female drone beneath him. Isaac Asimov, the science writer wrote, and I'm quoting here: "For the first time in history, we will be tapping the brain power of the other half of the human race. We will double our mental capacity without doubling our numbers."

It seems that there's going to be some fear on the part of the men. It will mean that there will be further competition in the economic market, but on the other hand, we will be tapping people we never have used before.

SNYDER: And, when he says, without doubling our numbers, there aren't going to be as many children. We've achieved Zero Population Growth in this country. The birth rate, we can expect, will continue going down. So the outlook is going to be for fewer children for couples, or possibly, no children at all.

WALTERS: We took an NBC poll to find out how you felt out there. And we asked whether you believe that a woman can be fulfilled without having children. You know what the answer was? The answer was: Overwhelmingly yes. From both men and women. Women don't have to be mothers to be fulfilled. And the younger the person answering, the greater the number who believed that.

SNYDER: And, if you think this is just Walters and Snyder quoting all this stuff, the people who know about the future, at least know about it in terms of their own research of the past, support all that has been said on this program.

2. A recent report made by Walter B. Miller of the Harvard Law School Center for Criminal Justice, on a grant from the Law Enforcement Assistance Administration, bluntly states that the six worst cities have at least 2,700 gangs with 81,500 members who average twelve to twenty-one years of age. These cities were identified as New York, Los Angeles, Philadelphia, Chicago, Detroit, and San Francisco.

231

The most frightening part of the report, however, is what it says about how these gangs terrorize the public schools: "Gang members have 'territorialized' the school buildings and their environments—gyms, cafeterias, sports facilities, and in some cases . . . the entire school." Students are shaken down and forced to pay for passing through a doorway, for using gym facilities, for protection from being assaulted, or even for the right to go to school.

The report quoted a Los Angeles official as saying that "gangs have completely taken over [some] individual classrooms. . . . Once the number of gang members in a class reaches a certain level, the teacher is powerless to enforce discipline." Philadelphia closed several high school cafeterias because gangs took control over access and eating.

3. Drug prevention officials say that, when alcohol and depressant drugs called "downers" are are taken together, they create an explosive "high" that may be five times as great as one of the drugs alone. The feeling is extreme numbness, often accompanied by hallucinations. The result may be respiratory and heart failure, deep coma, or death. One of the many casualties of the combination of alcohol and drugs is Karen Anne Quinlan, the New Jersey girl, who has been in a coma for many months and achieved national notoriety when her parents sought court approval to disconnect the life-supporting miracle machines.

4. The word *assassin* was originally derived from the Arabic word *hashshashin,* which means "eaters of hashish." This bit of etymology tells something about the world's practical experience with the dehumanizing effect on those who use hashish, one of the two products of the cannabis plant.

The other product of cannabis is marijuana. A mountain of scientific evidence has been accumulated that marijuana use results in massive damage to the cellular process, to the reproductive system, and to the respiratory system.

The principal ingredient in marijuana tends to accumulate in the brain and creates the serious possibility of brain damage, distortion of perception and reality, chronic passivity, and lack of motivation. These effects are all the more dangerous because its early use is deceptive: The marijuana user is not aware that an irreversible deterioration of mental functioning has begun.

Other scientific data show that marijuana causes genetic damage and mutation, weakens immunity to disease, has a "precancerous" effect on lung tissues, and severely damages the process by which cells are restored and replaced in a healthy body.

The myth of harmlessness was nurtured at Berkeley, where in 1967 Dr. Harvey Powelson, chief of the Department of Psychiatry in the Student Health Center at the University of California, was quoted in the campus newspapers as saying: "There is no evidence that marijuana does anything except make people feel good. It has never made anyone into a criminal or a narcotics addict. It should be legalized."

After treating more than 1,000 patients, both in consultation and in therapy sessions, Dr. Powelson came to the conclusion that his earlier statement was "totally wrong." He cites example after example of brilliant graduate students upon whom marijuana had the following effects: difficulty in concentration, loss of sense of time and memory, loss of will to do sustained work, inability to sleep regular hours, loss of normal appetite, sexual impotence, loss of ability to handle mathematics at a prior level of achievement or to follow logical arguments, hostile suspiciousness, and gullibility.

Dr. Powelson warns us that the early use of marijuana "is beguiling. Pot smokers are so enraptured by the illusion of warm feelings that they are unable to sense the deterioration of their own mental and physiological processes. Its continued use leads to delusional thinking."

The evidence suggests that marijuana is more dangerous than tobacco or alcohol. Marijuana damages the lungs and respiratory system ten times as fast as cigarette smoking. It usually takes years for a social drinker to become an alcoholic and drink himself to death or out of a job. Marijuana, however, can destroy our young people in a couple of years, before they ever have the chance to know life and the excitement of confronting its challenges.

The United States Senate Internal Security Subcommittee collected the findings of top scientific experts on this subject and summarized them in a report entitled *The Marijuana-Hashish Epidemic,* published in 1974. The principal findings were:

> (1) THC the principal psycho-active factor in cannabis, tends to accumulate in the brain and gonads and other fatty tissues in the manner of DDT.
>
> (2) Marijuana, even when used in moderate amounts, causes massive damage to the entire cellular process.
>
> (3) Tied in with its tendency to accumulate in the brain and its capacity for cellular damage, there is a growing body of evidence that marijuana inflicts irreversible damage on the brain, including actual brain atrophy, when used in a chronic manner for several years.
>
> (4) There is also a growing body of evidence that marijuana adversely affects the reproductive process in a number of ways, and that it poses a serious danger of genetic damage and even of genetic mutation.
>
> (5) Chronic cannabis smoking can produce sinusitis, pharyngitis, bronchitis, emphysema, and other respiratory difficulties in a year or less, as opposed to ten to twenty years of cigarette smoking to produce comparable complications.
>
> (6) Cannabis smoke, or cannabis smoke mixed with cigarette smoke, is far more damaging to lung tissues than tobacco smoke alone. The damage done was described as "precancerous."
>
> (7) Chronic cannabis use results in deterioration of mental functioning, pathological forms of thinking resembling paranoia, and "a massive and chronic passivity" and lack of motivation—the so-called "amotivational syndrome."

5. *McGuffey's Eclectic Readers* (New York: American Book Co., 1879), primer and grades one through six.

6. 143 U.S. 457 at 470 (1892).

7. *Humanist Manifestos I and II* (Buffalo, New York: Prometheus Books, 1973), pp. 13, 16, 17. Among the signers of the "Second Humanist Manifesto" are Corliss Lamont, Lester A. Kirkendall, Alan F. Guttmacher, Paul Blanshard, Lester Mondale, Joseph Fletcher, Betty Friedan, Julian Huxley, Vashti McCollum, and Gunnar Myrdal.

8. In *Torcaso* v. *Watkins,* 367 U.S. 488 (1961), the Supreme Court declared that neither the federal government nor any state can "aid those religions based on a belief in the existence of God as against those religions founded on different beliefs." The Court then went on to specify that "among religions in this country which do not teach what would generally be considered a belief in the existence of God are Buddhism, Taoism, Ethical Culture, Secular Humanism and others." In *Abington* v. *Schempp,* 374 U.S. 203 (1963), the famous case that prohibited Bible reading in public schools, the Supreme Court held that the state may not establish a "religion of secularism" by affirmatively opposing or showing hostility to religion, or by "preferring those who believe in no religion over those who do believe."

9. *National Review,* August 15, 1975, p. 887.

10. Parents have successfully demonstrated that excessive and unreasonable state regulations imposed on private religious schools are, in fact, an interference with their free exercise of religion. The big breakthrough came in *Wisconsin* v. *Yoder,* 406 U.S. 205 (1972), the case that established the right of the Amish to withdraw their children from public high schools. Important lower court cases have since been won for private religious schools in Ohio and in Vermont.

11. Senator James Buckley and Congressman James Delaney proposed a solution to remedy this unfair treatment—a bill to amend the Internal Revenue Code by allowing a tax deduction of up to $1,000 for each person whose tuition at a private school or college is paid by a taxpayer. Such a change would eliminate the present elements of discrimination and save money for everyone. It would ease the financial burden on public schools, on private schools, and especially on the taxpayers. It would restore a freedom of parental choice in schools that would be beneficial for educational standards. Most of all, it would give us the opportunity to seek alternative solutions to the current problems of the thirteen-year decline in scholastic achievement tests, the lack of moral training, and the rising crime and vandalism in our schools.

12. *U.S. News and World Report,* September 3, 1973, p. 28.

13. The myth that the new is always superior to the old is a major factor in the phenomenon called "modern art." If modern art is an

enigma to you, if you are one of the many millions whose reaction to ugly and incoherent shapes is to walk silently through museums and public places too embarrassed to criticize what you cannot understand, you will welcome the devastating expose by Tom Wolfe, *The Painted Word.* (New York: Farrar, Straus & Giroux, 1975).

With intimate knowledge of his subject and the light touch of exquisite sarcasm, Wolfe cuts up the sacred cow called modern art and leaves its carcass bleeding on the floor. Wolfe's book is the definitive description of the phenomenon called modern art, how it rejected the mission of art to be a mirror held up to man and nature, and enshrined instead the new god of the avant-garde and the new orthodoxy of futurism, cubism, abstract expressionism, surrealism, social realism, and all the other art "isms" that gained social chic during the last fifty years. Modern art was the product of several little cliques, each in pursuit of its own goals, including untalented nonconformists seeking notoriety, the nouveau riche seeking an entree into high society as patrons of the arts, those who inherited wealth but thought it was smart to hobnob with the proletariat, the socialists of the 1930s seeking to turn art into a propaganda weapon, and businesses trying to mask their corporate profit-making with a veneer of culture. The entire movement was invented and sustained by some 10,000 persons living mainly in Rome, Paris, London, Berlin, and New York.

Although twentieth century scientists built upon the wisdom of their predecessors and led man to soar through the air and out into space, the practitioners of modern art closed the door on true progress by rejecting everything that their predecessors, from Leonardo and Michelangelo on down, had discovered.

14. Rudolf Flesch, *Why Johnny Can't Read* (New York: Harper's, 1955).

15. The phonics system I used successfully with six children, and which I highly recommend, is Julie Hay and Charles E. Wingo, *Reading with Phonics, Revised* (Chicago, Philadelphia, New York: J. B. Lippincott Co., 1954). It is available with a teacher's edition, three workbooks, and three teacher's workbooks.

16. Among the many fine organizations working to improve the teaching of basic skills are the Council for Basic Education, 725 15th St., N.W., Washington, D.C. 20005, and the Reading Reform Foundation, 7054 East Indian School Road, Scottsdale, Arizona 85251.

17. *Saint Louis Post-Dispatch,* January 4, 1976.

18. April 8, 1976.

19. *Chicago Tribune,* December 19, 1975.

20. Associated Press Dispatch, May 29, 1976.

235

21. *Miller* v. *California,* 413 U.S. 15 (1973). See also the companion case, *Paris Adult Theatre* v. *Slaton,* 413 U.S. 49 (1973).

22. 96 S.Ct. 2440 (1976).

23. The February, 1974, issue of *Playboy* magazine carried the following letter from Sonia McCallum writing on behalf of E.R.A. Central in Chicago: "E.R.A. Central is an organization for Illinois supporters of the Equal Rights Amendment. . . . Without the help of the Playboy Foundation, E.R.A. Central would probably not be operating at its present level. We are deeply indebted to the Foundation." The contribution of "thousands of dollars" from Playboy was subsequently admitted by ERA supporters at an Illinois legislative hearing on ERA.

24. Albert Shanker, president of the AFL-CIO American Federation of Teachers and leader of the 1975 New York teachers' strike, testified for the Brademas-Mondale Bill at the June, 1975, congressional hearing, and strongly recommended a universal training program for children from the age of two or three.

25. This rationale was best described by Mack A. Moore, professor of economics at Georgia Tech, in an article called "Economics of the Equal Rights Amendment," published in *The Phyllis Schlafly Report,* October, 1974:

> By focusing primarily on the legal and social considerations, the controversy over the Equal Rights Amendment has largely overlooked the fact that the economic implications are an integral part of the question. For openers, it would be well if everyone could read an article in the November/December, 1973, issue of *Challenge: The Magazine of Economic Affairs,* entitled "Have Swedish Women Achieved Equality?" The article is not by a male chauvinist but by Nancy S. Barrett, an economics professor at American University. Some pertinent excerpts follow:
> "Five years ago . . . Sweden began a purposeful campaign to change the institution of the family and the attitudes that are associated with it.
> "It is true that labor unions have been successful in narrowing the gap between male and female wages.
> "[But] changes in the structure of taxes and in income-linked social benefits have in many cases forced women to work when they would have preferred to remain at home. And because equalization of wages in manufacturing has resulted in a relative deterioration of men's take-home pay, many Swedish families now claim that they can no longer afford to live on a single income.
> ". . . The Swedish experience is on the whole, disappointing; despite explicit recognition that equality cannot come without some change in family relationships, traditional attitudes and values remain deeply ingrained."
> The Day Care/Kindergarten lobby is part of the same campaign to get more women to work, regardless of whether they really need jobs or whether the economy needs their services. The more people work-

ing, the more money there is available for spending, including taxes to finance the "solutions" to the various crises. One must bear in mind that if a woman cares for her own children at home, no money changes hands and hence no taxes are paid. It is possible that a woman could wind up caring for her own children as a paid employee of a public day care center (or two neighbors caring for each other's children, in which case both would pay taxes).

In my opinion, this churning of the national money crock is clearly the objective of the professional reformists in Sweden and in the U.S., in order to drain the "foam" away and hence provide funds to support the problem solvers. Quoting again from the article cited:

"Despite the benefits of sexual equality, the effects of urging women into the labor force are at best uncertain if they are accompanied by a deterioration in the quality of family life. Pamphlets distributed by the women's committee of the Swedish Labor Market Board disconcertingly suggest that working women should avoid 'complicated cooking' and that 'there are nowadays so many prepared things to buy, for instance frozen food, ready-made dishes and canned nutriment.' In addition, institutionalized child care has mixed—and largely unknown—effects on children."

Again, it must be noted that when a woman "hires" her cooking done in the form of frozen food and ready-made dishes, more taxes are paid. It also means that money is available for union dues, charitable contributions, and for other causes which create careers for the professional reformists. In addition, the various delinquencies, and the divorce rate resulting from more working women, provide the clientele for the reformists.

Also, in my opinion, the tax question explains why some reformists (including Columnist Sylvia Porter a few months ago) have proposed that husbands be required to pay Social Security taxes on their wives, for "services rendered" as housewives. As government spending for day care and myraid other "supportive services" causes more inflation (which it would), and as higher taxes reduce family incomes, there would be more demand for government to create make-work jobs. This proposal is advanced under the cliche of the government as the "employer of last resort" (also suggested by Sylvia Porter and a host of other self-styled experts). This will mean even more inflation, and so on in a never-ending circle leading to more and more economic and social controls.

Admittedly, just as some parents mistreat each other, some mistreat their children, brutally so in some cases. Here again, however, we have separate laws already, so that the ultimate question is whether America wants the state or the parents to rear children. In some quarters of the Day Care/Kindergarten lobby, age 3 has already been proposed as the beginning age. Any success toward achieving that goal will mean a progressive lowering of the age even further, so that children eventually may be moved from the maternity ward directly to public day care centers.

Housewives are the last frontier for expanding the labor force (and hence the number of taxpayers), which is the essence of Woman's Lib. But Professor Barrett, recalling her research tour of Sweden, notes that:

"Talking with Swedish women, one gets the impression that they are less concerned with job satisfaction than they are disturbed at being forced to work."

This form of "forced labor" is due to taxes and inflation, as noted earlier. The fact that so many people are addicted to public spending on the various crises for a livelihood explains why our society is in a state of permanent emergency.

Like other parasites capitalizing on the public crises industry, the legal profession has a large economic stake in the "liberation" of women. An ad in the *Atlanta Constitution* of February 12, 1974 announces "Divorce in 24 hours. Learn all about liberalized divorce laws in the Dominican Republic. . . . Fast, low-cost, discreet legal proceedings—the same used by thousands of Americans already." Legalized abortion is likewise becoming a growth industry. Commercial billboards all around Atlanta urge: "Pregnant? For confidential help, call Georgia Family Planning Service." Here again it must be noted that no taxes are paid on illegal abortions. By making them legal, the state can perhaps collect enough additional taxes to support the abortion service, and maybe net enough "profit" to meet the "rising demand" for other public services.

Surely the biggest hoax in history lies in this latter shibboleth. For in fact the rising demand is not from people who would *consume* the services but from those who propose to *supply* them. In short, the alleged rising demand for public *services* is really a rising demand for public *spending*. Any relationship between the two is coincidental and is as likely to be negative (such as expenditures for the destruction of houses in order to make room for highways).

In fact, government's primary function has become that of providing a sheltered market place for suppliers of economic resources (including labor). With political forces being used to insulate suppliers from the discipline of consumer choice, there is an open conspiracy between political and economic powers. Rather than government by, of, and for the people, we have government against the people, as the myriad special private interests sponsor political candidates as hired mercenaries to exploit the common interest.

The above argument, which I refer to as *polinomics,* explains the make-work wars and all other public crises, since politicians can stay in power only by providing a continuously *expanding* market. Political sponsors are really investors in this neo-corporate state and expect regular dividends in the form of phantom markets and artificial prices. It also explains why the big cities are crying for "new sources of revenue" in order to meet the increasing demands of the blackmailers. It explains why we have posh public buildings growing like weeds while private citizens are forced into public housing and mobile homes. In short, we have private poverty amidst public extravagance, which is just opposite the theme which John Kenneth Galbraith parlayed into a fortune with his book *The Affluent Society.*

In order to provide this perpetually expanding market, government must have an increasing amount of taxes. The way to obtain such increase is to develop synthetic taxpayers. Under the banner of "human resource utilization," the exploiters cannot afford for women to waste their time in such unproductive activities as raising children unless monetary transactions are involved, as explained earlier. They must be kept busy producing taxes in order to finance the rising demand for public spending by the political sponsors. The same applies to the private sector, where women are needed to produce purchasing power. . . .

One method for gaining acceptance of state guardianship is that of promoting divisiveness *within* the family. A recent book "advocates the overthrow of parental authority." Indeed, divide and conquer is the hallmark of statism. Childhating is reportedly becoming wide-spread and even gaining an aura of respectability.

Thus by promoting divorce, abortions, and childless marriages, and by creating artificial jobs, the reformists may, to be sure, liberate women from men and from the boredom of caring for their own children. But in the process, all three groups may be transformed into quasiserfs watched over by an all-seeing but unseen eye.

26. Dr. Dale Meers, a child psychoanalyst affiliated with Children's Hospital in Washington, D.C., and with the Baltimore–District of Columbia Institute for Psychoanalysis, studied day-care in Eastern Europe and the Soviet Union. He is no longer an advocate of day-care as a solution to the problems of disadvantaged children, believing that it is "clinically dangerous" and results in damage from the "deper-sonalization" of infant care. He cites the high infant mortality rate in institutions. Dr. Meers stated:

> I know of few researchers who dispute the probability that mild to severe developmental failures derive from "institutionalization." . . .
> Why should we want to take over what the poorest of Europeans were trying to rid themselves of? In my own study and observation of Communist centers, I was singularly depressed by what I saw, so much so that it seemed inane to continue to photograph room after room, center after center, of passive and despondent youngsters.

Time-Life produced an excellent film, available through many public libraries, called "Rockabye Baby." It demonstrates by the scientific observation of monkeys that babies grow and develop better with their own mothers.

Dr. Rhoda L. Lorand, renowned practicing clinical psychologist in New York City, wrote the following letter to Senator James Buckley on May 26, 1975, which accurately pinpoints the fallacies and the follies of the Brademas-Mondale Bill:

> With reference to your request for comments on the Child and Family Services Act of 1975: the bill is characterized by puzzling contradictions and vagueness, some of its provisions based on misin-formation, others reflecting the dangers inherent in having only the most fragmentary knowledge of the dynamics of the emotional-cog-nitive development of the child and its connection with the parent-child relationship. . . .
> For example, the bill is presented as a measure designed to help the poor and marginal families, yet the children who are destined for private schools will not be excluded.
> The privacy and rights of parents will be safeguarded, the bill assures, but there are at least two provisions which give carte blanche to the Secretary to install any program or take any action which in his opinion furthers the spirit of the legislation. The con-cept of a partnership with the parents is a snare and a delusion. . . .
> The program is to be voluntary. If the poor do not apply, will they be subject to subtle or overt coercion or will those in command be satisfied with fulfilling the requests for services of more fortunate applicants?
> The primary purpose of the bill, it is said, is to give children of

mothers who are forced to work, the opportunity to develop to their fullest potential, and that one must avoid subjecting children to "mind-numbing custodial care." This means that the children must be cared for by people who like and enjoy youngsters, who understand what to expect of children at each age from infancy on, who are patient, kind, reliable, honest, conscientious and dependable and with whom the child can establish a long-term relationship. . . .

As if the above were not a tall enough order to fill, the proponents of the bill plan to combine it with the amelioration of the unemployment problem in depressed and deprived areas. As many of the local people as possible will be hired as paraprofessionals in child-care and for other positions which may bring them into frequent contact with the children. The sad fact is that many of these people, having themselves been treated with a combination of harshness and neglect as children have been rendered quite incapable of treating children any other way, because there is a compulsion in all of us, clinical evidence reveals, to handle children in the way we ourselves were handled. . . .

One cannot be too careful in the choice of one's parents, Mark Twain observed—and the same applies to the hiring of parent surrogates. A child's cognitive abilities are stimulated and enhanced by contact with people who make him feel happy. He is motivated to know more about them and the world they represent. He identifies with them, tries to live up to their demands on him in order to please them. The child who is hurt, neglected, unhappy or frightened withdraws into himself and tries to know as little as possible about the pain-giving world around him, or else may feel the need to continually attack it in order to overcome his feeling of helplessness or to express his rage and disappointment because of emotional frustration. Such attitudes are vitally important components in learning disabilities. The need to not know and the presence of unmanageable quantities of rage are among the prime causes of learning blocks. . . .

Over and over again it has been demonstrated that that which gives a child the greatest chance to achieve his maximum potential in life, a stated goal of this bill, is the opportunity to spend his first five years in the loving care of a normally devoted mother, yet Senator Mondale quotes with approval statements of the Director of Woman's Bureau of the U.S. Department of Labor who, in arguing strongly for day care for all classes of women's requirements, claims that it is of importance to middle class women to be able to upgrade their standard of living. She adds that "women with professional and technical skills can continue to contribute their skills and talents to fill the needs of our society in health, science, business and industry, politics and other fields. Day care, in fact, is a boon to women of all economic levels who want the freedom to choose for themselves their own life style and decide for themselves how they can best contribute (translation: how much they are willing to give) to the wellbeing of their families." Certainly none of these women can be considered poor and in need of government assistance, yet it appears that the proposed facilities will be at their disposal.

Those statements represent the position of the universal-day-care proponents and of Women's Lib (often one and the same), many of whose members openly express their belief that child care and homemaking are the most degrading of all human activities. How does this square with the statements of appreciation of the importance of the family and the desire to strengthen family life which are emphasized

240

in the bill as well as the Senator's introduction? The mother will be freed to make a contribution to the world of work while neglecting the opportunity to enhance the development and happiness of her own babies, toddlers, and preschoolers. The younger her children are, as clinical studies have definitely proven, the more damaged they will be emotionally, developmentally and cognitively by the impersonality and the changing personnel characteristic of institutional care. . . .

In his sponsoring address to the Senate, Mr. Mondale, in stressing the imperative need, in his opinion, for institutionalized child-care, cited statistics on the disappearance of the extended family, which left mothers without the needed help in caring for their children while they were at work. There seems, however, to be an information gap. According to the University of Michigan's Institute for Social Research which surveyed 5,000 families in 1973, "only 8 % of the families with young children and working mothers took their children to either a day care center or a nursery school. About half used some method which involved another family member as a sitter, and nearly a quarter either had husbands who worked a split-shift so that they could share in the responsibility of the child care, or had a job which they could do at home. *Almost half of the families interviewed did not pay anything for child care, including families in both low and high income strata.* (Emphasis added) Most of this 'free' care was provided either by parents or other relatives and might involve what amounts to a nonmonetary exchange system. . . ."

Recently the *Today* show featured an account of a cooperative day-care center in which parents, as well as grandparents, took turns caring for the children, at no cost to anyone. Of course there are neighborhoods where this system cannot work because there are too many troubled people. They are the ones who do require government assistance and other services which they usually reject, such as psychotherapeutic help. But it is a tremendous asset to a child's development to have parents who keep full responsibility for his well-being and are able to enter into and maintain cooperative relationships with other parents. It enhances the parents' sense of self-worth and the child identifies with the excellent self-image of the parent, thereby enhancing his own self-image.

Too many well-meaning social planners and legislators fail to understand this. While bemoaning the decline in the authority of the family, they promote all sorts of measures which deprive the parents of authority or encourage them to yield it to others. Instead there should be widespread encouragement of cooperative ventures through government citations of merit and widespread publicity. All available funds should be used for the intensive care of the deeply troubled people who really cannot function adequately without assistance. . . .

Should this Act become law, we may, to borrow the phraseology of Rep. Edith Green, soon be engulfed and overburdened with a runaway federal program—a diverse, overlapping, confusing array of governmental efforts whose faults are beyond remedy and whose abuses are beyond belief.

The evidence is conclusive that babies do need mothers. The Yiddish proverb must be correct: "God couldn't be everywhere, so He made mothers."

27. See pp. 85–86 above.

28. *Equal Employment Opportunity Commission* v. *American Telephone and Telegraph Company*, 365 F. Supp. 1105 E.D. Pa. 1973. The case resulted in a consent decree forced on AT&T and its associated Bell Telephone Companies by EEOC and the Department of Labor that specified "affirmative action programs," "goals and timetables," "intermediate targets and timeframes." The consent decree included this language:

> The Equal Employment objective for the Bell System is to achieve, within a reasonable period of time, an employee profile, with respect to race and sex in each major job classification, which is an approximate reflection of proper utilization. . . . This objective calls for achieving full utilization of minorities and women at all levels of management and non-management and by job classification at a pace beyond that which would occur normally. . . .
> An integral part of our Program is goals, intermediate targets and timeframes designed to change the race and sex profile particularly in those areas where there has been under-utilization of women and minority group persons. . . . [1 CCH Emp. Prac. # 1860, at 1533.]

As a result of this consent decree, the telephone companies have been forced to promote women who are less qualified and have less seniority over men who are more qualified and have more seniority, merely in order to meet the affirmative-action "targets." (For example, see the case of *McAleer* v. *AT&T*, Civil Action No. 75–2049, June 9, 1976.) When the telephone companies were unable to meet their affirmative-action targets for women climbing telephone poles and other outside work formerly considered men's work, the companies resorted to paying $500 bonuses to women to take those jobs and keep them for only five months. It is easy to see what an adverse effect this has on the morale of the men, who then earned less for doing men's jobs efficiently. Of course, the telephone companies had no trouble getting enough men to fill the affirmative-action quotas for such inside sit-down jobs as telephone operator. This is just another area where everyone suffers: women, men, and the community.

29. Comparisons of standards of living and purchasing power between the United States and foreign countries usually leave me wondering about their validity because of the obvious statistical barrier posed by the different money systems. The international journal *To the Point* (February 9, 1976, p. 23) published a meaningful comparison of eight major countries by showing the buying power of wage earners in different occupations expressed in the working time required to buy common consumer items. The resulting chart is a blockbuster that provides new proof of the superiority of the American system in providing more material goods to more people than any system in history.

Compare, for example, the purchase of twenty-two pounds of sugar by a nurse. An American nurse can buy the sugar with one hour of work, an English nurse with four hours, seventeen minutes, a Japanese nurse with four hours, fifty minutes, a Polish nurse with six hours, forty-eight minutes, and a Russian nurse with sixteen hours.

What if you are a skilled laborer trying to buy a pair of men's shoes? An American can buy them with six hours of work, a Japanese with ten hours, an Englishman with fifteen hours, and a Russian with forty-three hours, or an entire week.

Now take the case of an engineer buying a man's suit. In America, it takes him twelve hours of work, in England twenty hours, in Sweden twenty-two hours, in Japan thirty-four hours. A Russian engineer has to work 162 hours, or about a full month.

Anyone who wants to exchange our American economic system for socialism had better prepare himself for an abrupt reduction in standard of living caused by having to work up to sixteen times longer for ordinary consumer necessities.

30. Igor Shafarevich, "Socialism in Our Past and Future," published in Aleksandr Solzhenitsyn, *From Under the Rubble* (New York: Bantam Books, 1976), p. 51.

31. The Soviet military threat and the inadequacy of the United States response have been copiously documented in the books by Phyllis Schlafly and Rear Admiral Chester Ward, USN (Ret.): *The Gravediggers* (Alton, Ill.: Pere Marquette Press, 1964), *Strike From Space* (New York: Devin-Adair Co., 1965), *The Betrayers* (Alton, Ill.: Pere Marquette Press, 1968), *Kissinger on the Couch* (New Rochelle, N.Y.: Arlington House, 1975), and *Ambush at Vladivostok* (Alton, Ill.: Pere Marquette Press, 1976).

32. James 1:22–25.

33. Isaiah 40:31.

Index

249